The Shepherd King

The Shepherd King

Learning from the life of David

Roger Ellsworth

EVANGELICAL PRESS

EVANGELICAL PRESS
Grange Close, Faverdale North Industrial Estate, Darlington,
Co. Durham, DL3 0PH, England

First published 1998

British Library Cataloguing in Publication Data available

ISBN 0 85234 412 0

Printed and bound in Great Britain by Creative Design and Print
Wales, Ebbw Vale.

Once in a while in the desert sand,
we find a spot of fairest green…

(Nixon Waterman).

The following chapters are lovingly dedicated to Immanuel
Baptist Church, my place of 'fairest green'.

Acknowledgements

The chapters that follow were originally delivered in sermon form to the Immanuel Baptist Church of Benton, Illinois. I am profoundly grateful for the appetite these believers consistently manifest for the Word of God. The same grace that worked in David's life has worked in these dear saints as well.

I also appreciate the kind assistance of my wife Sylvia and my secretary Sheila Ketteman in making these chapters possible.

Contents

Introduction

Any pastor who dares to dip into the Old Testament for a series of messages finds himself confronted with a sharp question: 'Why should we study anything from the Old Testament?' We live in a time in which even Christians have been known to lightly dismiss passages by saying, 'That's Old Testament.'

The best response to this attitude comes from no less an authority than the apostle Paul himself: 'All Scripture is given by inspiration of God, and is profitable for doctrine, for reproof, for correction, for instruction in righteousness, that the man of God may be complete, thoroughly equipped for every good work' (2 Tim. 3:16-17). 'All Scripture,' says Paul. That includes the Old Testament.

The prominence of David

Once we are clear on the continuing validity of the Old Testament, we have no trouble understanding why it is necessary to study the life of David. He receives, to put it mildly, a lion's share of the Old Testament, and is repeatedly mentioned in the New Testament. In fact, David's name is recorded 1,127 times in Scripture, fifty-eight of which are in the New Testament.

On top of that, sixty-one chapters of the Bible are devoted to him (1 Sam. 16 - 1 Kings 2; 1 Chron. 11-29).

In addition to the Scriptures *about* him, there are those *written by* him. Most of our Bibles attribute seventy-three of the 150 psalms to David, and it is possible that he wrote some of those which name no author. For example, Psalm 2 is attributed to David by the early church (Acts 4:25).

All of this forces us to ask why God should see to it that such a significant portion of Scripture was connected with David. Much of the answer is to be found in David's unique position in God's scheme of redemption. That plan of redemption is the centrepiece, the unifying theme of all Scripture, and must govern our interpretation of all its parts. How easy it is to forget this! Before we realize it, we are looking at the men and women of the Bible in a psychological sort of way. We are interested in how they solved their problems so we can figure out how to solve our own. While there are legitimate conclusions to be drawn along these lines, we must never make them primary.

Let's stop and think about God's plan of redemption for a moment and try to determine David's place in it.

This plan was, of course, in place before the foundation of the world (1 Peter 1:20). Even before God created Adam, he knew sin would enter the human race and he and the other persons of the Trinity agreed upon a plan to redeem a portion of Adam's fallen race. This plan called for the Second Person of the Trinity, the Son of God, to step into human history as a man. He could provide redemption for humankind only by becoming a man.

Now stop and think about what was necessary for the Son of God to become a man. He had to be part of a nation. That part was settled when God chose Abraham (Gen. 12:1-3), and made him the father of the Jewish people.

As the nation developed, it was divided into twelve tribes. It was necessary for the Messiah to come from one of those tribes. That part was settled when God designated the tribe of Judah (Gen. 49:8-12).

But each tribe consisted of several families. From which family would the Messiah spring? That part was settled when God made a covenant with David. We find Jesus, therefore, being referred to as 'the seed of David' (Rom. 1:3-4; 2 Tim. 2:8) and 'the son of David' (Matt. 9:27; 15:22; 20:30; Mark 10:47; Luke 18:38).

But David's pivotal role in the plan of redemption goes far beyond ancestry. He was also set apart as a special type of Christ. In other words, his reign was, in the wisdom of God, to anticipate and even prefigure the kingly reign of the Messiah. To David, God said, 'And your house and your kingdom shall be established for ever before you. Your throne shall be established for ever' (2 Sam. 7:16).

The repeated use of 'for ever' in that promise removes fulfilment from any earthly king and attaches it to the eternal King, the Lord Jesus Christ.

The major divisions of David's life

With the importance of David's life in place, we can turn our attention to the three major periods of his life.

The future king

In the first of these David is the *future* king (1 Sam. 16-31). Here he exhibits the preserving grace of God. Although he was anointed as the future King of Israel, it appeared that he would never come to the throne. Goliath, King Saul and his armies and the Philistines all posed enormous threats to David from time to time, but God graciously preserved him in the midst of them all and brought him to the throne.

The triumphant king

In his second phase David is the *triumphant* king (2 Sam. 1-10). Here he not only comes to the throne, but begins piling one impressive victory upon another. God's blessings rested upon him in such a stunning way that we can say he was at this time a token of the enriching grace of God.

The troubled king

The third stage of David's life contains much sadness and tragedy. It begins with David committing adultery with Bathsheba and having her husband Uriah killed, and it ends with David's death (2 Sam. 11 - 1 Kings 2). While David found forgiveness for his sin (Ps. 32), the consequences of that sin lingered in his family. This is not to say that David had nothing but trouble during this portion of his life, but Scripture definitely shifts the emphasis from his triumphs to his troubles.

This shift entitles us to refer to David as 'the troubled king' through the last years of his reign. Even David's sin could not eradicate the grace of God. During the last stage of David's life, we are able to see the overruling, forgiving grace of God on display. As horrible as it was, David's sin could not thwart God's covenant with him or his purpose for him.

How the periods of David's life typify Christ

David's life was designed to be a type of Christ. How do these major parts of his life typify, or point to, Christ?

It is easy enough to see the Lord Jesus portrayed in the first two parts. Those early years in which David's battles for Israel were rewarded by the hatred and hostility of Saul picture the Lord Jesus coming into this world to fight the great battle of redemption, only to be hated without a cause.

The era in which David served triumphantly as king pictures the victorious reign of the Lord Jesus Christ.

But how does the third part of David's life point to Christ? It shows us that even though David was a type of Christ, he was only a very imperfect and flawed type. Daniel M. Doriani summarizes this part of David's life by saying, 'It showed Israel's need of a righteous king who would lead his people into incorruptible righteousness.'[1]

David's life as an encouragement to believers

In addition to foreshadowing the life of Christ, each of the major periods of David's life also provides strong encouragement for the people of God. Each does so, as we have noted, by pointing us to some aspect of the grace of God, and together they all point us to the sufficiency of that grace.

Do we today need the truth of *the sufficiency of God's grace*? Yes. We need the truth of God's preserving grace hammered powerfully home to our hearts. So often in these days our hearts tremble within us. The power of modern-day Goliaths, the militant paganism of modern-day Philistines, the disdain of modern-day Nabals, the treachery and hostility of modern-day Doegs and Sauls — all swirl around us in such a frightening mix that we often find ourselves wondering if our Christ really reigns at all and if he will be able to preserve us in such a time as this. The early life of David fans the flame of our faith by showing us the certain fulfilment of God's promises and the sufficiency of his grace.

We also need the truth of God's *enriching grace*. The truth is that God's people are often found living beneath their privileges. One would never know by looking at many of them that their Christ has already begun his reign in heaven, that victory is already his, that he is even now at the right hand of God to pour out the power of the Spirit upon his people in showers of blessing.

If the truth of God's enriching grace grips us, we will understand that we are not to be content just to get through this life with our faith intact, but as we go through life we are to demonstrate the riches of God's grace and the reality of his power.

We also need the truth of God's *overruling grace*. We all, like David, are feeble and flawed, and we often fall into sin. When we do Satan always stands ready to point an accusing finger at us. But God's grace continues to triumph even when we fail. God's purposes are so certain and sure that they cannot even be thwarted by the failures of his people.

As we work our way through the major episodes of the life of David, we will continue to look for truths about our Lord Jesus Christ and encouraging truths for our own walk as the people of God, and we will pray as we do so that God will fan the flames of our faith in such a mighty way that the riches of his grace will shine forth from our lives.

1.
When God intends great mercy for his people

1 Samuel 16

The Lord always shows mercy to his people. Not a day goes by that is not hedged about with his blessings. But there are times when the Lord, in his own sovereign wisdom, decides to smile more graciously upon his people. Such a time came in Israel of old when God gave her David. God never smiled more broadly in Old Testament times than he did at that time.

What an incredible man David was! What a blessing for Israel! A warrior to fight her battles, a king to lead her to unprecedented glory, an inspired poet to fill her worship with songs of praise — David was all this and more.

One of the reasons for studying the life of David is to kindle within us a desire to see the Lord abundantly shower his mercies upon us in these days. I hope the life of David will cause us to say, 'If God so smiled upon his people then, perhaps he will be pleased to smile more broadly upon us.'

One thing ought to be as clear as day to us. We urgently need that broader smile. The society in which we live continues its steady march into ruin. Our churches are wracked with dissension, turmoil and apathy. Homes, even Christian homes, continue to disintegrate. Christians easily succumb to the prevailing moods and mores of the day.

What is the problem? We may rightly trace much of our trouble to an inept, ineffective church. But why is the church so inept and ineffective? Some suggest it is because she does

not put on the right kind of activities or use the right methods
— that the church machinery is just not functioning as it ought
and a little tinkering with it will produce the desired results.
The real problem, however, can be put as baldly as this — the
church is ineffective because God has hidden his face from
her. She has grieved him and he is withholding his power and
blessing.

It appears that many are beginning to see that the great
need of the church is revival. Revival is the work of God, not
the work of men. We cannot produce it by just pressing a few
buttons. We are completely shut up to God's own time if we
are to have the revival we so urgently need. Revival is God
taking the initiative. It is God breaking into the lives of his
apathetic and indifferent people to bring new vigour and
strength.

One aspect of revival is reformation. Thomas J. Nettles
defines this as 'the recovery of biblical truth which leads to the
purifying of one's theology. It involves a rediscovery of the
Bible as the judge and guide of all thought and action, cor-
rects errors in interpretation, gives precision, coherence, and
courage to doctrinal confession, and gives form and energy to
the corporate worship of the Triune God.'[1]

The fact that revival is God's work does not mean we should
just sit on our hands and do nothing. We find in 1 Samuel 16 a
couple of important truths which shed light on this matter of
the time when God's people can realistically expect him to
smile more broadly upon them. If we are willing to occupy the
ground described here, we have much more reason to hope
revival is near than we do if we refuse to occupy it.

God gives a sense of burden and heaviness

From these verses, we can say that when God intends great
mercy for his people he first fills them with a sense of burden

and heaviness over the conditions in which they find themselves. In other words, God gives his people an awareness of the evil of the times.

As this chapter opens, we find the nation of Israel in a wretched condition. Her king, Saul, had massively demonstrated his unfitness to rule. Though called to be the leader of the people of God, he had made it clear he had no heart for God. Saul's aversion to the things of God cast a spiritual chill over the land. The prophet Samuel deeply mourned Saul's lack of spiritual vitality (15:35), and the people in general seemed to live in terror of what the unstable king might do (v. 4).

The people themselves were far from the Lord. Their desire to be like other nations (8:5,20) indicated a shocking elevation of worldly standards over God's revealed will (8:10-20).

It was against this backdrop that God spoke to Samuel these words: 'Fill your horn with oil, and go; I am sending you to Jesse the Bethlehemite. For I have provided myself a king among his sons' (v. 1).

'I have provided myself a king.' The king of Israel was to be for God himself. He was to rule on God's behalf and in accordance with his will. Saul had miserably failed to be God's king, but God, speaking of the future as already accomplished (such is his sovereign power), said he had provided a king who would not fail.

Against a backdrop of evil and failure, then, God determined to bless Israel in a surpassingly remarkable way. This always seems to be God's *modus operandi*. History is replete with instances in which it looked as if all was hopeless, but then God moved in to unleash a fresh burst of mercy upon his people.

We want to know if we are near such an outpouring of mercy today, but that is the wrong question for us to be asking. The right question is this: do we feel the evil of the times? Are we burdened and distressed over the condition of the church today? Until we are conscious of such a burden we need not scan the horizon for the thunderclouds of God's mercy. They only break upon the heads of those who feel the burden of the times. We have no right to expect the mercy-drops of revival if we are content to lightly dismiss the evil of our time by saying, 'Our time is no worse than other times. We just hear more about the evil.' Nor do we have any right to expect the showers of blessing if we are content to believe our problems are political in nature and can be straightened out at the next election.

Samuel mourned over Saul and what he had unleashed upon Israel, and we may be sure other godly Israelites mourned as well. How many mourn today? But did not God tell Samuel not to mourn over Saul? (v. 1). Yes, but it was only when he was ready to give David to the nation. We too can stop our mourning, then, when revival breaks loose.

God bypasses our devices

This brings us to a second lesson from these verses: when God intends great mercy for his people, he invariably bypasses those things on which we are most likely to depend (vv. 6-13).

Samuel arrived at Jesse's house and invited his sons to attend the sacrifice (v. 5). When Samuel saw Jesse's first-born, Eliab, he was duly impressed. Eliab was tall and striking in every way.

But God said, 'Do not look at his appearance or at the height of his stature, because I have refused him. For the Lord does not see as man sees; for man looks at the outward appearance, but the Lord looks at the heart' (v. 7).

Thus rebuked, Samuel does not seem to have jumped to any more conclusions as the sons of Jesse passed by. The second, the third, the fourth and, finally, the seventh were all paraded by Samuel and there was still no king.

Samuel was puzzled. The word of the Lord was clear. There was a king among Jesse's sons, but he was not to be found among these seven men. There had to be another. So Samuel asked Jesse, 'Are all the young men here?' And Jesse's response seems to amount to saying, 'Well, there's the youngest who is out keeping the sheep, but, surely, you wouldn't be interested in him?' (v. 11).

But God was interested in him and, when David arrived on the scene, the Lord said to Samuel, 'Arise, anoint him; for this is the one!' (v. 12).

We should not picture God in these verses as a frustrated shopper who goes over item after item and finally has to settle on something because nothing else strikes his fancy. David was the one God had sent Samuel to anoint. Why David? Because, even though he was not as striking physically as Eliab, he had the right heart. Why was his heart right for what lay ahead? Because God, in grace, had already put the right things in his heart.

It is surprising that Samuel needed to be cautioned about looking on the outward appearance. If anyone should not have been taken in with outward appearance it was Samuel. Saul was an imposing and striking physical specimen (10:23), but he had turned out to be a spiritual pygmy, and Samuel had seen all of this from a front-row seat.

The fact that Samuel needed this caution tells us how inclined we are to rely upon mere human wisdom when it comes to the things of God. Start talking about the crying need of the hour for revival, and someone will invariably pop up to suggest a committee be appointed to study the need and bring back a recommendation. Someone else will suggest we bring in a Christian rock group, a film star, or an athlete with 'a good testimony'. Someone else will chime in with a suggestion that we do a study of the demographics of the community and plan a multi-media campaign that will arrest attention. It should be obvious to all of us by now that these things have been tried and have failed. We have seen what human wisdom can produce, and it is not much. But, like Samuel, we still have the tendency to flirt with Eliab even though we have been burned by Saul.

How differently God does things! Down through the centuries, he has consistently sent revival to his people through unlikely, ordinary instruments. He usually begins it in a small place with a very ordinary group of people. He did so in the two great 'awakenings' in America (the former occurring in the 1730s and 1740s and the latter in the 1780s), the revivals in Wales in 1904 and 1905 and the revival in Ireland in 1859. Jonathan Edwards and George Whitefield, hardly famous as the world considers fame, were God's instruments in the first of the two American awakenings. Far lesser known are the names of James McGready, Barton Stone, Evan Roberts and James McQuilken, the men God chose to use in the other revivals mentioned above.

God did the same thing when he sent his Son into this world. Jesus came, not to the hustle and bustle of Jerusalem, but to tiny Bethlehem. And when Jesus began his public ministry, he bypassed those who were the movers and shakers of the day and surrounded himself with ordinary fishermen and tax-collectors.

God's saving work to this very day is primarily carried on in those who are not mighty or noble, but who are weak and plain. Why? Paul gives the answer. It is so that all the glory for his mighty works will go to him rather than to men (1 Cor. 1:29).

We can be sure that God will protect his glory as much in his reviving work as he does in his saving work. He will not allow us to take a shred of it for ourselves, and we would do exactly that if we could produce a revival through our stars, our promotions and our committees.

With all our slickness and cleverness, we have been unable to produce what we so desperately need — namely, a true work of God in our midst. Maybe, just maybe, God has almost brought us to the end of ourselves so that we can now stand in awe of the mercy he is about to unleash upon us.

2.
Grace on top of grace

1 Samuel 16:14-23

The keynote of David's life is grace. The grace that was at work in his life pictures for us the grace God demonstrated in the life of Christ and the grace he continues to demonstrate in the lives of his people today.

It was the grace of God that reached down, singled David out from among his brothers and designated him as the future King of Israel. In doing this, the grace of God bypassed human wisdom and dignity. Grace surprised Samuel, Jesse and all David's brothers.

That same *surprising grace* was at work when the triune God mapped out the plan of redemption. That plan designated the Son of God to step into human history as a man, to live in perfect obedience to God's holy law and to pay the penalty for sinners by dying on a cross.

Human wisdom would never have guessed eternal salvation could be provided in such a way. The idea of eternal salvation through a man dying on a cross seemed utterly ludicrous and foolish when Christ died. And such is the assessment of many today. They look at that cross and say, 'To receive salvation from our sins we must bow in submission and repentance before a man crucified in agony and blood on a cross? Such a thing is beneath us! It does not make any sense! It is undignified!'

The apostle Paul was aware of this mentality when he wrote to the Corinthians. In effect, he said that all those who despise and disdain the cross of Christ as utter foolishness had better think again. What looks to the human eye to be ridiculous is really nothing less than 'the power of God and the wisdom of God' (1 Cor. 1:24).

That same surprising grace of God has worked in the life of each and every believer. Was David chosen by the grace of God? The Bible says the same is true of all those who believe. Our minds are far too feeble to penetrate the mysteries of God's election, but our inability to understand it does not invalidate it. The teaching of Scripture is that the eternal salvation of God's people is not their own work. It is God's work, and it is a work he put in place before the world began. There in eternity past, God the Father chose to redeem from the ravages of sin a people to share his eternal glory. This redeeming work was to be accomplished through the Second Person of the Trinity taking their humanity unto himself and receiving in their stead the penalty for their sins. Further, these same people were to be brought to saving faith in the redeeming work of Christ through the Holy Spirit working in them. All of this was to be done for these people, not on the basis of any foreseen merit in them, but entirely as a matter of his grace (Eph. 1:3-6).

We should also notice that God's choice of David bypassed human wisdom, and the Bible assures us the same is true in the salvation of God's people. Not many mighty, noble, powerful people are called. God's surprising grace generally bypasses such people and focuses on common, ordinary, unimpressive people (1 Cor. 1:26-28).

Another example of the surprising grace of God is to be found in those instances in which he has poured out revival upon his people. He invariably bypasses those things we are most inclined to depend on for revival and uses unlikely instruments in unlikely places.

Why does God operate in this manner? Why does he delight to demonstrate his grace in such surprising, unpredict-
able ways? One succinct phrase from the apostle Paul gives us
the answer: 'that no flesh should glory in his presence' (1 Cor.
1:29).

God's grace, then, always goes hand in hand with his glory.
It paves the way and opens the door for his glory to shine
forth. In the passage before us, we see more of the grace of
God at work in the life of David.

The sad spectacle of evil

To appreciate and understand this aspect of grace, we must
first look at the very sad spectacle these verses bring before
our eyes. Here we see the blackness of evil. Saul, that promis-
ing man who was given such a golden opportunity to shine for
God, is here in the clutches of evil thoughts and broodings of
despair. Scripture puts it most succinctly: 'A distressing spirit
from the Lord troubled him' (v. 14).

This 'distressing spirit from the Lord' has raised difficult
questions for many who read this passage. Does this mean
God is the source of evil? Could a God of love do such a
thing? How are we to explain this? Gordon J. Keddie offers
this word of explanation: 'This does not mean that God is the
source of evil spirits. It simply emphasizes that when the Holy
Spirit withdraws from someone, that person is easy prey for
Satan and, indeed, for his own self-destructive sinfulness.'[1]

Saul is left here, then, to the consequences of his own
choices. Time after time he had made it clear that he did not
want to bear the yoke of obedience to God, and God finally
granted his desire by withdrawing from him.

Don't think this was some special form of judgement that
was reserved just for Saul. God employs this same judgement

with all those who throw off all restraints and plunge reck-lessly and greedily after sin. This is confirmed by Paul's three-fold use of the dreadful phrase 'God gave them up' in his de-scription of Gentile sin (Rom. 1:24,26,28).

What irony there is in this sad description of Saul! He oc-cupied the throne because the people of Israel had insisted that they have a king 'like all the other nations' (1 Sam. 8:5,19-20). Their wish has now been fully realized. In this man from whom God had withdrawn, the people indeed had a king like all the other nations around them, a king without God. The great sadness is that Israel was not intended to be like all the other nations. She was called by God to be a special nation, one that was to demonstrate the glory of belonging to God. But now through her sinful insistence and Saul's sinful living, the nation had stepped off the high pedestal on which God had placed her. Oh, the sadness, the tragedy of the sinful life that drives God away and invites trouble and distress in!

Saul, Judas Iscariot, Cain, Korah, Lot, Esau — Scripture abounds with the names of those tragic figures who rebelled against God and reduced the once-promising edifices of their lives to bombed-out ruins.

May God help all of us who take his name upon ourselves to understand that no tragedy mortal man can ever experience compares with the tragedy of the distressing spirit that fol-lows hard in the wake of a withdrawn God.

The bright ray of grace

All is not bleak in this passage. There is also here a bright ray of grace to pierce and relieve the gloom.

Saul's servants said to him, 'Surely, a distressing spirit from God is troubling you' (v. 15). Isn't it interesting that these men were able to diagnose the problem correctly? We should not be surprised. Saul's sins were written so large in Israel that it did not require theologians to see the heavy hand of God's judgement on him. Mere servants could see it.

One would think that correct diagnosis would lead these servants to suggest to Saul that he should go before God in true brokenness and repentance, but they did not. Their remedy was music (v. 16). Keddie observes: 'Having diagnosed the need for heart surgery, they proceeded to prescribe a sedative!'[2] The soothing powers of music are well known and certainly have their place, but Saul needed much more than mere music could provide.

The servants not only had music in mind as the cure for Saul. They also had a musician in mind — David (v. 18). So David came for the first time into the service of Saul. When Saul was distressed, David played on the harp for him, and the soothing strains of those strings smoothed Saul's furrowed brow and lifted his heavy heart. Music was indeed a temporary sedative, but the heart trouble remained.

Crucial truths

Crucial truths are embedded in this simple story of a troubled king and a shepherd boy, truths about the grace of God. First, we catch a glimpse of the *restraining grace* of God at work here. By playing for Saul, David kept him from being completely disabled.

S. G. DeGraaf writes, 'Thus David was a blessing to Saul and thereby also to Israel. Because of David's presence, Saul's mind was not immediately and wholly disabled, and Israel's affairs were not completely thrown into confusion.'[3]

This same grace of God is at work today. The world, like Saul, is devoid of God. She has thumbed her nose at his laws and despised his name, and he is deeply troubling her with judgement.

The only thing that keeps this world from total collapse is the presence of God's people, who serve as salt and light — salt to retard the moral corruption that pervades our day and light to dispel some of the darkness (Matt. 5:13-14).

Another aspect of God's grace that was at work at this particular time was God's *equipping grace*. What strange feelings must have surged through David as he ministered to the man he had already been anointed to replace! David must have realized that God had placed him in the shadow of the throne so he could learn some valuable lessons.

What was there for David to learn from Saul? The main thing was to learn about the importance of obedience to God. Saul sat there as a monument to the power of sin to ravage and destroy. Surely, David took this to heart and vowed not to play fast and loose with God's laws.

David must also have been given deep insight into what his role as king was to be. He had been anointed, but he was thrust into a position of not only having to wait patiently for God's time to arrive, but also having to humbly serve the very man he was to replace. DeGraaf says, 'Such service was already preparation for the throne, for a king was not to be a man who used power for his own benefit. He was to use the throne to serve the Lord and to be a blessing to others.'[4]

This entire chapter, then, holds up the jewel of God's grace and slowly turns it so we can catch the glimmer of its various facets. That same surprising, restraining, equipping grace of God is at work today. How we need to realize this! Even though the darkness and distress of sin hang as heavy over this world as they did over Saul, the grace of God is still at work. It is sufficient not only to sustain us in this dark world, but also actually to make us a source of blessing to those around us.

3.
David and Goliath

1 Samuel 17

Prior to the events described in this chapter there was probably very little agreement among the Israelites on the greatest problem facing their nation. The city gates and the market-places may very well have resounded each day with lively debate on that issue.

A Philistine named Goliath changed all that. Great problems have a way of wonderfully focusing the mind, and Goliath's presence on the battlefield focused the minds of all Israel. No longer was there any need to debate what their greatest problem was. All agreed it was Goliath.

Why was Goliath suddenly such a problem for the nation of Israel? For forty long days (v. 16) he had challenged the Israelite army to send a man out to fight with him. If Israel's champion defeated him, the Philistines would become their slaves, but if Goliath won the match the Israelites would become slaves of the Philistines (vv. 8-9).

It sounded like a fair challenge. But there was a problem. Goliath was no ordinary man. He was over nine feet tall with a suit of armour weighing 125 pounds. Just the sight of his spear was enough to strike terror into the heart. The shaft of it was like 'a weaver's beam' and the head of it weighed fifteen pounds (vv. 4-7). In addition to all of this, as if he were constantly in mortal danger, he had a shield-bearer to walk in front of him (v. 7).

So massive and terrifying was Goliath that all the army of Israel was completely nonplussed. 'They were dismayed and greatly afraid,' says it all (v. 11).

Yes, most in Israel would readily have agreed that Goliath was their greatest problem, and the topic of debate rapidly shifted to how to deal with this walking fortress.

The real problem in Israel

But was Goliath really the problem in Israel during the forty days in which he ritually flung out his challenge to the cowering Israelite army?

No, not at all. He was just a symptom or manifestation of a much larger problem in Israel — lack of faith in her God.

What is faith? Many equate it with mere positive thinking. They would have us believe defeating Goliath was simply a matter of an Israelite 'psyching himself up' until he believed he could actually defeat such a brute. By such positive thinking this Israelite would activate powers he did not even know he possessed, and — hey presto! — Goliath would fall.

Faith today is often taken to mean faith in ourselves. But faith in the Bible is not just optimism, or positive thinking, or believing everything will somehow or other turn out all right. Faith in the Bible is a very precise matter — it is believing what God has revealed.

Had God said or done anything that the people of Israel could have applied to Goliath's challenge? He most certainly had. If they had just taken time to think, they would have realized that their forefathers had allowed the fear of giants to keep them from entering the land of Canaan. Forty years later, after that fearful, unbelieving generation died off, the people of Israel trusted God's promises to give them victory over their enemies and conquered the land. The giants in the land of Canaan were still there. The difference was that the new generation of Israelites were not afraid of them. They believed God's promises about giving them the land and defeating their enemies while the fearful generation refused to believe those same promises. When a person has the Almighty pledged to help him, he does not care how big his enemies are.

I am sure that if someone had pointed out this part of their history to the Israelite soldiers as they cringed before Goliath they would have all said, 'But that was a long time ago. Times have changed.'

Jonathan, the son of King Saul, did not think times had changed when he and his armour-bearer placed their trust in God and defeated a whole garrison of Philistines (14:1-14). That happened just a few short years before Goliath strode onto the stage of Israel. But Jonathan seems to have faltered in faith for he is nowhere to be found in this account.

Distant history and recent history joined their voices, then, to give one clear testimony — when the people of God walk in complete reliance upon his promises he enables them to defeat their enemies.

The problem in Israel in the face of this new challenge can be put very simply: there was much more talk about Goliath than there was about God.

Incredible as it sounds, Goliath himself seems to have grasped the lack of faith in Israel far more clearly than King Saul and all his soldiers. Daniel M. Doriani suggests Goliath was essentially saying in verse 8: 'Am I not a pagan, God-hating Philistine? Then why won't any of you men of "the living God" fight me? You must not really believe in him at all! In fact, you must believe that a nine-foot warrior is actually stronger than your "living God" when it comes to a real battle.'[1]

The flame of faith burning brightly in David

The flame of faith may have been flickering feebly in the nation of Israel as a whole, but it was burning brightly in David.

Sent by his father Jesse to take food to his brothers, David arrived upon the scene just at the time that Goliath chose to issue his daily challenge.

David was astounded. He saw the giant's challenge for what it actually was — a defiance of Israel's God and a challenge to her faith in him (v. 26). Had faith declined and deteriorated so badly in Israel that no one was willing to take up the challenge? Were God's great promises regarding the chosen nation of Israel suddenly null and void? Had God suddenly been toppled from his throne?

David's faith responded with a resounding 'No!' to all these questions, and it compelled him to take up the giant's challenge (v. 32).

The rest, as they say, is history. Spurning the heavy armour offered him by Saul, David went forth to meet Goliath with only his shepherd's sling and five smooth stones (vv. 38-40). In reality, he went forth with far more than those simple items. He went to the conflict with a blazing concern for the honour of God, with confidence in the certainty of his promises and with the power of the Spirit of God.

Goliath was insulted that such an unlikely warrior would take up his challenge (vv. 42-44) and supremely confident that he would win the battle. King Saul and his soldiers, on the other hand, must have been gratified that someone had finally accepted the giant's challenge, but they undoubtedly trembled with dismay over the outcome of the battle.

But Goliath did not stand a chance. One stone did it. Guided by the unseen hand of the God who sovereignly reigns over all, it hit Goliath in the forehead and felled him (v. 50).

That one stone shattered something else besides Goliath's skull. It shattered the coldness that had crept over many an Israelite heart. God was still on the throne! His promises were still in force! In addition to these things, it was clear that God had great things in store for his people. He had not cast them off, but had sent them a deliverer.

Valuable lessons

We often think of the account of David slaying Goliath as nothing more than an entertaining story for children, but it abounds with meaning for even the most seasoned saint of God.

For one thing, it gives us a faint glimpse of *the work of the Lord Jesus Christ* who has triumphed over the whole kingdom of darkness. And he, like David, did it with an unlikely instrument — a Roman cross. Who would have thought a Jewish rabbi dying in such agony and shame could have delivered the crushing blow to Satan and his forces? But that is exactly what took place. Those of us who know the Lord do well, therefore, if we rejoice over the triumph of our Lord Jesus Christ as we read this account of David's triumph over Goliath.

We also do well if we see this as a picture of *the situation in which we find ourselves today*. The church of today is hardly robust. We can point to statistical success here and there, but the church is having little impact on society. The truth is that the church seems to have scarcely any impact on the lives of her own members. The sinful thinking and doing of society show up with alarming frequency in professing Christians. Such things lead us to conclude that we Christians are, as someone has observed, many but not much.

What is the problem with the church today? Many say it is Goliath. They point to the difficulty of the times in which we live. They wring their hands over the militant secular spirit of the time. They speak mournfully over the steady deterioration of the Judeo-Christian heritage.

But is our problem really Goliath? Is it really the times in which we live? Or is it our own lack of confidence in our God and in the redeeming message of the gospel?

Has God toppled from his throne? Is he limited to working only when the circumstances are favourable? Has the gospel been shorn of its power? Has Paul's fervent declaration been deleted from our Bibles: 'For I am not ashamed of the gospel of Christ, for it is the power of God to salvation...'? (Rom. 1:16).

The nub of the matter is this — our problem is not Goliath but ourselves and our own lack of faith. And what is the answer? Is it to try to create a more favourable climate for Christians through political processes? Or is it to fall on our faces before God to confess our lack of faith and to plead for the spirit that moved in David to move mightily in us? Is it to take up the cumbersome armour of Saul, or to take up the message of a crucified Saviour and hurl it into this dark age by the power of the Spirit of God?

4.

Grace prized and despised

1 Samuel 18:1-9

The grace of God was truly at work in David. His stunning victory over Goliath left no room for debate on that issue. A burning concern for the glory of God, an unflinching faith in the promises of God and a steady dependence on the Spirit of God are infallible indicators of the grace of God. All were written too large in David's defeat of Goliath to be denied.

Everyone rejoiced in what the grace of God had achieved through David. Goliath had posed a problem that seemed to be without solution until David came along.

But after the initial burst of euphoria subsided it became clear that Israel had a problem of a different sort: what to do with David? God had obviously raised up a champion for the people, and that constituted a serious challenge. Would they now receive him as their champion? Would they allow the faith that flamed so brilliantly in him to burn brightly again in their own hearts? Or would they continue to walk with the chilled hearts that had almost brought them under the iron heel of a pagan nation? The people of Israel were glad to be rid of Goliath, but were they ready for what David represented?

This is a dilemma we meet with time and time again. The Gadarenes were happy enough to be rid of the legion of demons that tyrannized and terrorized their community, but they were not ready to accept Jesus. They wanted what Jesus could produce without having Jesus himself (Mark 5:1-17).

It is also an ongoing dilemma. Many want the stability and tranquillity Christianity has produced down through the centuries, but they want these things without having to submit to the demands of Christ. They want the results without having that which produces the results.

In the last chapters of 1 Samuel, David was a sword of division in the nation of Israel. His victory over Goliath gained him the support of everyone at first (v. 5), but much of that support evaporated, or went underground, as Saul began to make his hostility known. Nowhere was the sharpness of that sword felt more keenly than in Saul's own household.

One who prized grace

What Jonathan did

Jonathan, Saul's son and heir apparent, was in no doubt about how to respond to the grace of God at work in the life of David. The opening verses of this eighteenth chapter record an amazing and astonishing thing. Here Jonathan enters into an agreement with David (v. 3) and gives him his robe, armour and weapons (v. 4).

What did this agreement consist of? It was quite obviously a covenant of friendship. By surrendering these personal items to David, Jonathan was clearly pledging to be his friend for ever. If others spoke evil of David, Jonathan would speak kindly of him. If others took up their weapons against him, Jonathan would not.

Jonathan's act also indicates that he understood David was going to be the next king of Israel. The throne was Jonathan's natural right, but here he relinquishes his claim to it and gladly and freely submits to David.

The covenant Jonathan made with David that day was enlarged some time later when Jonathan completely cast himself

and his family upon the mercy of David (1 Sam. 20:14-16). It
was customary for kings of that day to consolidate their position by immediately eliminating all rivals. In asking David not
to follow this custom, Jonathan was pledging never to be a
rival to his friend.

Even as he made this commitment, Jonathan must have
known that his father Saul and David were on a collision course,
but he would not even allow his natural allegiance to his father
to cause him to turn against David. When that inevitable collision finally came and Saul's hostility towards David was out
in the open, Jonathan stood by his friend and spoke well of
him to his father (19:4). What a great act of surrender this
was! Self-interest and natural allegiances were laid aside as
Jonathan freely cast himself and his family upon David.

Why Jonathan did it

Why would Jonathan do such a thing? The answer is that
David's heroic act of defeating Goliath had won his heart.
Jonathan's covenant with David followed hard on the heels of
David's victory. David brought the head of the Philistine to
Saul (1 Sam. 17:57). Saul enquired about his parentage (1 Sam.
16:18-19 reveals that Saul already knew David was Jesse's
son. Saul's question here was probably intended to determine
if such heroic deeds ran in his family). Immediately after David's
conversation with Saul, we are told that the soul of Jonathan
'was knit' to David, 'and Jonathan loved him as his own soul'
(18:1).

What are we to carry away from this? Is Jonathan's act
recorded here merely to extol the virtues of friendship? Is this
passage intended to inspire us to be more friendly to all, or to
form a special friendship with one person?

We might be inclined to think along these lines if we forget
what we noted at the beginning — namely, that the grace of
God was at work in David. But if we keep this in mind, we

will take a far different view of Jonathan's act. If the grace of God was at work in David, Jonathan's submission to him was nothing less than a surrender to that grace.

The pressing question for us

When we look at Jonathan's act from this angle, this passage suddenly has profound and immense spiritual significance for us. It thrusts this question squarely before each of us — have we surrendered to the grace of God in the same way that Jonathan surrendered to David?

The grace of God was presented to Jonathan in the person of David. It has been presented to us in the person of Jesus Christ. As David slew the giant Goliath with the unlikely instrument of a sling and a stone, so the Lord Jesus has dealt the mortal blow to Satan and his whole kingdom of darkness with the unlikely instrument of a Roman cross.

Has that deed won your heart as David's deed won Jonathan's heart? Have you surrendered fully and freely to Christ? Has his deed caused you to renounce your self-interest? Has it caused you to subjugate your natural desires and allegiances to him? Do you see that he has the authority to pass the sentence of eternal death upon you and that your only hope is to cast yourself upon his mercy? Have you come to him also to seek mercy for your family?

Like it or not, these are all marks of true conversion to Christ. Ours is a day in which the gospel has been so cheapened that we think it is possible to have Christ while we still wrap ourselves in the robe of self and carry the weapons of sin. But Jesus says, 'If anyone desires to come after me, let him deny himself, and take up his cross, and follow me' (Matt. 16:24). Have you thrown your robe of self at his feet? Have you surrendered the weapons of sin in true repentance?

David's deed was certainly worthy of Jonathan's admiration and respect. It was worthy of the commitment Jonathan made. The people of Israel were staring at hard, oppressive bondage under the iron heel of oppressive taskmasters when David came on the scene and shouldered the burden.

But the Lord Jesus Christ is even more worthy of the devotion of those of us who know him as Lord and Saviour. The Bible tells us that we were not merely facing the possibility of slavery under a cruel taskmaster when the Lord Jesus went to the cross. We were already enslaved to Satan (Eph. 2:1-3) and already part of his dark dominion (Col. 1:13) when the Lord Jesus shouldered our burden. By his death on the cross he paid for our sins, freed us from Satan, and made us part of the kingdom of God. He did not have to come and he did not have to die, but he did. We owed a debt we could not pay, and he paid a debt he did not owe. And it was all because of his great, incomprehensible love for sinners. David's act was great, but it cannot compare to what Christ did.

One who despised grace

We cannot leave Jonathan without comparing him to his father Saul. What a vast difference there was between these two men! Yes, Saul was glad David won the battle with Goliath, and he sought to show his appreciation to David by giving him a position of leadership (v. 5).

But Saul never gave his heart to David. He never saw David as God's gift of grace to deliver him and his nation from a terrible fate. The truth is that there was no room in Saul's heart for anything except himself. He could tip his hat to the benefits the grace of God produced through David, but he could never give his heart to that grace. He was willing to tolerate David as long as he did not have to renounce his own self-interest.

When Saul heard the women giving David greater praise than himself (v. 7), his self-interest seemed to be in danger and he lashed out at David.

When it comes to the work of the Lord Jesus on behalf of sinners, there is no middle ground. We either associate with Jonathan and surrender ourselves and our hope for eternal salvation completely to Christ, or we join with Saul and refuse to submit.

Many have cast their lot in with Saul. They have heard the call of the gospel to lay down the robe of self and the armour and weapons of sin, but that call has only made them wrap their robe more tightly around them and grip their weapons more firmly. If they could have Christ along with self and sin, they might be willing to accept him, but they will never accept a Christ who calls for total surrender. They will tip the hat to the benefits of Christ but never surrender the heart to his demands.

All who have cast their lot in with Saul would do well to consider his end. He opposed David at every turn, but God still brought David to the throne of Israel, and Saul came to ruin. Opposition to God never works. It did not work for Saul when David was the issue, and it will not work for us on the issue of Christ. Refusing to submit to Christ will in no way thwart him, but it will certainly bring all who engage in it to utter ruin.

5.
Mastering the art of spear-dodging

1 Samuel 18:10-16

The spear of Goliath must have been an impressive sight. The head of it weighed fifteen pounds. David probably expected that massive spear to come his way as he approached the giant, but so far as we know it never did.

The expected spear did not come, but in the verses which form the subject of this chapter an unexpected spear did come.

The day after the women had chanted their chorus about Saul slaying thousands and David ten thousands, David was back at the palace to play his harp for Saul. Suddenly Saul hurled his spear at him. David managed to elude it and dash out.

Shortly after this episode David was called back to play for Saul. Have you ever wondered why he was willing to go back? The answer is not all that hard to come by. Saul was David's king, and kings had absolute authority. David had great respect for the office and, from all indications, genuine understanding of, and affection for, the man who held it.

Furthermore, it is very likely that Saul apologized profusely for the incident and assured David it would never happen again. But it did happen again. Without warning the spear suddenly came straight at David, but he was again able to dodge it and get away.

David must have been completely mystified and perplexed. He and Saul were supposed to be on the same side. Both professed to belong to God and to have the cause of God uppermost in their thoughts and deeds, and here one is throwing a spear at the other.

The spears that came at David and his skill in dodging them contain some lessons for us. The truth is that there are still plenty of spears around, even though that dreaded weapon of ancient warfare has all but passed off the scene. It is not at all uncommon for us to find spears dropping around us as we go along life's way. Someone says something that is painful and cutting, or perhaps one whom we counted as a friend begins speaking evil of us to others. These are spears. We could dismiss those that come from a Goliath, but what do we do about those from people who are supposed to be on the same team as we are?

David, the masterful spear-dodger, can help us. As we look at his spear-dodging episodes we can discern four helpful lessons.

Refusing to be a spear-thrower

First, David teaches us not to be spear-throwers ourselves.

This passage seems to picture for us a great option in life. On one side sits Saul, brooding with a spear in his hand, and over there sits David quietly strumming on the harp. If you had to choose one of these two items as an emblem of your own life, which would it be? Are you among the spear-carriers or the harp-players?

The fact that Saul twice threw a spear at David indicates he was a man who enjoyed having a spear in his hand. He carried it with him as he walked through the palace. He slowly turned it in his hand as he sat on his throne. The spear was an instrument of destruction, and he enjoyed having it near him at all times.

Is this a picture of you? Are you one of those who enjoy carrying around destructive thoughts? Are you one who continually rolls destructive, bitter thoughts around in your mind? Do you nurse resentment and bitterness? Are you one of those who can at any moment hurl that spear of destruction at a family member or friend? Are you one who carries a spear in his hand even when he walks into the house of God and slowly turns and twirls it around even while worship is going on? Are you one of those who come to church simply to find fault?

Or is the harp, an instrument of peace and tranquillity, a more fitting emblem for you?

Jesus says, 'Blessed are the peacemakers, for they shall be called sons of God' (Matt. 5:9). Are you a peacemaker? Or are you a destroyer of peace? It is true, of course, that spear-throwers can strum the harp and harp-players can throw the spear. The question for us to ponder is this: what is the general tenor of my life? Even the harp-player can say things that are wrong and hurtful, but that is not typical of him. Even the spear-thrower can be pleasant at times, but that amiability is not characteristic of him.

Making sure we do not deserve spears

A second lesson we learn from David is to be sure that we do not deserve to be on the receiving end of spears.

If David had been actively opposing Saul and seeking to subvert his leadership and take his throne, he would have been guilty of treason and would have deserved Saul's wrath. But all David had ever done in relationship to Saul was good: playing the harp for him, conquering Goliath, serving as captain of

Saul's army (18:5). In each of these capacities, David was either doing good *to* Saul or *for* Saul. The last thing he deserved was to have a spear hurled at him.

Why did Saul twice throw a spear at David? It was simply because David was a success in all he did and Saul was a failure. Instead of taking responsibility for his own failure, Saul blamed it on David.

David's goodness is a model for all of us. Sometimes we complain about another person for throwing a spear at us when we have not been practising goodness. We give the impression that we have just been innocently strumming on the harp when someone suddenly flung a spear in our direction. If the truth were known, however, we were far from innocent. When we have been up to our elbows in meanness, we have no right to complain about the spears that are thrown at us. In such cases, what we call a spear may be nothing more than a well-deserved rebuke!

The apostle Peter wrote to some Christians who were in the crucible of suffering. Part of his advice to them was this: 'But let none of you suffer as a murderer, a thief, an evildoer, or as a busybody in other people's matters' (1 Peter 4:15).

Refusing to retaliate

The most obvious thing David teaches us is this: don't throw the spear back, but just concentrate on our duties.

How easy it would have been for David to do this! He had already proved himself to be a fearless warrior. When that spear went whizzing by, he could simply have seized it and hurled it right back at Saul. Saul would not have stood a chance.

David could then have legitimately pleaded self-defence and stepped right into the kingship of Israel. Furthermore, he could have justified the whole thing in his own mind by simply saying that this was the way in which God intended him to come to the throne.

Retaliation is the way of the world. You throw a spear at me, and I'm going to throw it back at you. But the Christian is different. He is in the world, but he is not of it. He is a citizen of a higher world and subscribes to a higher standard (Matt. 5:38-41; Rom. 12:17-21).

The fact that we are not to retaliate when others throw spears at us does not mean we must do nothing at all. There is something for us to do when others make life miserable for us. We are to do what David did. He 'behaved wisely in all his ways' (v. 14).

In other words, David responded to the spears thrown by Saul by just going about his business. He did not go around talking about what Saul had done and defending himself. He knew that if he focused on doing what he was supposed to do God would take care of his reputation.

Forgiving the spear-thrower

Finally, David teaches us to forgive the spear-thrower.

As Saul's hostility increased, it became apparent to David that he would not be able to stay in close association with him, but David never allowed that hostility to make him bitter and hateful towards Saul. On a couple of occasions, David could very easily have taken Saul's life (1 Sam. 24:1-15; 26:1-20), but he refused to do so. He continued to speak highly of Saul even though Saul hated him. It seems that David subscribed to this simple principle: people who hate us only win if we hate them back.

The great question in all human relationships is not whether spears (that is, offences) will come to us, but rather how we will handle them when they do come. The Bible answers that question in these words: 'And be kind to one another, tender-hearted, forgiving one another, just as God in Christ also forgave you' (Eph. 4:32).

Some think those who have remained loyal to the church down through the years are very fortunate because no one has ever offended them. In reality, all those who have stayed faithful to the church have been on the receiving end of plenty of spears. They stay in the church not because they are never offended, but because they have learned to handle offences in the biblical way. They have forgiven the spear-throwers.

There are many things in this life that we are unable to control. We cannot stop others from throwing spears at us. However, there are things we can control. We can be harp-players instead of spear-throwers. We can make sure we do not deserve to be a target of the spear-throwers. We can refuse to retaliate. And we can forgive.

The Lord Jesus Christ is, as always, our model here. He, the sinless one, did nothing to deserve hostility but had to endure it (Heb. 12:3) to a degree unknown by anyone else. While the spears of hostility fell around him, he strummed the chord of peace on his harp and refused to retaliate. Then he went to Calvary's cross and there cried, 'Father, forgive them...' (Luke 23:34). Through his atoning death, his people are drawn from their hostility to embrace him as their Saviour and Lord.

6.
God's preserving grace

1 Samuel 18 - 19

The eighteenth and nineteenth chapters of 1 Samuel are ugly and repulsive. Here we have Saul, King of Israel, seeking to take the life of one of his subjects, David.

What had David done to deserve such mean, spiteful treatment? He had walked with God and God had blessed and used him. The blessing of God upon his life was amply and powerfully proved by his stunning victory over Goliath.

That victory over Goliath had kept the nation of Israel and Saul himself from a terrible fate. If Goliath had defeated David, the people of Israel would have become slaves of the Philistines and Saul himself would have been dragged through the streets of the Philistine cities as a trophy of war and then would have been unceremoniously dispatched from this life.

We would have expected, therefore, that Saul would have rejoiced mightily in the blessing of God upon David, but he did not. I have found that many of God's people have a hard time rejoicing in the success of their brothers and sisters in Christ. We find it easier to weep with those who weep than to rejoice with those who rejoice.

God preserving David

Instead of rejoicing over what God had done for him and his

nation through David, Saul despised and detested David so much that he sought to take his life.

Are we shocked that Saul was capable of this kind of intense hatred? We should be. At the same time we should be aware that Saul's hatred is always lurking outside our own hearts and is ready to dash through the door in that one unguarded moment. Have you ever thought how much easier your life would be if it were not for this person over here, or that one over there? Look out! Saul's hatred is making a dash for the door of your heart.

The first manifestation of Saul's hatred came in the form of a spear hurled at the unsuspecting David (18:11). It is interesting that David was simply engaged in doing something for the benefit of the king when Saul threw that spear.

What he failed to accomplish with his spear, Saul attempted to accomplish in other ways. He promised to give David his daughter Merab, on the condition that David would fight the Philistines. If Saul had been a man of integrity he would simply have given David his daughter. He had evidently promised as much to the man who defeated Goliath (17:25), but here he adds the condition that David fight further battles against the Philistines (18:17).

What was all this about? Saul was not planning David's wedding, but his funeral! By sending David out against the Philistines Saul hoped he would catch an enemy arrow or spear (18:17).

When that ploy failed, Saul resorted to another stratagem. He gave the daughter he promised to David to another man. This was nothing less than a deliberate attempt to provoke David to do something rash, something that could have been used to bring about his formal execution.

When David did not explode with outrage, Saul had another thought. He would give another daughter, Michal, to David. This gave Saul the opportunity to send David against the Philistines for yet another time (18:25-27).

The eighteenth chapter of 1 Samuel comes to a close with David having avoided all the traps Saul set for him and with Saul being much afraid of David (v. 29). Saul afraid of David! David should, it would seem, be afraid of Saul, but Saul was afraid of him.

The nineteenth chapter brings more of the same. Jonathan, Saul's son, was able to stem his father's hostility against David for a short time (v. 7), but that soon vanished. Saul threw another spear at David (vv. 9-10), but missed him again. He then sent some executioners to David's house, but Michal helped him escape (vv. 11-12).

By this time Saul was so eaten up with hatred and envy of David that he did not even bother to disguise his intent to take his life. He commanded messengers to carry David into his presence on his sickbed so he could kill him. When David again escaped with the help of his wife, Saul threatened to kill her, his own daughter (vv. 13-17).

The nineteenth chapter closes with Saul going to Ramah to pursue David, who had gone there to seek the counsel and protection of the prophet Samuel. Saul's murderous intent was thwarted when the Spirit of God fell upon him and caused him to lose his faculties (vv. 18-24).

God preserving his Christ and his cause

These chapters read very much like a fast-paced, entertaining novel, but what do they have to do with us? Are they here just to give us a titbit or two on how to deal with human conflict? Or is there more?

I have no hesitation in affirming that there is much more here than two men having a personality conflict. In fact, I would go so far as to suggest that God has embedded in the ore of these two chapters a gleaming vein of truth that each generation of Christians sorely needs to be reminded of — namely, that God will preserve his Christ and his cause.

We must always keep in mind that the grace of God was mightily at work in the life of David. Saul's hatred for David was, therefore, hatred of the grace of God. And his attempts to murder David were nothing less than attempts to eliminate the grace of God.

Hostility towards the grace of God

As we look carefully and closely at this man Saul we can see the dark, leering countenance of Satan himself in the background. Satan has always hated the grace of God and has ceaselessly busied himself in stirring up opposition to it. His efforts have been so successful that we can truly say there is a deep and unremitting hostility in the world today for the grace of God.

That hostility is expressed and manifested in much the same way as it was when Saul attacked David. Open persecution of Christians is not hard to find today. Saul's spears of destruction and his messengers of death are still with us.

Christians also find themselves the targets of much subtle opposition, and in that we can see Saul's Merabs and Michals. How we Christians need to be on our guard in these evil days! A world without God can talk of weddings, but it never ceases to plan the funeral of Christianity.

The hostility of the world often causes Christians to be deeply distressed and depressed. Some find it in their employment. They cannot earn a living for their families without having their faith either openly or subtly attacked. Some find it in the school they attend. Some find it in their own homes.

No matter how great the hostility, no matter how severe the attacks, no matter how dark the gloom, we can take refuge in the knowledge that God's cause is going to prevail.

Because of that those who fight against it are engaged in utter folly.

The means by which God preserves

God preserved David in various ways and through various means. As we look at these chapters, we can see the Lord using three different means to preserve David. First, he used *Michal*. From all indications, she certainly was not a child of God, but he still used her to protect and preserve David.

We must not forget that David's marriage to Michal was due to the crafty, evil devising of Saul. Saul's evil schemes backfired him on when his daughter sided with David. Here we have God using the craft of the wicked to confirm and preserve his own truth.

Do we not see the very same thing today? The more the world rejects Christian teachings and values, the worse the world becomes, and thus proves the validity of Christian teachings and values. Even the wrath of man works to God's praise.

Secondly, God used *Jonathan* to preserve David. These splendid words summarize what Jonathan did for David: 'Now Jonathan spoke well of David to Saul his father...' (19:4). The essence of what Jonathan said to Saul was this: 'David has done you good. Why should you do him harm?'

Jonathan had surrendered to the grace of God at work in David (18:1-4). So his testimony to Saul is emblematic of the testimony of a child of God to the truth of God.

This is the main way in which God preserves his truth. Yes, he can and does use the evil designs of the wicked from time to time, but God primarily preserves his cause through his children testifying of the grace of God to a dark world. We can say of Christianity what Jonathan said of David: 'It has done you good. Why should you do it harm?'

The final means God used to preserve David was *the direct intervention of his Spirit*. When Saul went to Ramah the Spirit

of God fell upon him and caused him to prophesy. This intervention of the Spirit did not make Saul a child of God, but it
did temporarily suspend his evil designs against David.

As we read the history of the church, we find it is replete
with sudden, surprising interventions of God's Spirit. We have
a word to describe such interventions. We call them 'revival'.
J. I. Packer defines the term in this way: 'It is an experience in
the life of the Church when the Holy Spirit does an unusual
work. He does that work, primarily, amongst the members of
the Church; it is a reviving of the believers... Suddenly the
power of the Spirit comes upon them and they are brought
into a new and more profound awareness of the truths that
they had previously held intellectually, and perhaps at a deeper
level too. They are humbled, they are convicted of sin, they
are terrified at themselves. Many of them feel that they have
never been Christians. And they come to see the great salvation of God in all its glory and to feel its power. Then, as the
result of their quickening and enlivening, they begin to pray.
New power comes into the preaching of the ministers, and the
result of this is that large numbers who were previously outside the Church are converted and brought in.'[1]

When a revival comes it does not convert all who are unbelievers, but it does so change the whole tone of society that
evil is put on a chain and hostility towards Christians is temporarily suspended.

Saul's attempts on David's life must have been very perplexing and distressing to David, but they are full of comfort
and encouragement for us. From those attempts we see how
we should respond to the hostility of our own time. We should
trust God to overrule and use the evil of men for his own
purposes. We should continue to bear witness to our Lord
even in the midst of hostility. And we should pray fervently for
God to intervene in such a mighty revival that evil will subside
and hostility will be temporarily suspended.

7.

When God's arrows fall beyond us

1 Samuel 20

David stood by the stone Ezel. There he waited and watched. It was his stone of destiny. Jonathan was to determine whether his father, Saul, still harboured murderous intentions towards David. If so, David would have to flee. If not, David would be able to return to his normal routine.

David and Jonathan had agreed upon a signal. If it was safe for David to return Jonathan would shoot three arrows and call out to the lad with him, 'Look, the arrows are on this side of you; get them and come...' (v. 21).

But if Saul still harboured malice towards David, Jonathan would shoot the arrows and shout to the lad, 'Look, the arrows are beyond you...' In that case David would know he must flee (v. 22).

In either case, it was important that David should not be seen in the field with Jonathan. This was obviously important if Saul still harboured hatred towards David. Saul knew how Jonathan and David felt about each other and he certainly would not have hesitated to send someone to follow Jonathan to David's hiding-place with orders to seize David.

It was also important even if Saul was ready to forgive and forget. David and Jonathan had contrived a lie about David's whereabouts. David was supposed to be in Bethlehem at this time (v. 6). If his presence in the field were to be reported to

Saul, the king would resent the deception and probably forget his new resolve and return to his old hostility towards David. Let this remind us that deception is never the right course for the child of God.

The hours must have dragged slowly for David as he waited by the stone Ezel. There was nothing he wanted more fervently than to return to his wife and to his service to his nation and his king. Yes, he had been anointed to be King of Israel, but he harboured no evil intent towards Saul. He was quite content to wait for the throne to become his and to simply serve Saul while he waited.

How he must have hoped Jonathan's message would be: 'The arrows are on this side of you.' But what if that was not the message? What if Jonathan called out, 'The arrows are beyond you'? Jonathan had made it clear that this message would mean that David must flee. And Jonathan had tacked on seven little words that David could not get out of his mind: 'for the Lord has sent you away' (v. 22). In other words, if the arrows were shot beyond the lad, it would mean God's plan was for David to flee and to be pursued as a fugitive.

What a life! Living with constant pressure, never knowing when he might be sighted and the sighting reported to Saul, separated from his wife and from his dear friend Jonathan, forced to stay in isolated, desolate places — David would face all of this if he became a fugitive. It was a life of emotional distress and physical hardship.

God's strange providence for David

David's hours of waiting finally came to an end. He could hear the voices of Jonathan and the lad in the distance, and he knew it would not be long now before he had his answer. Hope must have welled up within him. If only the message was favourable,

he would slip back to Bethlehem, be seen there and then report to Saul. Surely, God did not want him to go through the
hardship and suffering of a fugitive.

David could hear the arrows whizzing by. Then came those
dreaded words: 'Is not the arrow beyond you?' (v. 37).

Could this be God's plan for his life? Why would the God
who had selected him to be king and so signally blessed him
with the victory over Goliath now consign him to such a terrible
life? Why should a child of God face hardship and disappointment? God had the power to remove Saul quickly! With one
stroke he could spare David much hardship and fulfil his promise to bring him to the throne. Why did not God do the one
thing that seemed to make so much sense? Why did he allow
something that did not make any sense at all — permitting
Saul to reign and David to live as a fugitive?

But there was no time for such thoughts now. He knew he
must be on his way, but he could not bring himself to do so
without saying farewell to Jonathan. So ignoring his intention
not to be seen, he ran to Jonathan for a tearful goodbye
(vv. 41-42).

God's strange providences for us

We know about this stone Ezel, don't we? We all spend a
good bit of our time waiting, watching and hoping there. And
so very often we find, like David, that the arrows of God's
providence fall beyond us — beyond our ability to understand,
beyond our prayers for a different direction, beyond our desire to simply serve the Lord in the peaceful pattern of normal
living.

Sometimes the arrow that goes whizzing by has the words
'serious illness' written on it, and we wonder why the Lord
would send us into a life like that. Sometimes that whizzing

arrow carries on it the words 'loss of a loved one', and again we wonder why. Or it may have on it the words 'financial hardship', 'loss of career', 'misunderstanding of friends', or 'relocation in a community far from family and friends'.

What are we to do when the arrows of God's providence fall beyond us?

Trust the loving purpose of God

One thing we must do is trust the loving purpose of God in the strange providence.

As far as David was concerned, he did not need the experience of a fugitive. We always think we know what we need and what we do not. But God did not see things as David did.

It was true, of course, that God had already anointed David to be Saul's successor, but that did not mean David was ready to take the throne. There was this matter of going through God's finishing school. David had already given ample proof that he needed to matriculate in this school. His faith, so strong when he stood before Goliath, had faltered under Saul's relentless pursuit.

As this twentieth chapter opens we find David filled with fear. God has just miraculously intervened by sending Saul sprawling in a fit of prophecy. That in itself should have been enough to convince David that he had nothing to fear, that God would always preserve him in some way or other. But David's response to this intervention was to flee to Jonathan.

His conversation with Jonathan graphically depicts the slippage in his faith. He had little to say about God, but talked instead about being very close to death (v. 3). Evidently, David had reached the point where he was no longer sure God could be counted on to keep his promises.

So it was off to the wilderness with David. There God would wean him away from relying on his own wisdom and teach him to rely wholly on his word. The promise that David would become king would be fulfilled despite all the machinations of Saul and all the deprivations of the wilderness. Those who saw David during his months as a fugitive would probably have laughed at the suggestion that he would some day rise to the throne of Israel, but the power of the Word of God is such that it will prevail, no matter how unlikely this may seem.

We may be sure David did not want the life of a fugitive and he did not go happily into it, but he came to have a deep appreciation for it. That strange providence worked for his good. He was not very far into this life as a fugitive before he was able to write:

> You number my wanderings;
> Put my tears into your bottle;
> Are they not in your book?
> When I cry out to you,
> Then my enemies will turn back;
> This I know, because God is for me.
> In God (I will praise his word),
> In the Lord (I will praise his word),
> In God I have put my trust;
> I will not be afraid.
> What can man do to me?
>
> (Ps. 56:8-11).

Seek God instead of an explanation

Another thing that will help us when God's providence mystifies and baffles us is to remember to seek him instead of an explanation.

'The chief end of man,' says the *Westminster Confession*, 'is to glorify God and enjoy him for ever.' We are easily trapped into thinking God can only be our priority when our circumstances are good, but he is to be our priority no matter what our circumstances are. We are to love him and serve him when times are good and when times are bad.

David learned this. During his fugitive days he reached the point where he could say:

> O God, you are my God;
> Early will I seek you;
> My soul thirsts for you;
> My flesh longs for you
> In a dry and thirsty land
> Where there is no water...
> Because your loving-kindness is better than life,
> My lips shall praise you.
> Thus I will bless you while I live
>
> (Ps. 63:1,3-4).

May God help us to come to that point where we see what David saw — God is what counts, no matter whether our circumstances are calm and peaceful or boisterous and turbulent. May God help us to reach that point where we can say with Paul, 'For to me, to live is Christ ... ' (Phil. 1:21).

When we do arrive at the point where we occupy ourselves with God and his glory instead of with our own trials, we find the trials are much easier to bear.

Are the arrows of God's providence falling beyond your ability to understand today? Don't try to read the book of his providence. He will read that to you later in heaven. Instead read that book in which he declares his love for you, the Bible, and know he has a loving purpose for the trials that come your way. And when the trial comes seek to occupy yourself with him.

If we do these things we shall be able to see the wisdom of William Cowper's lines:

Judge not the Lord by feeble sense,
But trust him for his grace;
Behind a frowning providence
He hides a smiling face.

8.
Christians at Nob

1 Samuel 21

I don't mind admitting that I am afraid of some places. High-crime areas, the office of a tax auditor, places where bitterness and dissension reign — all scare me. I am also afraid of Nob. Yes, Nob scares me.

The village of Nob was just a wide spot on the road in ancient Israel. The tabernacle of God was located there after having been moved from Shiloh. The priests of the tabernacle and their families lived there. As David fled from the withering hatred of Saul, he stopped at Nob to seek food and a weapon.

When David came to Nob he was a man who was going downhill spiritually. Even though God had preserved him at every turn, his faith had begun to flicker and falter. He was filled with fear and spoke as if God had died and as if he, David, were about to follow suit (20:3).

We always pick up speed going downhill, and David definitely picked up speed at Nob. He did not hit rock bottom there, but we can safely say he left there with a full head of steam.

What David did at Nob

At Nob, this great man David acted in a very distressing way.
A child of God, who so obviously had the hand of God upon
his life, stooped to vile, foul behaviour, behaviour that was
completely out of keeping with his calling as a child of God —
disgusting behaviour. What did David do?

The compromise of convictions

For one thing, he compromised his convictions on what is right
and wrong. David knew and loved the law of Moses. And the
law of Moses said, 'You shall not bear false witness...' (Exod.
20:16).

But David bore false witness at Nob. When Ahimelech
the priest opened the door to David it was with a trembling
hand. Everyone in Israel knew about Saul's hatred of David.
Everyone knew, therefore, that befriending David was taking
the fast lane to the cemetery. Well might Ahimelech tremble!

David knew Ahimelech was afraid and he knew he had
every right to be afraid. Integrity demanded that David say,
'Ahimelech, I am in desperate need of help, but helping me
may be the same thing as signing your death warrant.'

But David did not speak with integrity. He looked Ahimelech in the eye and essentially said, 'There's nothing to be afraid
of, Ahimelech. The hostility between me and Saul? That is all
in the past. In fact, the king has sent me on a secret mission'
(v. 2). These are shocking words from a man who had been so
blessed and used by God!

The lack of concern for others

Nob was not only the place where David compromised; it was
also the place where he shrank his world down to his own
size.

It was bad enough for David to put the life of Ahimelech in jeopardy, but Ahimelech was not alone at Nob. Other priests were there and their wives and children as well (22:19). David's presence endangered all of them, but David did not care.

All that mattered to David was David. At this point, David's world began at the top of his head and ended at the soles of his feet. These are very small parameters for the world of one who had been anointed to rule those who were to be a blessing to the whole world (Gen. 12:1-3).

The ignoring of hostility

Nob was also the place where David forgot about the scrutiny of a hostile, unbelieving world. He completely ignored what Christians down through the centuries have called their 'testimony'.

Doeg the Edomite was there. Later David would say, 'I knew that day, when Doeg the Edomite was there, that he would surely tell Saul' (22:22). Tell Saul he did, and Saul in a fit of rage sent him to Nob and had all the priests and their families slaughtered (22:18-19).

So Nob is the place of the backslider. I have been to Nob. Have you? Have you ever compromised your convictions and gone against what you knew to be the clear teaching of the Word of God? Have you ever shrunk your world down to the same size as yourself and acted without regard to the well-being of others? Have you ever forgotten that Christians are constantly observed by an unbelieving, hostile world eager to discredit us? If so, you have also been to Nob.

Why David did what he did

Why did David do it? Why did he throw integrity to the wind and tell a bare-faced lie? Why did he, who had once voiced such deep concern about the whole nation of Israel (17:26), suddenly shrink his world to his own size? Why did he ignore the malevolent, hostile presence of the pagan Doeg? Yes, a thousand times, why?

If we had been there and if we had been able to crawl inside David's mind and peer into his innermost thoughts, we probably would have heard the 'rationalizing machine' churning away: 'I have been so hurt and so mistreated and so misunderstood that I am justified in doing this.'

If that sounds familiar it is because we all have a 'rationalizing machine' that cranks out the same message from time to time: 'My situation is such that it justifies a new standard of conduct. My situation is such that it justifies lying. My situation is such that it justifies selfishness. My situation is such that it justifies ignoring my responsibilities.' And before we know it we have accepted a standard of conduct that we would once have found totally repugnant.

Living at Nob today

Are you at Nob today? Can you list all the slights, all the hurts, all the mistreatment, all the misunderstandings that have come your way? Do you now use these things to justify behaviour you would once have scorned? Are you forgetting all about the welfare of your family and your friends because your world is no longer large enough for anyone except yourself? Are you ignoring your testimony as a Christian and engaging in behaviour that allows unbelievers to discredit the gospel?

If so, I have two words for you. The first is a word of warning. David's actions at Nob led to destruction. Nob is always the place of loss and sorrow. Stay there for a while and you will find it to be true. Compromise the clear teachings of

God's Word, live selfishly, ignore your testimony, and you will some day be made painfully aware of Nob's high price tag. Nob's bills pour in long after our stay there is over.

A man named Lot had his Nob, but it went by the name of Sodom. There Lot compromised his convictions, lived for himself and neglected his testimony. And there Lot picked up an exorbitant price tag. He lost all of his family except two daughters, and they lived only to heap disgrace and heartache upon him (Gen. 19:1-38).

Bob Jones puts it like this: 'Oh, what Lot lost! He lost all his cattle, all his land... His wife was gone. He lost his honour, lost his good name. He lost his reputation. He started a stream of sin and damnation that has come across the ages. But he lost something else... He lost fellowship with God.'[1]

Oh, backslidden Christian, Nob promises great things, but it delivers nothing but anguish and pain!

If you are living at Nob today, I also have a word of consolation and encouragement for you. Nob is not greater than God. God's grace is so great that he forgives the Christian who visits Nob. What a glorious word this is! Our God will forgive when we compromise our convictions, when we live for ourselves, and when we damage our testimony. The apostle John assures us of this truth with these priceless words: 'If we confess our sins, he is faithful and just to forgive us our sins, and to cleanse us from all unrighteousness' (1 John 1:9).

But be careful about this. Don't presume upon the grace of God. Don't be guilty of reasoning like this: 'If God forgives me when I sin, I can sin all I want and just ask God to forgive me.'

David would not allow us ever to think this way. He would have us understand that sin in the life of the Christian is always a very serious matter. Some of the saddest words in all the Bible were spoken by David after his actions in Nob came to fruition. He said to the only survivor of Saul's slaughter,

Abiathar, 'I have caused the death of all the persons of your father's house' (22:22).

It is true that the Bible never mentions this matter again, but it would be a grave mistake for us to think David simply wiped his actions at Nob from the slate of his mind with those words to Abiathar. We may rest assured that Nob stayed with him. It was there in those years in which he was driven from place to place by Saul. It was there when he finally came to the throne of Israel. It was there when he lay his body down to sleep.

There is a great and abiding lesson here for all of us. We can get out of Nob, but Nob may never get out of us. Do we understand this? We get out of Nob by repenting of our compromise and our selfishness, but the consequences of Nob may remain for a long time. Think of David's later affair with Bathsheba. He received God's forgiveness for that as well (Ps. 32), but the consequences of that sin lingered long after he was forgiven.

Think long and hard about this, dear Christian. Pulling away from godly living may seem very attractive and harmless enough. Don't be deceived. One minute in Nob is too long. If you are there today, get out. Tell God about your downhill slide, renounce it, ask his forgiveness and rejoice in his cleansing.

9.
A backsliding observed

1 Samuel 21:10 - 22:2

The closing verses of the twenty-first chapter of 1 Samuel are incredibly sad. Here a saint of God hits rock bottom.

It is sad when any child of God backslides, but no case of backsliding could be sadder than this. David was no ordinary man. In addition to being anointed of God to serve as the next king of Israel, he had been singularly blessed by God. God had given him a stunning victory over the fear-mongering Goliath. God had shielded him from the murderous machinations of King Saul. God had given him the friendship of Saul's son Jonathan to encourage and strengthen him.

Backsliding — a shocking thing

One would think such blessings would have been more than enough to keep David walking with God, but such was not the case. Like a stubborn mule, David took the bit in his mouth and forged blindly ahead into incredibly startling behaviour.

How are we to explain such a thing? We look at one page of David's life, and it seems all is well. Yes, he has his burdens and problems, but he is walking in faithful obedience to God. Then we turn the page, and all is different. This man who has been walking with God is suddenly running headlong down the path of ruin.

Every Christian can identify with David's abrupt shift. One Sunday we stand before our church family to declare our intention to serve the Lord. The next Sunday we find it difficult even to go to church.

What causes us to vacillate so much in our commitment to the Lord? In most cases, there is probably a combination of factors at work, but in David's case there seems to have been a single moment when he abruptly shifted to the wrong road. It was that moment when the arrows of God's providence fell beyond him (1 Sam. 20). Up to that moment, David had fondly nurtured the idea that the breach between him and Saul could be healed and their relationship restored. David wanted nothing more. He fervently hoped that Saul could be won over, that he could faithfully serve Saul until the latter died a natural death. At that time, David would be glad to be king.

When the arrows fell beyond David, he knew his hopes would not be realized. He was suddenly a torn man. On the one hand, he had a definite promise from God that he would serve as king. On the other hand, however, it looked as if he would perish by the hand of Saul (1 Sam. 20:3).

The providence of God seemed, therefore, to be at variance with his promise. Do we not often find the same thing to be true? Is it not true that our circumstances often make the promises of God seem uncertain?

We can visualize a war taking place in David. Faith argued that the promise of God was secure, that he must simply continue to seek God's face and do whatever God led him to do. But fear rushed in to tell David he had been a fool ever to believe the promise in the first place. If God intended him to be king, he would not be going through all this difficulty.

The battle was fierce but brief. Fear came out the winner, and David began to run. First, it was to Nob, where he not only lied to Ahimelech, but also showed callous disregard for the safety of all the priests and their families. And then it was on to Gath, a province of the Philistines and the home of Goliath!

What ironies there are in the life of sin! There was a time when David's zeal for his own nation was such that he disdained the land of the Philistines, but here he leaves the land of promise to take up residence among the Philistines. There was a time when David had such great confidence in God that he did not fear the sword of Goliath, but now God is far from his thoughts and he carries that same sword with him (1 Sam. 21:9). That sword could not help Goliath, but David now expects it to help him.

What did David hope to achieve by going to Gath? Only two things could result from his taking up residence there, and neither was good. If the Philistines took umbrage over the man who had killed their champion seeking refuge among them, they would either seek his life or run him out of their country. If, on the other hand, they accepted him he would be entrapped in an alliance with those who were the sworn enemies of his own people.

It was not long before the Philistines made their choice. The King of Gath evidently saw some political advantage in having David as a resident and was prepared to welcome him, but to the king's servants David was about as welcome as an outbreak of typhoid fever.

Backsliding — a painful thing

Terror

When David realized the Philistines were less than overjoyed to see him, he was terror-stricken (v. 12). He knew he had to do something at once or his hosts would quickly dispatch him from this life into eternity.

Such a fertile mind is seldom at a loss. So it was with David. He began to slobber and drool on himself and to scribble on the doors of the gate (v. 13). His actions achieved their desired result. The king was convinced David was mad and, having no shortage of madmen on his hands, quickly sent David on his way back to Israel (vv. 14-15).

We might find ourselves inclined to chuckle over David's clever ploy and the wry comment of Achish, but this whole episode is unspeakably sad and depressing. Here is the future king of Israel acting like a madman in the presence of his enemies! The man who stood calmly before Goliath because he was possessed with faith now acts like a maniac because he is possessed with fear.

Bitter recrimination

This, then, is the story of David's backsliding. It began when David allowed his circumstances to override his faith, when he began to walk by sight rather than by faith. It carried him to the depths of deception and callousness. When it was all over it left him as the object of scorn and ridicule of the pagan Philistines and, we may be sure, the object of self-loathing and bitter recrimination. How he must have winced when he looked back on his little sojourn in Gath, a sojourn that surely caused the Philistines to gloat! The God of David was evidently unable to comfort and sustain his servant in the midst of difficulties!

Backsliding — a temporary thing

We should rejoice that we can use that phrase 'when it was all over'. Children of God can and do backslide and, in the course of backsliding, they can sink to incredible depths. But backsliding is not the final word in the life of the child of God.

Gordon Keddie says of David's experience in Gath, 'Like Jonah in a later generation, David was to find his flight arrested by an unseen hand and his steps redirected to the path of God's purpose.'[1]

Daniel M. Doriani puts it even more bluntly by saying, 'The Lord drove David out of Gath.'[2]

This is not to say that God approved of David's drooling and scribbling. The fact that something works does not mean it is of God. God used this evil to deliver David from the Philistines, but he could just as easily have used a calm, dignified statement from David on how wrong it was for him to seek refuge among them in the first place.

But how do we know God had anything to do with David's leaving Gath? The passage before us has absolutely nothing to say about God. But Psalms 34 and 56 do. And the superscriptions of those psalms tell us they were written by David about his experience in Gath.

Read Psalm 34 and you will find David saying:

The righteous cry out, and the Lord hears,
And delivers them out of all their troubles...
Many are the afflictions of the righteous,
But the Lord delivers him out of them all
(Ps. 34:17,19).

Do those verses sound as if there was any doubt in David's mind about how he escaped from Gath?

Look further at these two psalms, and you will find David stressing other truths such as the importance of trusting the Lord (34:8-11; 56:3,10-11), and the importance of telling the truth (34:12-13). Nob and Gath proved to be good teachers!

When David left Gath he went to the Cave of Adullam. This cave, near his boyhood home, not only provided David a place to hide from Saul, but also a place to experience personal renewal.

David penned two psalms there in the dark recesses of that cave, Psalms 57 and 142. In the former, David says:

I will cry out to God Most High
To God who performs all things for me.
He shall send from heaven and save me...

(Ps. 57:2-3).

Later in the psalm he adds: 'My heart is steadfast, O God, my heart is steadfast; I will sing and give praise' (Ps. 57:7).

In the second psalm written in the cave, David cries to the Lord, 'You are my refuge, my portion in the land of the living' (Ps. 142:5).

The words of these two psalms are, then, not just pleasant, theoretical words that sounded good to David as he whiled away his time in the lap of luxury. They were born in the crucible of hard, bitter experience. For a while David had doubted whether God would indeed perform all things for him, and he had relied upon his own wisdom. For a while his heart was not steadfast in devotion to the Lord. For a while David had not made the Lord his refuge and portion. In writing these psalms, then, David was admitting that he had been a colossal fool.

Every time we let our difficult circumstances obscure the loving-kindness of our heavenly Father and his faithfulness to his promises, we are, like David, playing the fool.

We may be inclined to think Nob, Gath and Adullam are just names on the maps in the back of the Bible, but they are, in fact, God's shorthand for a great spiritual truth — a true saint of God can sink to a dreadfully low state, but God's grace will pursue, preserve and, finally, renew him. If you have played the fool and run to Nob or Gath, I urge you to cast yourself afresh and anew on that grace today.

10.
Tiny pictures of tremendous realities

1 Samuel 22:1-5

We are often surprised as we read the Bible. When, for instance, we think we are simply reading unimportant historical details, we suddenly find ourselves face to face with great spiritual truths. We might say there are veins of gold gleaming and glittering in the rock of biblical history.

So it is with these verses. At first glance there seems to be nothing unusual or significant here. A group of malcontents gather around David as their captain. David spirits his parents away to Moab for refuge from Saul's hostility. At first sight, this seems to be just a straightforward account of events of no particular interest, but a closer look at these verses reveals glittering gold in the ore.

A picture of the sinner coming to Christ

Two rich veins of interpretation present themselves for our consideration. First, we may see in these verses a picture of the sinner coming to Christ.

This passage tells us the distressed, the discontented and those who were in debt flocked to David when they learned he was in hiding in the Cave of Adullam. We may gather, therefore, that the rule of Saul had engendered a great deal of hardship and stress among the people of the kingdom.

Those who joined themselves to David were seeking relief from the anguish and stress unleashed by Saul. They saw David as their rightful king, even though he was in exile, and they fled to him for refuge.

The situation in Israel at that time mirrors great spiritual realities. Just as there were two kings at that time, so there are in the spiritual world. The Bible calls Satan the god of this age. He rules and reigns over all of us by nature. When we come into this world, we are already part of his kingdom and under his dominion. The apostle Paul says we are 'by nature children of wrath, just as the others' (Eph. 2:3).

Satan's kingdom, like Saul's at the beginning of his reign, is impressive enough. It promises great things, but it delivers only hardship and anguish. Scripture affirms that the way of the unfaithful is hard (Prov. 13:15).

Most are content just to go along in Satan's kingdom. They see the wreckage and ruin caused by sin, but they simply choose to ignore it and forge ahead.

Others, however, find themselves growing increasingly dissatisfied and discontented with it all. The shiny gloss of sin has grown dim. They find themselves disillusioned and dissatisfied with what Satan's kingdom has to offer. And they start thinking there must be something more to life, something far better. They realize they must some day leave this world, and they wonder where their allegiance to the kingdom of Satan will leave them at that time.

How is it that citizens of Satan's kingdom become dissatisfied and disillusioned with it? Is it a result of their own keen insight and understanding? The Bible attributes all to the grace of God. It is God who creates disillusionment with Satan's kingdom. It is God who convicts the sinner of sin, righteousness and judgement (John 16:7-11). It is God who causes the sinner to see the depth and guilt of his sin. It is God who makes the sinner to understand that he can never hope to stand in God's holy presence while still in his sins. It is God who points the sinner to the garment of perfect righteousness that has been provided by Jesus Christ, the Son of God. It is God who causes the sinner to see that Satan is a defeated foe, that he is destined to an eternity of woe and that he, the sinner, must either break with Satan or share his woe. It is, of course, possible for a person to become disillusioned and dissatisfied with the things of this world and not be undergoing a work of God's grace, but everyone who experiences a true work of grace will experience this discontent.

As God's work of grace creates dissatisfaction with this world it also causes the sinner to hear and rejoice in the good news that there is another king and another kingdom. This King is not recognized by this world even though he is its rightful King. He is, as it were, a king in exile. But those who are familiar with his kingdom say that, unlike the kingdom of Satan, it is a kingdom of peace and joy. It is none other than the kingdom of the Lord Jesus Christ.

There is a period of intense struggle but, finally, the sinner who, by God's grace, becomes discontented and disillusioned with Satan's kingdom makes the break and flees to Jesus Christ.

It is, to be sure, a most costly decision. Those who left Saul's kingdom to join David left behind many comforts and conveniences and entered into a life that entailed sacrifice and suffering, but the peace and joy of being a follower of David far surpassed the hardships involved.

So it is with all those who, by the grace of God, leave Satan's kingdom for Christ's. They must leave the world behind and enter upon a life of cross-bearing, but the peace and joy the followers of Christ find far outweigh the difficulties of the Christian life.

The question that confronts each of us is this: which kingdom are we in? There are only two, Satan's and Christ's, and all of us belong to one or the other. If you are in Satan's kingdom, I beseech you to open your eyes to take a long, hard look at it. Are you really finding deep peace and abiding joy under Satan's rule? Or are you finding that the life of sin does not satisfy?

I have good news for all citizens of Satan's kingdom who find their deepest longings are unsatisfied. King Jesus stands with arms open wide saying, 'Come to me, all you who labour and are heavy laden, and I will give you rest. Take my yoke upon you and learn from me, for I am gentle and lowly in heart, and you will find rest for your souls. For my yoke is easy and my burden is light' (Matt. 11:28).

We must not leave this matter without observing one more thing. The Bible emphatically declares of all those who left Saul for David that the latter 'became captain over them' (v. 2). So it is with Christ. If you come to him, he becomes your captain. You cannot live as you want. He is your Lord and Master, and you must constantly seek to obey him.

A picture of the saint walking with God

If the discontented gathering around David pictures the sinner coming to Christ, David going down to Moab pictures for us the saint walking with God (vv. 3-5).

What a profound renewal David experienced in the Cave of Adullam! Prior to arriving there, he was sadly backslidden. But there in the dark recesses of that cave the frostiness of his heart melted away and he began again to walk as a child of God should.

We may note three things about David at this point in which he was walking with God.

Communing with the Lord

As we saw in the previous chapter, David penned two psalms while in the Cave of Adullam. A quick glance at these psalms reveals that the floodgates of prayer were opened in David's

life there in the cave. In one of these psalms he writes, 'I will
cry out to God Most High, to God who performs all things for
me'   (Ps. 57:2)

In the other of these two psalms, he says:

I cry out to the Lord with my voice;
With my voice to the Lord I make my supplication.
I pour out my complaint before him;
I declare before him my trouble

(Ps. 142:1-2).

It is a fundamental law of the Christian life that there is no
spiritual renewal apart from earnest, fervent prayer that con-
fesses sin and lays hold of the mercy of God.

Trusting God for the future

Secondly, we can see David trusting God for the future. As
we look at David taking his parents to Moab, we find him
freely acknowledging God as the director of his paths. This is
evident in his words to the King of Moab — words to the
effect that he was waiting to see what God would do for him
(v. 3).

When spiritual renewal comes, the language of faith re-
places the language of doubt. While in the grip of doubt, David
went to Nob and Gath, and in each place he acted in unbeliev-
ably vile ways. But now David is walking with God again and
there is absolutely no doubt in his mind that God is going to
fulfil all his promises.

David now understands his role to be almost that of a spec-
tator. God's promises are so certain and sure that he can simply stand on the sidelines and watch God work. What a refreshing way to look at life! My life is God fulfilling his promises and achieving his purpose!

Obeying God

Finally, we can see David obeying God. The prophet Gad was one of those who had joined himself with David. In these verses we find Gad giving David a word from the Lord and David obeys without hesitation (v. 5).

The three traits David demonstrated in verses 3-5 will be characteristic of all of us who are walking with God. We will realize God is providentially working all things together for his glory and our good and we will not question his working but will rejoice in it. We will have great faith that God is guiding us, even though we may not be able to see his hand at work. And we will be quick and ready in our obedience to the Word of God.

The two pictures we have drawn from these verses deal with each and every one of us. There are only two categories of people in this world — those who do not know the Lord and those who do.

The first picture is for those who do not know the Lord. It beckons all such to break with the unsatisfying kingdom of Satan and make Christ their captain. Please heed its voice!

The second picture is for those who know the Lord. It beckons us to walk as Christians ought to walk. May God help each of us to heed its voice.

Together these pictures present the key to finding true happiness and joy in this life. It is a matter of submitting to Christ as our captain and walking with him in gratitude, faith and obedience.

11.
Coping with sour, vexing circumstances

1 Samuel 23:1-13

David was a man with a serious dilemma. His own king, Saul, was murderously devoted to chasing him down and ending his life. If David had harboured the slightest hope that Saul might relent in his hostility, it was dealt a fatal blow when Saul ordered the slaughter of all the residents of Nob (1 Sam. 22:6-23). (What sharp pangs of conscience David must have felt over Nob! His irresponsible conduct there had caused Saul's bloody rage.)

David's situation was worsened by the fact that his status as a fugitive had brought great hardship upon others. His parents had been obliged to pull up roots and go to Moab (1 Sam. 22:3-4).

His situation was made still worse by the responsibility that had devolved upon him. Hundreds of men and their families had cast in their lot with him, and he felt responsible for their well-being. The pressure of making good decisions must have weighed very heavily upon him.

If a team of consultants could have been dispatched to do a study of David's circumstances at this time, they might very well have said, 'David, one thing is in your favour — things can't get any worse.'

David was, then, in the midst of what one writer has called 'desolate, trying times'.[1] Have you found yourself in such times?

Are you in such times now? Are your circumstances contrary? Do you find yourself saddled with the double burden of personal hardship and awesome responsibility? Do you find yourself drawing some meagre comfort from that well-worn line: 'Things can't get any worse'?

This passage of Scripture comes to burdened, vexed people to give principles that will strengthen and encourage them.

The danger of losing sight of others

The first principle that emerges from this account is this: we must not let our circumstances blind us to the needs of others.

While David was pressed on every side by problems, he received, like a bolt from the blue, disturbing news that the village of Keilah was being raided by the Philistines.

In normal times we would expect the man who had earlier expressed fervent zeal for the nation of Israel (1 Sam. 17:26) to be concerned about even a small part of it. But David was not in normal times, and we would not be inclined to blame him if he had dismissed the situation at Keilah with these words: 'I've got enough problems of my own. I don't need this.' Or he could have said, 'Why come to me? Saul is the King of Israel. Let him deal with it.'

Excuses were ready at hand for David, but he did not let his personal problems and pressures cause him to lose sight of the needs of others.

Have we learned the lesson David teaches here? Or do we allow our burdens and responsibilities so to occupy us that we scarcely have a thought about the needs of others? When trials and afflictions pour in upon us, the temptation is great to withdraw from others and sit in lonely misery while we lament and bemoan what has befallen us.

In so doing, we close to ourselves an avenue of strength

and help. Those who do as David did soon discover that in helping others we help ourselves. As we give ourselves to meeting the needs of others, we find ourselves gaining a new perspective on our own problems. And, mysteriously enough, in expending strength to help others we find renewed strength to deal with our own difficulties.

David's action in freely taking on himself the plight of the village of Keilah ought to cause us to think of the Lord Jesus Christ who freely took on himself the plight of his people. As David girded on his sword to defeat the Philistines and become the saviour of Keilah, so Christ, the mighty captain of our salvation (Heb. 2:10), girded on his sword to decisively defeat Satan on the cross to become the Saviour of his people (Col. 2:15).

While David's protection of Keilah was just for a short time, Christ's protection of his people is constant and never-ending. Although defeated, Satan still conducts a warfare against the people of God. The world, the flesh and death menace them as well. But no enemy shall finally have the victory over them because of their protecting Christ. He is 'mighty in battle' (Ps. 24:8). He is in the midst of his people as 'the Mighty One' who will save (Zeph. 3:17). He is the one whose garments are red with the blood of his enemies, so red that his appearance is like that of someone who has been treading grapes in the winepress (Isa. 63:1-6). He gives his people the strength and the grace to do combat against their enemies. He provides an armour that is sufficient for their spiritual warfare (Eph. 6:10-20).

The church is in hostile territory now, but she will not remain there. Her mighty, protecting Christ will finally come to receive his bride unto himself. He will come from his ivory palaces with his sword girded upon his thigh; his arrows will be sharp in the hearts of his enemies as he administers their final defeat, and he will take his people past those enemies to be with him for ever (Ps. 45:3-5).

The danger of wrong counsel

That brings us to a second principle for this matter of dealing with difficulties — that is, refusing to let our circumstances cause us to listen to wrong counsel.

As soon as David received word about the crisis in Keilah, he sought the guidance of the Lord. When David went through the spiritual blackout that took him to Nob and Gath, God was far from his thoughts, but his experience of renewal in the Cave of Adullam had caused him to walk again with a keen consciousness of God.

How did David seek God's guidance? We know the prophet Gad had provided guidance for him when he was still in the cave (22:5), and we assume that David made use of him again on this occasion.

There is some debate over whether the priest Abiathar was with David at this point. The closing verses of chapter 22 indicate that he was, but we are later told that Abiathar 'fled to David at Keilah' (v. 6). Hebrew scholars Keil and Delitzsch take that phrase to mean that Abiathar arrived as David was deciding to go to Keilah and accompanied him there.[2] If so, no doubt David made use of the ephod that Abiathar carried with him. We know David made use of it after he arrived in Keilah (v. 9).

The ephod was a garment that included what was known as the 'Urim and Thummim'. This was a small pouch containing two flat objects. One side of each was called 'Urim', which means 'curse'. The other side of each was designated 'Thummim', which means 'to be perfect'. If both sides turned up 'Urim' when the priest drew out the objects, the answer was negative. If both turned up 'Thummim', the answer was positive.

This was one form of guidance God employed in the Old Testament. The primary way God guides his children today is through his written Word. When David needed guidance, he was able to say, 'Bring the ephod here' (v. 9). When we need guidance we are able to say, in the words of Matthew Henry, 'Bring hither the Bible.'[3]

When David posed the question of whether he should attack the Philistines, the answer was positive. The guidance he sought had been provided. But just then he was also given guidance he had not sought. Some of his men sidled up to him with these discouraging words: 'Look, we are afraid here in Judah. How much more then if we go to Keilah against the armies of the Philistines?' (v. 3).

David, then, had competing counsels ringing in his ears. On one hand was the voice of divine guidance. On the other hand was the voice of human wisdom. And the great question he had to settle was this: 'Which voice do I heed?'

David did a wise thing. He went back to enquire of the Lord to be sure he had not misunderstood the Lord's message (v. 4). But when he determined that the Lord had indeed commanded him to attack the Philistines, he did what the Lord said.

This experience finds parallels in our own lives. We no sooner find God's Word clearly laying out the path we should follow than we immediately hear voices that contradict it. They are reasonable and persuasive voices that tell us we are mistaken to believe the Word of God. They either suggest there is no such thing as a word from God, or they suggest we have misconstrued or misinterpreted it.

What shall we do when we are faced with competing voices? There certainly is nothing wrong with going back to the Word of God to make sure we have not misinterpreted it, but our final resting-place must be the same as David's — if God's Word clearly prescribes a certain course of action, we are to obey it regardless of what other voices say.

Are you surrounded with perplexing, vexing circumstances?

There is guidance, strength and comfort to be found in the Word of God. Believe it. Make use of it. Read and study it in private. Go to the house of God where it is preached and taught.

Through my years as a pastor, I have been astonished to see many Christians stop going to the house of God when difficulties set in on them. We always need to be in the house of God, and especially in times of trial.

God did not design Christianity to be a fair-weather faith. In other words, he does not intend us to practise our faith only when things are going well and then cast it aside in times of difficulty to embrace messages that contradict it. God designed Christianity as a sea-worthy vessel that can withstand the storms of life.

One would never know this by looking at some professing Christians. As soon as a storm hits, they seem to abandon ship. They run from God and the church at the very time they most need to be running towards both. David arises from the pages of Scripture to remind us to heed the Word of God when we are in the midst of vexing circumstances.

The danger of bitterness

There is one more principle for us to glean from David on this matter of dealing with trying circumstances: we must not allow the failures of others to embitter us.

An astounding thing happened to David after his victory over the Philistines at Keilah. The Lord told him the men of Keilah would hand him over to Saul if he stayed in the city. Such gratitude!

Although he was the Lord's anointed king, David had to travel the road of suffering. In doing so, he prefigures the Lord Jesus Christ, who endured indescribable sufferings in the very world over which he is finally to rule in glory.

David could have allowed this act of betrayal to lead him to take revenge upon the men of Keilah, or he could have allowed it to plunge him into depression and gloom. But David maintained his trust in the Lord. Hard on the heels of this experience and immediately after a similar experience of betrayal by the Ziphites, David wrote these words: 'Surely God is my help; the Lord is the one who sustains me' (Ps. 54:4, NIV).

When our circumstances are sour, it is very easy to expect others to sympathize with us and support us. And Scripture clearly teaches us to bear one another's burdens. But if your friends and your church fail — as they invariably will — don't get a chip on your shoulder. Remember your greatest resource in every situation of life is God himself.

We all have sour circumstances from time to time even as David did. David's handling of his difficult circumstances is full of instruction for us. It teaches us to serve others, to stay ourselves upon the Word of God and, if others fail us, to resist the temptation to add bitterness to the burden. Most of all, David's handling of his difficulties points us to the Lord Jesus Christ, who endured far greater sufferings.

12.
Reassuring grace

1 Samuel 23

If someone could have crawled into David's head in the days described in this portion of 1 Samuel, he could very well have found things somewhat chaotic and confused.

Why would David have been confused? On one hand, he had a clear and distinct promise from God that he was going to succeed Saul as King of Israel. On the other hand, he had circumstances that made the promise seem implausible and maybe even impossible.

It would have been easy enough for David to believe that promise when he killed Goliath and led Israel to victory over the Philistines, but things had gone steadily downhill since. David's circumstances were such that it looked as if he might very well not even survive, let alone rise to the throne.

What did David think about God's promise in these times of hardship and trial? Did he tell himself God was true to his promises, but that he had assumed something God had not intended? Maybe God had only intended his anointing to indicate that he would do something special for Israel (such as killing Goliath) and nothing more.

Or did David find himself revolving a more sinister notion in his mind? Could it be that God could not be trusted, that he had made a promise he had no intention of fulfilling? Or did God mean well, intending all the while to fulfil the promise he had made, but did he lack the power to do so? Perhaps God, like his creatures, made plans only to see them 'blown out of the water' by unforeseen circumstances.

In his darkest moments, David may even have wondered if there was a God at all. Maybe the whole business of Abraham, Isaac, Jacob, Moses, Joshua and Samuel was nothing more than the elaborate result of clever and vain imaginings. Perhaps the fathers of the faith had never heard from God or experienced him at all.

If these were indeed some of the thoughts that surged through David's mind, it is not hard to see the relevance of this part of his life. Most of us have to admit that similar thoughts have gone racing through our heads from time to time. Although none of us can claim a promise from God that we are going to rule a nation, all who are Christians do have promises from God. We also have our circumstances. And sometimes the circumstances make the promises seem shadowy and uncertain.

Before we know what has happened great questions and doubts are making themselves heard in our minds. Perhaps we misunderstood. Perhaps God is unfaithful or lacking in power. Perhaps Christianity is a farce.

All of us who have been assailed by such doubts should praise God for this twenty-third chapter of 1 Samuel. This chapter shows us some of the resources our gracious God makes available to his saints in the midst of their trials and afflictions. It shows us what God did for David and, in doing so, urges us to believe that God has resources for us in our times of trial. In this chapter God confirms his promise for David in several ways.

The gifts of royalty

First, the Lord gave David some things that could only be associated with royalty (vv. 1-13).

Before we ever come to these verses, we find David had already been blessed with one of the trappings of royalty — namely, the presence with him of the prophet Gad (22:5) and the priest Abiathar (22:20-23).

We should not take their presence lightly. The King of Israel was to be like no other king. He was to rule the nation according to the Word of God and, therefore, in close association with the prophets and priests.

The fact that David had these two men with him becomes very significant when we place it alongside the fact that Saul had neither prophet nor priest. He had alienated the prophets by invading their community to capture David (1 Sam. 19:18-24), and he had mercilessly commanded the slaughter of the priests (1 Sam. 22:18-19). This was a significant token that God was gradually stripping the kingdom away from Saul in order to give it, as he had promised, to David.

The opening verses of this twenty-third chapter add another indication that God's promise was intact. Word came to David that the people of Keilah were being raided by the Philistines. The protection of Keilah was a task that properly belonged to Saul, but God assigned the task to David. A man who callously butchered one village in his domain (1 Sam. 22:18-19) was obviously unfit to protect another!

It did not take much thought for David to realize what this meant. The fact that the Lord had assigned him a task logically belonging to Saul proved that God had not forsaken his promise.

The gift of a confirming visit

The second thing the Lord did to confirm his promise to David was to send Jonathan to visit him in the forest around Ziph (vv. 15-18).

Jonathan's visit came at just the right time for David. He had obeyed God's command to deliver Keilah, but his victory there was tempered by the stunning readiness of the inhabitants of Keilah to deliver him to Saul (vv. 12-13).

It is not hard to visualize doubt once more seizing hold of David's mind. The people of Keilah were from David's own tribe of Judah. If his near countrymen were willing to betray him, what chance did he have to survive?

David did not have long to brood over such things before Jonathan appeared on the scene. What did Jonathan do for David? The Bible says he 'strengthened his hand in God' (v. 16). How did Jonathan do this? He emphatically stated his own conviction of the truthfulness of God's promise: 'Do not fear, for the hand of Saul my father shall not find you. You shall be king over Israel… ' (v. 17).

We may rest assured that David was greatly helped by this visit, because weak, trembling faith is always strengthened by being in the presence of strong faith.

Jonathan's visit is recorded for us so that we might marvel at the tender grace of God towards David, grace that followed him into the depths of despair and lifted him out. But we are remiss if we do not also come away from this passage with an understanding of how vital it is for us to be doing for others the same thing that Jonathan did for David.

This vital ministry of encouragement is often much neglected among us. We are all so absorbed with ourselves and our own needs and problems that we fail to note those who desperately need our encouraging presence.

In addition to teaching us the value of encouragement, Jonathan teaches the means of encouragement. He did not merely tell David to think positively about his situation, but he pointed him to the Lord and urged him to keep trusting in the Lord's promises.

Dale Ralph Davis uses Jonathan's visit to David to make

this observation: 'We best encourage not by being cuddly with people but by reminding them of the promises of God. Encouragement from God for the people of God comes from the word of God.'[1]

The gift of continuing protection

The things we have looked at were more than enough to confirm God's promise to David, but God went even further and gave David protection from Saul (vv. 14,19-29).

Verse 14 gives us a general statement about this protecting care of God. Each day the Lord surrounded David with his protecting care. Saul sought David each day, and each day the Lord frustrated his plans.

In addition to that general statement, this chapter includes a special, remarkable instance of God protecting David from Saul (vv. 19-29).

This episode took place as a result of the Ziphites' betrayal. The upshot of it is that David and his men escaped Saul and his superior force by a hair's breadth. Only a mountaintop separated the two when news of a Philistine invasion compelled Saul to give up the chase.

Was this sheer luck for David? Some might think so, but the believer knows better. The unbeliever's 'luck' is the hand of God to the believer.

Keith Kaynor mentions five things that had to happen in order for David to escape what seemed to be certain death. First, the Philistines had to decide the time was right to invade. Second, a messenger had to be dispatched to fetch the king. Third, when the runner learned that the king was absent from the palace, someone had to be on hand who knew where he was. Fourth, the runner had to have additional directions when he arrived in Ziph, or he would not have known to continue south to Maon. Finally, the messenger had to arrive at precisely the right time. A few minutes later and it would have been all over for David. [2]

David and his men knew exactly what had happened. They knew Saul was breathing down their necks and he was suddenly taken away. They knew because they named that place '*Sela Hammahlekoth*', the Rock of Escaping (v. 28).

David's battles with doubt and uncertainty were not entirely over (27:1), but at that particular time in his life he must have felt a great sense of calm sweep over him. God had demonstrated in unmistakable ways that his word was true and secure. And it was all because of God's gracious concern for his servant.

That grace of God is our resource today. Yes, we live in difficult times, times in which scepticism and doubt are running high. In such times, it is all too easy for us to waver in our faith and to vacillate in our commitment. But the grace of God that worked in us to make us his children will never let us go. God will continue to work in us until he finally brings us before the throne of his glory. Our faith may waver, but the grace of God will see to it that we persevere, and he will even use that wavering to make us conscious of how weak we are and of how much we need him.

13.
Restraining grace

1 Samuel 24

The grace of God is a many-splendoured thing. We need look no further than the life of David to see that.

We are unlike David in many respects. He occupied a unique and unrepeatable place in God's plan of redemption. David's reign in Israel was designed by the Lord to portray something of the nature of Christ's kingship. Specifically, David's conquering his foes and establishing the kingdom over which Solomon reigned pictures Christ conquering his foes and establishing the kingdom over which he himself rules. It was to David that the Lord gave the promise that his kingdom and throne would be established for ever (2 Sam. 7:16), a promise that was fulfilled in the Lord Jesus Christ.

While David held a place no other child of God can ever hold, the same grace that worked in his life is at work in each and every Christian.

With this chapter we come to a new section of 1 Samuel, and with it we are enabled to see a fresh aspect of the grace of God. Chapter 24 tells us of an opportunity David had to kill Saul. Chapter 25 relates the opportunity David had to take vengeance on the churlish Nabal. Chapter 26 lays before us another opportunity that David had to take Saul's life. In each of these instances the restraining grace of God is on display.

We do not often celebrate this restraining grace. It is not as glamorous and flamboyant as some of the other manifestations of grace. The grace of God that restores a prodigal saint from the depths of sin catches our attention and moves us, but the grace of God that holds the saint back from ever becoming involved in such sorrow and woe often escapes our notice.

One writer calls our attention to the greatness of restraining grace in this way: 'Suppose a house is on fire. We are glad if firemen, through heroic efforts, can save the building from total destruction. But wouldn't it be better if there had been no fire? ... We should never plunge into sin just to experience being pulled out of it. It is a great mercy of God when He keeps us from sin.'[1]

The evils from which David was restrained

As we look at the first instance of God's restraining grace in this portion of David's life, we must first note the evils from which God kept David.

Vengeful hands

First, we may say God kept David from the evil of vengeful hands. Saul, who had recently abandoned his pursuit of David to deal with an attack of the Philistines, was back on the trail with three thousand men in tow. He and his men were in an area honeycombed with caves, and David and his little band of men just 'happened' to be hiding in the very cave Saul chose to enter. Someone will say, 'What a coincidence!' Christians have another word for it — providence.

Many of David's men had no trouble interpreting God's design in this particular providence. God had steered Saul to that very cave so David could kill him. Someone whispered, 'This is the day of which the Lord said to you, "Behold, I will deliver your enemy into your hand, that you may do to him as it seems good to you." ' And all the other men whispered, 'Amen.'

But wait a minute! When did God ever say such a thing to David? There is no record of it. God had promised David would be King of Israel. He never said anything about when or how this would take place. He certainly had not said he would deliver Saul over for David to do with him as he pleased. Someone had apparently taken it on himself to read that into the promise.

I can hear the powerful voice of temptation whispering sweetly in David's ear: 'Saul doesn't deserve to live. He has tried to kill you on several occasions and he has already killed several innocent people in Israel. The sooner you come to the throne, the sooner you can bring to an end the chaos and hardship Saul has created.'

Humanly speaking, this would have been a case of 'justifiable homicide' if ever there was one. But the invisible hand of God reached down and restrained David. One corner of Saul's robe was cut off and that was all. David could go no farther.

Deceptive words

The second evil from which God restrained David is the evil of deceptive words (vv. 16-22). When Saul realized David had spared him, he tearfully admitted he had been wrong and openly acknowledged that David would one day become king over Israel.

Such words might have inclined David to think the breach had been healed and that he could once again resume a normal life, but he refused to be convinced by Saul's emotional confession and remained in the safety of the wilderness (v. 22).

Had David fallen for Saul's enticing words and gone back to Jerusalem, he would certainly have found himself in greater danger. The fact that he did not go is another testimony to the restraining grace of God.

The means by which David was restrained

That brings us, in the second place, to consider the means God used to restrain David.

A tender disposition

In the first instance — David's refusal to kill Saul — God restrained David by first giving him a tender, merciful disposition.

Refusing to kill Saul was proof enough of this disposition, but an even greater proof comes from what David said to his men after he had done nothing more than remove a small corner of Saul's robe: 'The Lord forbid that I should do this thing…' (v. 6).

Steadfast convictions

Regarding this matter of David's action in sparing Saul, we can also say God restrained David by working certain strong convictions or principles into his mind.

What were these convictions? A quick look at David's address to Saul (vv. 9-15) gives us the answer. For one thing, David was convinced that Saul was not on the throne by accident. God had placed him there. David by this time probably had very little respect for Saul as a man, but he had deep respect for the office he held.

On top of that, David had the conviction that God would eventually take care of Saul. He said, 'Let the Lord judge between you and me, and let the Lord avenge me on you. But my hand shall not be against you' (v. 12).

We often hear it said these days: 'Don't get mad, get even.' Those with that mentality are treading on ground God has reserved for himself. 'Vengeance is mine, I will repay,' says the Lord. Our minds naturally gravitate towards the New Testament when we hear those words (Rom. 12:19), but God taught this principle to the people of Israel long before David ever came along (Lev. 19:18; Deut. 32:35).

We can well imagine that ancient teaching flashing into David's mind as he nervously fingered his sword. His sparing of Saul was not just a sudden burst of noble idealism. It was a mind fed and informed by the Word of God that stayed his hand.

We surely cannot leave David's refusal to take revenge on Saul without seeing him here as a type of the Lord Jesus Christ who, although he was reviled, did not revile in return (1 Peter 2:23).

Discernment

Regarding the evil of deceptive words, we can only say God restrained David by giving him discernment. Saul's speech was, as we have noted, quite moving and persuasive, but David did not fall for it. He knew Saul had a long history of paying lip service to God and righteousness when it was expedient for him to do so. When his great resolves were inexpedient, Saul could turn just as quickly back to his wicked course.

We may attribute all of this to shrewdness on David's part, but David himself, in a psalm written at this time, gives all the credit for his safety to God: 'I will cry out to God Most High, to God who performs all things for me' (Ps. 57:2).

As we look at God's restraining grace at work in the life of David, we have to say this grace made him as harmless as a dove and as wise as a serpent (Matt. 10:16).

The harmless dove fluttered in his heart when the sword was in his hand. The wise serpent coiled its way through his mind as Saul spoke flattering, persuasive words. Those two qualities kept David from a double jeopardy. On one hand, they kept him from doing evil to Saul. On the other hand, they kept him from suffering evil at the hand of Saul.

Those of us who are Christians will never be able to appreciate all of this unless we understand that we are confronted with a situation very much like that which David faced. King Saul died, but his spirit lives on. There is in the society around us a deep, unremitting hostility towards all those in whom the grace of God is evident. What is this but the spirit of Saul?

Most of us have no trouble seeing it and feeling it. Our dilemma is how to deal with it. The answer is that the same combination that worked in David must work in us. We too must have harmless hearts and wise, discerning minds. We must so confront this godless age with the gentle spirit of Christ that those who oppose us will be completely disarmed and will have to admit that God is at work in us.

When the world is so disarmed by our goodness that it can no longer say anything evil of us, we must still be wise and discerning. Christians are often found in greater danger when Saul speaks with smooth words than when anger and hatred flash in his eyes. Kind words from an unbelieving world only mean its innate hostility towards the gospel has gone temporarily underground, not that it has gone away.

This combination of harmlessness and wisdom is one we are unable to produce at will. It is born in us as we, like David, inform our minds with the Word of God and as we walk in close fellowship with him.

14.
Restraining grace in the face of Nabal's insult

1 Samuel 25

The grace of God has three primary manifestations in our lives. The first of these is *redeeming grace*. Every Christian knows about this. This is the grace that reached down into the pit of our sin and condemnation, lifted us out and elevated us all the way to the spiritual riches and blessing we enjoy as part of God's family.

Then there is *restoring grace*. Those who experience the redeeming grace of God are not entirely freed from sin in this life. It is true that sin has been decisively defeated in their lives but, though defeated, it still conducts something like guerrilla warfare against the Christian, and it often succeeds in defeating him. Sin always interrupts and disrupts the Christian's fellowship with God. But God's grace is sufficient to restore to fellowship any Christian who comes to him in true confession.

The facet of God's grace that often escapes our attention is the one that is celebrated in chapters 24-26 of 1 Samuel. Here we find the *restraining grace* of God.

We have already looked at how God restrained David from killing Saul in the cave and from falling for his deceptive words (1 Sam. 24:1-22). With chapter 25 we come to another demonstration of that same restraining grace. Four times in this chapter we find explicit reference being made to God's restraining grace (vv. 26,33,34,39).

We might be inclined to think David had arrived spiritually after he stood so strongly against the temptations of chapter 24. But, lo and behold, the strong man of chapter 24 suddenly becomes very weak and faltering in chapter 25.

The stupidity of Nabal

It was all due to a man named Nabal. It is interesting that we are not told his name until verse 3. Verse 2 tells us that he was a rich, successful businessman, and only after that do we learn his name. Walter Brueggeman says, 'This way of introducing Nabal is precisely on target because Nabal's possessions precede his own person. His life is determined by his property. Nabal lives to defend his property, and he dies in an orgy, enjoying his property. Only after being told of his riches are we told his name.'[1]

And his name, strangely enough, means 'fool'. We are not told how he came to have such a name. We can perhaps imagine his parents becoming so exasperated with this lad that they began to call him by this derogatory name, but it is doubtful whether they would have given him such a name at birth. Perhaps his acquaintances gave him this name and it stuck.

The word 'fool' makes us think of silliness and crazy behaviour, but the word carries a quite different connotation in Scripture. Daniel M. Doriani says the word 'implies viciousness, atheism, and materialism'.[2] Dale Ralph Davis is more blunt. He calls Nabal 'a thick-headed clod' and 'a spiritual, moral, and social disaster'.[3]

Just what did the thick-headed Nabal do to provoke David? He refused to give David and his little band of men a small portion of his great bounty — and this at the traditional time for generosity, sheep-shearing time, and after having received protection and a very polite request from David (vv. 4-9,16,21).

The stupidity of David

David might have let the whole thing pass if Nabal had merely refused. But Nabal used the request as an occasion to 'vent his spleen' about David: 'Who is David, and who is the son of Jesse? There are many servants nowadays who break away each one from his master' (v. 10).

In other words, Nabal was suggesting that David was nothing more than a rebellious slave who had run away from his master. This was too much for David. He would take vile treatment from Saul because he was, after all, the anointed King of Israel. But Nabal was just an ordinary citizen of the kingdom — and not a very good one at that.

So the spark of an insult ignites the dry tinder of David's wrath, and he orders four hundred of his men to strap on their swords (v. 13). What were David and his men going to do? Were they just going to go down and take the food they so desperately needed? Were they going to take the food and also relieve Nabal of his head?

Consider this: David was not going to be content with mere food, or even with Nabal's head. In his anger, he swore that he and his men would kill every male in Nabal's household! (v. 22).

Let's step back and think about this for a minute. The King of Israel was to be like no other king. He was called to rule the people of Israel on behalf of God and in accordance with the Word of God (Deut. 17:14-20).

Saul had miserably failed in this sacred calling, and he failed because he was always putting his personal honour and feelings above the good of the kingdom.

David, on the other hand, was to be better than Saul (1 Sam. 15:28). He was to be the man 'after God's own heart'.

But here he is acting very much like Saul. Just as Saul had butchered the innocent priests of Nob because he was insulted by their supposed support of David (1 Sam. 22:6-23), so David stands ready to butcher innocent men in Nabal's household because their master has insulted him!

The wisdom of God

The same invisible hand that reached down and stayed David's hand in the cave reaches down again. There God used a tender disposition and a mind informed by scriptural principles to restrain David. Here he uses human instruments.

The first was an unnamed servant who discerned the danger and reported Nabal's insult to his wife Abigail (vv. 14-17). The second, of course, was Abigail herself, who collected a generous supply of food, rushed to meet David and encountered him blustering towards the accomplishment of his announced threat (vv. 18-31).

Abigail completely disarmed David and, it is to be hoped, shamed him. She readily took the blame, though none of it was hers (v. 24), freely acknowledged her husband's stupid, loutish behaviour (v. 25) and graciously offered the food she had brought (v. 27).

But she even went beyond all this to assure David that he would indeed become King of Israel just as the Lord had promised, and she urged him to come to the throne with a clear conscience (vv. 28-31).

David, then, received far more than food from Abigail. He received what he so critically needed at that moment — namely, the restraining grace of God in that she helped him come to his senses before committing a terrible act.

That would have been in and of itself more than enough to cause David to give praise to God, but God also gave him another dose of reassuring grace in that Abigail stated her firm faith that God's promises regarding him would definitely be fulfilled. There is always a surplus in God's bounteous grace.

This whole affair comes to an end with Nabal's sudden death (vv. 36-38) and David's marriage to Abigail (vv. 39-42). The Nabal that David had turned into a great crisis was, in the providence of God, nothing more than a temporary blip on the radar screen, and David was reminded of the truth that had guided him in the cave — vengeance belongs to the Lord.

Points of contact between then and now

What is there for us to gain from this account? What does it have to do with us?

One point of contact between this passage and us is this matter of *calling*. All Christians, like David, have been called to a high calling. No, we are not going to ascend to a throne and reign as he did. But we are called to be the people of God, people who demonstrate in their lives that they have received the mercy of God and are, therefore, made entirely new and different (1 Peter 2:9-10). Do we realize what an enormous privilege this is? There is in fact no higher privilege. It is better to be one of God's people than to be a king or a president without God.

Another point of contact has to do with *pressures and tensions*. As we seek to live in a manner consistent with our high calling, we are inevitably going to run into circumstances and people that exert pressure on us to forget our calling and give in to our feelings.

How many Christians have let some insulting Nabal so vex and disturb them that they have laid aside the Lord's work? How many Christians are staying away from God's house because they have been hurt by some thoughtless word or deed from someone else?

The sad thing is that those who have excused themselves from service because they have been hurt have themselves, if the truth were known, hurt and insulted others. Even sadder is this — hurt Christians who have laid aside their service to the Lord are even now hurting others. Sometimes they have right there in their own home children who do not know the Lord. A hurt Christian has little chance of bringing his children to the saving knowledge of Christ.

The final point of contact is this matter of *the restraining grace of God*. No Christian is prepared to live the Christian life and face all the pressures it entails until he understands that he can do absolutely nothing apart from the grace of God. We must daily remind ourselves of this. We must daily cast ourselves upon the words of Jesus: 'Without me you can do nothing' (John 15:5). We must cast ourselves daily upon God's promise to Paul: 'My grace is sufficient for you, for my strength is made perfect in weakness' (2 Cor. 12:9).

And we must daily cast ourselves upon God, pleading with him to strengthen us for our tasks and, when we, in our self-will, are about to plunge off into some calamity, to send an Abigail to restrain us.

15.
Restraining grace again preserves the life of Saul

1 Samuel 26

This chapter brings us to the end of a section in which the author exalts and magnifies the restraining grace of God. In chapter 24, God restrained David from killing Saul. In chapter 25, he restrained David from killing Nabal. In this chapter, he once again restrains David from killing Saul.

This account is so similar to the one in chapter 24 that many have concluded it is just a divergent account of the same incident. This view fails to take into account the substantial differences between the two accounts but, most of all, it fails to come to grips with an extremely crucial point. The temptation David faced in chapter 26 was greater than the one he faced in chapter 24. If David had killed Saul in the cave, everyone would have known it, and David would have come to the throne of Israel with a public taint upon him. But in the camp David could have killed Saul (or simply let Abishai do the work) and only his most trusted men would have known. This chapter, therefore, presents us with a greater temptation and a greater instance of the restraining grace of God than the first.

Let's set the scene. Saul has received another report from the Ziphites concerning the whereabouts of David. He sets out in hot pursuit with his army of three thousand men, enters the wilderness of Ziph and sets up camp 'in the hill of Hachilah' (v. 3). Through spies David has monitored Saul's movements and marked the place of his encampment (v. 4).

Then a daring scheme suggests itself to David — namely, making a night-time visit to the camp of Saul. Abishai readily agrees to join him in this risky venture, and the two of them set off (vv. 8-9).

Quietly and steadily they make their way through the camp until they come to where Saul is soundly sleeping. Abishai pleads for permission to take Saul's spear, perhaps the very one David had to dodge on a couple of occasions, and drive it right through Saul's heart. But just as the Lord had stayed David's hand in the cave, David now stays Abishai's hand.

What restrained David from giving Abishai permission to slay Saul? David gives the answer in verse 10: 'As the Lord lives, the Lord shall strike him, or his day shall come to die, or he shall go out to battle and perish.'

With that truth firmly fixed in his mind, David takes the spear from Abishai's hand, picks up Saul's jug of water and makes his way out of the camp (vv. 11-12). It seems it was no mere accident that David selected these two items. The spear was the symbol of protection. The refreshing water represented comfort. The removal of these items was a mute and solemn testimony to the fact that the power and comfort of the kingdom were to be removed from him and he was powerless to prevent it.

From a safe distance, David awakens the camp, calls Saul's attention to the spear and water-jug and hears Saul admit again that he had been wrong (vv. 13-21).

A sustaining truth

What does this passage offer us? First, it gives us a truth to comfort and sustain us in difficult times — namely, the truth of *God's sufficiency for his people*. There was no need for Abishai to pave the way to the throne for David by killing Saul. The Lord himself would take care of Saul in due time.

It is safe to say David's confidence in God's ability to overcome evil and preserve his own cause had been greatly confirmed by his recent experience with Nabal. Just as God 'struck
down' Nabal (1 Sam. 25:38), so he could 'strike' Saul. Dale
Ralph Davis says that David had learned that God can be trusted
'to handle both fools and oppressors when such matters are
left in his hands'.[1]

If God chose, on the other hand, not to strike Saul as he
had Nabal, there were still plenty of other ways for Saul to be
removed from the scene without David's hand being against
him. David mentioned the possibility that Saul might die a
natural death as well as the possibility that he would die in
battle (v. 10), which was in fact what would soon transpire
(1 Sam. 31).

If David was inclined to doubt God's sufficiency in taking
care of Saul, all he had to do was look at Saul's sleeping men
as he and Abishai made their way through the camp. This was
no ordinary sleep.

Think about this for a moment. Three thousand men were
in that army. Some of these men were obviously in the category of those who should not have been asleep. No army
sleeps without guards posted. Others would undoubtedly fall
into the category of those who could not sleep.

But on this night they all slept with a very sound sleep. It
was as if they had been anaesthetized. How are we to explain
such a widespread, deep sleep? The Bible gives us the explanation in these words: 'A deep sleep from the Lord had fallen
on them' (v. 12). As David and Abishai made their way through
those sleeping men, they must have realized God was working on their behalf.

The God who was sufficient for David is sufficient for us.
He says the same thing to us that he said to the apostle Paul:
'My grace is sufficient for you, for my strength is made per-
fect in weakness' (2 Cor. 12:9).

No matter what the people of God are called upon to face, they may rest on the sufficiency of God to do whatever he deems wise and best, and to give them strength in the process.

A much-needed balance

The truth of God's sufficiency is wonderful and glorious but, as is the case with all other truths, it can be distorted and misused. Some are inclined to use the doctrine of God's sufficiency, or God's sovereignty, to completely obliterate and remove man's responsibility. In other words, they argue, if God is sufficient there is nothing for us to do except sit back and let God do everything.

Sufficiency does not preclude difficulty

The account of David's visit to Saul's camp provides us with a much-needed balance on this matter. First, we can see that David did not take the sufficiency of God to mean he should have no difficulties.

David was in the crucible of many harsh difficulties, but the thing that bothered him most was the fact that he had been driven away and cut off from public worship at the tabernacle (v. 19). David's anguish over this poses quite a test for us. How much anguish do we feel over missing public worship?

David did not blame God for his difficulties. He did not say, 'God, if you really are sufficient for me, why am I going through all this hardship?' He recognized that God's sufficiency is channelled to his people, not in the way that seems best to them, but in the way he deems best.

Some have great difficulty here. They take a problem or a trial to the Lord and ask him to remove it, and it only gets worse. Suddenly, they find themselves wondering if God really is sufficient. Such people fail to understand that God often demonstrates his sufficiency for us in the midst of the trial, not through the removal of it.

Why did David have to race around the wilderness for months on end? Was it because God was not sufficient to remove Saul and fulfil his promises to David? No, it was because God was determined to demonstrate his sufficiency for David in the midst of hardship. He was not only interested in David coming to the throne of Israel, but rather in a man of God coming to the throne. The wilderness was an essential part of grooming that man.

Sufficiency does not negate the need for prudence

We can also learn from David this truth: God's sufficiency does not preclude the need to be prudent.

David trusted God, but he also used common sense. He waited until he was safely out of the camp and had put a good distance between himself and Saul's army before he called out to them (v. 13). It was also common sense to try to get Saul to understand that he, David, harboured no ill designs against him and to urge him to give up his foolish crusade. This David did (vv. 18-20). David was also being sensible when he refused to trust Saul on the mere strength of what the man said. So, after another moving speech from Saul, David refused the king's invitation to return home (v. 21) and 'went on his way' (v. 25).

A good example of trusting God and still acting responsibly is found in the life of Paul. In the midst of a great storm, Paul assured his shipmates that God would see to it that none of them would perish, but then he went on to tell them they must stay with the ship. In other words, they were not to respond to God's promise by saying, 'Oh, God is going to take care of us? Good. I'll throw myself into the sea and just let the waves carry me safely to shore.' The end, their safety, was to be achieved through the means God had established — staying with the ship (Acts 27:23-24,31).

It is also interesting to note that David did not take the sufficiency of God to mean he should not pray or trust God. In his words to Saul, he prays that his sufficient God will indeed deliver him out of all his tribulation (v. 24). Someone invariably wonders why we should pray if God already knows our needs and is sufficient for them. The answer is again this matter of ends and means. God does indeed know our needs and he is sufficient to meet them, but he has designed his sufficiency to flow to us through the diligent use of the means of prayer.

How are we to explain David's resting on the sufficiency of God without distorting or abusing it? It was the restraining grace of God that enabled him to do so. That same grace is at work in his people today.

16.
A fainting fit

1 Samuel 27-29

It would seem that David had every reason to be encouraged about his situation. He was fresh from a remarkable experience. Although Saul was surrounded by an army of three thousand men, David and Abishai had walked right into his camp and made away with his spear and water-jug.

This could not be explained in merely human terms. God had caused a deep sleep to fall on all Saul's army and, in doing so, forcefully demonstrated a great truth. Just as Saul was powerless to stop David from taking his spear and water-jug, so he was powerless to stop David from coming to the throne.

Saul seems to have fully realized this. The last thing he said to David was this: 'You shall both do great things and also still prevail' (1 Sam. 26:25).

David's faith should have been greatly bolstered by his visit to Saul's camp and by the king's subsequent confession. These were just the latest in what was now an impressive string of confirmations from the Lord. Yes, David was in the midst of significant hardships and afflictions, but it was abundantly clear that he would eventually come to the throne of Israel just as the Lord had promised. All he needed was patience. All of which is to say that David should have been very strong in his faith at this particular time.

But he was anything but strong. Hard on the heels of this latest spectacular confirmation of the certainty of God's promise, David — astonishingly enough — says, 'Now I shall perish some day by the hand of Saul' (27:1).

I could well imagine Saul saying, 'Now I shall perish some day by the hand of David.' But, in the light of all that God had done for David, the one thing I find it impossible to imagine is David saying he would perish at the hand of Saul.

If I may picture it in this way, David had two books in his hands. One was the book of God's promise that he would indeed become King of Israel, a book that had been abundantly confirmed. The other was the book of his own heart which told him the promise would not be fulfilled. David chose to read the book of his heart.

David certainly was not the only one to battle with this tendency. All Christians often find themselves inclined to rely on what their hearts say instead of relying on what the Word of God says.

Sadly enough, when David read the book of his heart he became a classic example of what former generations of Christians were prone to call 'a fainting fit'. This occurs when children of God have lapses in their faith and begin to walk far from God even though they have been signally and continually blessed by God.

The sad portion of David's life presented in this chapter is not here to cause us to heap criticism on David. It is here for us to learn some valuable and vital lessons, which, if diligently learned, will translate into great joy and peace, but if not learned, will translate into misery and woe.

The frailty of God's children

The first lesson we should learn is how frail all of God's children are. David was a great man, but here he has another fainting fit. I say 'another' because this was not the first and, as we shall see, it certainly was not the last.

Go back to chapter 21, and you will find David travelling to Nob where he lied to Ahimelech the priest. From there he went to Gath where he brought reproach upon the name of God by acting like a madman.

What was true of David is true of all of us who know the Lord. One minute we are on the mountaintop; the next we are in the valley. One minute we are rejoicing over God's care of us; the next minute we are doubting it. One minute we are firmly convinced of the truth of his Word; the next minute we are questioning it.

Oh, the vacillations and fluctuations that are possible in this life of faith! Every child of God knows about these things and grieves that although he is saved by grace, there is still within him a principle of sin that wars against him every step of the way.

Some would have us believe it is possible to 'arrive' spiritually. If we just walk by faith, they tell us, we can have continual victory in the Christian life. True enough! But how to walk in faith? Ah, there's the rub!

The ugliness of backsliding

Another lesson for us to learn from David's fainting fit is how ugly backsliding is. Would you see how ugly it is? Gaze upon David in this chapter.

Ugly words

First, his backsliding made him say some very ugly things. Feast your eyes on the words David spoke immediately after Saul left him. What incredible words they are! It was incredible that David should say he was going to perish some day at the hand of Saul. But what he went on to say is even more incredible: 'There is nothing better for me than that I should speedily escape to the land of the Philistines…'

The Philistines were inveterate enemies of Israel and her God, and here is the anointed King of Israel saying there was 'nothing better' in his life than to go down and join himself to these who were bitterly opposed to everything that he stood for.

Ugly behaviour

Secondly, his backsliding led him into some very ugly behaviour. David was not well received on his first trip down to Gath, but this time the red carpet was rolled out. The fact that he had six hundred fighting men with him may have had something to do with that. The Philistines were evidently happy to add this significant fighting force to their number.

After spending a short time in Gath, David requested King Achish to station him in a town by himself. He claimed to be unworthy to live in the royal city with the king, but he secretly desired to be away from the prying eyes of the king and his officials.

Here is where the ugly behaviour comes in. In Ziklag, David began to lead a double life. While professing loyalty to the Philistines, he began conducting raids against enemies of his own nation, some of whom were allies of the Philistines. All the while he was alleging that he was in fact fighting against his own people (27:10).

Such duplicity is despicable enough, but David went even further. In order to keep his double life hidden, he made sure there were never any survivors from any of his raids (27:9).

It is true that the people against whom David conducted these raids were among those upon whom God had pronounced judgement, but it is also obvious that David's actions against them were motivated by concern for himself rather than the glory of God.

An ugly dilemma

Thirdly, David's backsliding led him into a very ugly dilemma, which is detailed in chapter 29. The Philistines decided to launch an all-out assault against Israel, and Achish expected David and his men, as loyal Philistines, to carry their share of the load (29:1-2).

Fainting fits lead to fearful fixes! On one hand, David knew he could not fight his own people, the people over whom he was to rule! But if he refused to join the assault, the Philistines would know he was not the loyal subject he professed to be.

Child of God, look long and hard at the ugliness of David's backsliding and know that it is just as ugly and repulsive in our lives as it was in his. Backslide and you will say things that are completely inappropriate for a child of God, you will do things that are shameful and repugnant and you will finally end up in disaster!

The graciousness of God

We should be grateful that there is yet another lesson we can learn from David's fainting fit — namely, how kind and gracious God is.

Where do we find God in this episode? The only references to God in chapters 27 and 29 do not come from David at all but from the pagan Achish (29:6,9). In fact, it can be said that the whole reason David was in Gath is because God was not in his thoughts. Prior to this, he had been much occupied with God (23:2,4,10,11; 24:6,10,12,15; 25:32,34,39; 26:9,10,11, 16,19,20,23), but after chapter 26 David became occupied with his circumstances.

God may have been absent from David's talk and thought, but he was not absent from his life. God had special designs on this man, and he was not about to let Saul, the Philistines, or David's own pigheadedness keep him from realizing those designs.

But let's go back to the question. Where is God in these chapters? He is there in the question the Philistine lords spat at Achish: 'What are these Hebrews doing here?' (29:3). (By the way, the people of the world are always quick to see the incongruity when a child of God lives like the world.) God is also there in the angry statement of these Philistine lords: 'Make this fellow return ... and do not let him go down with us to battle...' (29:4). And he is there in their resentful recollection: 'Is this not David, of whom they sang to one another in dances, saying: "Saul has slain his thousands, and David his ten thousands"?' (29:5).

Yes, it was the invisible hand of the Lord that swept over the thinking of these men and caused them to demand David's dismissal. Through them the Lord extricated David from the predicament his backsliding had created. Such is the greatness of God, he can use even wicked people to accomplish his purposes. Dale Ralph Davis is right in saying of the Lord: 'He can make the enemy serve us as a friend. He not only prepares a table for us in the presence of our enemies but also has the knack of making the enemies prepare the table!'[1]

There was no doubt in David's mind about how he got out of the terrible dilemma he was in. After he and his men left the Philistine army they were confronted with another crisis, and we immediately read that David 'strengthened himself in the Lord his God' (1 Sam. 30:6).

We should not take this to mean that David just gave himself a good 'pep talk'. This was not David 'psyching himself up' or engaging in positive thinking. This strengthening was 'in the Lord his God'.

What we have here is David deliberately fastening himself on the Lord and his promises by doing for himself what

Jonathan had done for him on a previous occasion. When David was in the Wilderness of Ziph, Jonathan came to him and 'strengthened his hand in God' (1 Sam. 23:16). Jonathan did this by reminding him of the reliability of God's promise that he would some day rule over the nation. Jonathan said to him, 'Do not fear, for the hand of Saul my father shall not find you. You shall be king over Israel, and I shall be next to you. Even my father knows that' (23:17).

It is interesting that Jonathan added to the promise of God. God had indeed promised that David would reign over the kingdom, and that came to pass. But God had not promised that Jonathan would be 'next' to David during his reign, and that did not come to pass. Jonathan was killed in battle the same day as his father (31:2).

This shows us that God is not obligated to do what he has not promised, but he will always do what he has promised. Because God is faithful to his promises, the way for God's people to encourage or strengthen themselves is by rehearsing those promises.

God's promises are so abundant that the child of God, no matter what his situation, has a promise to rehearse. Does he feel alone and forsaken? God has promised never to totally abandon his children (Heb. 13:5-6). Does the future look bleak and uncertain? God has promised to be a refuge and strength to his people even though the earth be removed and the mountains slip into the midst of the sea (Ps. 46:2). Does the heart tremble at the thought of death? God has promised that at death the soul of the believer will go immediately into his presence and the body will eventually be raised to inhabit realms of glory (John 11:25-26; 1 Cor. 15:51-53; 2 Cor. 5:6,8; 1 Thess. 4:13-18). Does wickedness seem to be invincible? God has promised that it will finally be judged and the righteous will be vindicated (Dan. 12:1-3; Mal. 3:17-18).

Where do we go to find these marvellous promises? They are all in the Word of God, the Bible. Therefore, if we who know the Lord want to receive the encouragement and strength of his promises, we must thoroughly and constantly study the Word of God.

When facing the enervating problems and crises of life, many Christians often lament that they do not have more faith. This is indeed an understandable and appropriate lament. The greater our faith, the greater our spiritual strength. But how does faith grow and become strong? The apostle Paul answers in these words: 'So then faith comes by hearing, and hearing by the word of God' (Rom. 10:17). If we want increasing faith, we must increase our intake of God's holy Word and the promises that it contains.

But why would David suddenly turn to the very one he had been so grievously neglecting? The answer is that he had seen the hand of God at work in freeing him from his dilemma and, fresh from that experience, he could only look to the Lord in the face of this new crisis.

Child of God, you can run from the Lord, but you can never get away from him. He has special designs on you just as he had on David. His purpose is ultimately to bring you before the throne of his glory as a completed token of his grace (Phil. 1:6; Jude 23). Rest assured that he will never cease to follow you even into your backslidings and bring you back to himself. And in the process, he will make you wiser about yourself and more dependent upon his grace.

17.
When life falls apart

1 Samuel 30

This long chapter may seem at first glance to have no meaning or relevance to us. Amalekites, an ephod, Egyptian slaves — it all sounds hopelessly out of place in a world in which we 'surf the internet'. But closer inspection will reveal that it is far more relevant than we ever thought possible. This chapter connects with our lives at four major points.

An experience with which to identify

First, it begins with an experience with which we all can identify (vv. 1-6).

This chapter opens with David and his six hundred men returning to Ziklag after having been dismissed from the Philistine army. That constituted a harrowing experience in and of itself. It looked for a while as if David was either going to have to lead his men into battle against his own countrymen, or admit that he was not as loyal to the Philistines as he had pretended to be.

After he and his men were dismissed from the Philistine army, David may well have thought no experience could be more harrowing than the one through which he had just passed. He was in for a shock. When he and his men caught their first sight of Ziklag, their hearts fell into their sandals. Their village was not there! It had been burned, and all their wives and children were gone (vv. 1-3).

'Then David and the people who were with him lifted up their voices and wept, until they had no more power to weep' (v. 4). That says it all. It would seem that things could not possibly have grown any worse. For David they did: 'Then David was greatly distressed, for the people spoke of stoning him...' (v. 6).

It was David who had decided that he and his men should seek refuge in the land of the Philistines (27:1). It was David who had left Ziklag defenceless by taking all his men when the Philistines were massing their forces against Israel (28:1-2). There was no doubt, therefore, in the minds of David's anguished men that he was to blame for the terrible calamity that had befallen them.

In this passage, then, we find David hitting rock bottom. His whole life seems to disintegrate right before his eyes.

We have no trouble identifying with David at this point. Some of us have seen the lives of those near us falling apart. Some of us have seen our lives falling apart. Maybe it was the loss of a loved one. Maybe it was serious illness. Maybe it was a child who broke our hearts. Maybe it was financial disaster. Maybe it was a combination of many things. There are many ways in which life can fall apart.

We don't like to hear this, but it is sadly true — one thing that can make life fall apart for the child of God is backsliding.

The sober truth is that David would never have been in this situation if he had not been walking far from God. For sixteen long months, he had kept the company of the sworn enemies of his people. For sixteen long months, he had practised deception. For sixteen long months, he had suppressed and silenced every protest from his conscience. But he could go no further. God will not be ignored by his children, and he will not allow them to continue in backsliding without chastising them. In this passage, David finally has to face up to it. His life had fallen apart because he had allowed his commitment to God to fall apart. He lost his family because he had lost his faithfulness to God. How many Christians have done the very same thing? How many have seen things at home fall apart while they were out in the world?

A resource to which we must turn

That brings us to another vital way in which this chapter connects with us — namely, there is a resource to which we must turn (vv. 6-8)

What do you do when life falls apart? Many would probably have to answer in these terms:

> When in trouble, when in doubt,
> Run in circles, scream and shout.

David shows us a better way. The Bible says he 'strengthened himself in the Lord his God'.

We know from our earlier studies that it is possible for others to strengthen us in God. This is what Jonathan did when he visited David for the last time (1 Sam. 23:16).

How did Jonathan do this? The account tells us Jonathan said to David, 'Do not fear, for the hand of Saul my father shall not find you. You shall be king over Israel...' (23:17). In other words, Jonathan assured David that God's promise would be fulfilled. He may very well have gone on to talk to David about both God's faithfulness and his power. His faithfulness means he will do as he promised. His power means nothing can prevent him from doing what he promised.

It could very well be that David remembered Jonathan's visit as he stood there in the ruins of Ziklag, and reminded himself that God's faithfulness and power were still intact. Yes, his problems were great, but his God was greater.

To strengthen ourselves in God means we remind ourselves of what Scripture says about God and his promises, and we bring those truths to bear on the situation. Every trial causes opposing voices to ring in the ears of the child of God. One is the voice of our circumstances, telling us that our situation is hopeless. The other is the voice of faith, telling us that our God is sufficient for the trial.

In addition to strengthening himself in God, David sought guidance from God (vv. 7-8). It has been a long time since we found David doing this (1 Sam. 23:2). But we should not be surprised to find him doing it here. David had been doing the steering and had nothing but a mess to show for it. Here he hands the controls back to God.

Has your life fallen apart? Take a long, hard look at David. Strengthen yourself with what you know of God's character and promises, and seek his guidance.

A hand to trust

The third connecting point between this ancient episode and our own lives is that in this passage we see a hand at work that we all need to trust (vv. 11-20).

Assured of victory, David and his men set out. They must have wondered how they would locate this band of raiders. The answer came in the form of a discarded Egyptian slave whom some of David's men just 'happened' to come across. After a little food and a little negotiation, David and his men had a sure guide to the camp of the raiders.

No, the Bible does not explicitly attribute the discovery of this slave to the providence of God, but there can be no doubt about it. God had promised that David and his men would both catch and defeat the Amalekite raiders. When God assures his people of certain ends, he always supplies the means to that end.

That same invisible hand is still at work today on behalf of all God's children. That hand ensures that 'All things work together for good to those who love God, to those who are the called according to his purpose' (Rom. 8:28).

We do not have to be able to see God's hand to know it is there. We do not have to understand how something can be for our good in order for it to be so. Those of us who are parents often have to allow painful things to come to our children in order to accomplish something that is good for them. The parent with a sick child may even allow painful surgery to come the child's way in order to finally achieve a restoration to health.

We understand these things in our parenting, but we have a hard time accepting them when God is doing the parenting. How much easier it would be to bear our trials and afflictions if we could just fix it in our hearts and minds once and for all that our God loves us with a love that far surpasses our ability to comprehend and, because of that love, he will never, never, allow anything to touch us that is not for our good.

Once this truth is firmly grasped we can believingly and gladly sing with Carolina Sandell Berg:

Day by day and with each passing moment,
Strength I find to meet my trials here;
Trusting in my Father's wise bestowment,
I've no cause for worry or for fear.

He whose heart is kind beyond all measure
Gives unto each day what he deems best —
Lovingly, its part of pain and pleasure,
Mingling toil with peace and rest.

Help me, then, in every tribulation
So to trust thy promises, O Lord,
That I lose not faith's sweet consolation
Offered me within thy holy Word.

Help me, Lord, when toil and trouble meeting,
E'er to take, as from a Father's hand,
One by one, the days, the moments fleeting,
Till I reach the promised land.

A principle by which to operate

As we look at this passage, we finally have to say there is a principle here by which we must all operate (vv. 21-25).

Because of the Father's hand, David and his men were able to overtake and decisively defeat the Amalekites and recover all they had lost (vv. 16-20).

That crisis was over, but it was replaced with another. Two hundred of David's men had to be left behind because they were so weary they could go no further (vv. 9-10). This caused some of those who had gone to battle to insist that those who stayed behind should not share the spoils (v. 22).

David responded by articulating a principle that was to govern Israel from then on — namely, that those who stayed behind to guard the supplies would share just as much in the spoils as those who fought (vv. 23-25).

One phrase explains how David arrived at this principle: 'what the Lord has given us' (v. 23). All was of grace as far as David was concerned. The victory was not what he and his men had achieved, but what God had given. Because they had been the recipients of God's grace in battle, they must now demonstrate that grace to those who stayed behind.

A great lesson leaps out of this passage for us — those who have experienced the grace of God in salvation cannot now refuse to show that grace to others. The grace that saves us must also dominate our thinking and doing each day.

From this Old Testament passage, then, spring several principles that are vital for us. This passage reaches across the years of time to show us how to handle our trials, how to react when life falls apart. We must stay ourselves on God. We must trust his hand. We must channel his grace to others.

18.
Two approaches to life

2 Samuel 1

The closing chapters of 1 Samuel are shrouded in darkness and gloom. Israel's king, Saul, finally comes to the end of his long, unchecked descent into disobedience and rebellion. After seeking guidance from the witch of Endor (1 Sam. 28), he dies by his own hand in the ensuing battle against the Philistines (1 Sam. 31).

And what of David, the anointed successor of Saul? As we have already seen, the closing chapters of 1 Samuel find him, of all places, in the land of the Philistines. There he compromised his principles and acted in ways totally unbecoming to a child of God.

There also David tasted the bitter fruit of his backsliding. Disaster struck! While he and his men were away, their city was burned and their families carried away. This calamity brought David to his senses and caused his spiritual darkness to lift as he began to strengthen himself in God (1 Sam. 30:6).

After pursuing the raiders and recovering their families, David and his men returned to Ziklag. Two days later they received the deeply troubling news that Israel had been defeated by the Philistines and Saul and Jonathan were both dead.

This news came to David from an Amalekite who claimed to have come across a severely wounded Saul on the battlefield. The Philistines were closing in and, according to this man, Saul begged to be killed, a request that this Amalekite claimed to have honoured because he was sure Saul was going to die any way. As proof of his story the man had carried Saul's crown and bracelet to David.

The story was, of course, pure fabrication. Saul had indeed pleaded for someone to take his life, but his plea was directed to his armour-bearer, not to this Amalekite. And the armour-bearer had refused to raise his hand against the king. So Saul, in desperation, took his own life by falling on his own sword, and the poor armour-bearer did the same (1 Sam. 31:3-5).

Evidently the Amalekite came upon Saul shortly after this and hastily formed a plan. Assuming David would rejoice over the death of Saul and would welcome his killer, he pocketed Saul's crown and bracelet and beat a path to David's door.

It was all perfectly logical. Saul had spent the better part of his latter years hating David and trying to eliminate him. So it only stood to reason that David would hate Saul and desire to see him eliminated. This was the way of the world. It was as predictable as sunrise and sunset.

The Amalekite reckoned correctly that this was indeed the way of the world, but he was completely wrong in assuming that David would follow the world's way of thinking and doing.

How dreadfully wrong he was! The first clue that he had seriously miscalculated came when David and his men began, not to rejoice, but rather to mourn over the news about Saul and Jonathan, a mourning that evidently lasted for a period of several hours (vv. 11-12). This would seem to have been a good time for the Amalekite to creep silently away out of the camp, but he evidently persisted in believing he would be rewarded for what he claimed to have done. He did indeed receive the reward due to his actions, though it was not the kind he had expected! David abruptly turned his attention back to the Amalekite and commanded one of his men to execute him.

After this, David continued to mourn the deaths of Saul and Jonathan by composing 'the Song of the Bow' (vv. 19-27).

What does all this have to do with us? It might be said that this Amalekite and David represent two ways of approaching life that are still very much with us today.

The Amalekite's approach

On one hand, there is the 'Amalekite' approach to life. This is the approach of self-serving expediency. This Amalekite saw in Saul's death a chance to get ahead. He would take credit for it, David would be grateful to him for taking Saul out of the way, and then, he hoped, he would probably be given a position of influence in David's kingdom.

This is the approach that says there are no absolutes, that each person is free to make up his own mind on what is right and wrong on the basis of what his own comfort and convenience dictate.

This approach to life has flourished in our society for a long time. Does a pregnancy impede a woman's comfort? She can do away with the baby, and justify the decision with such high-sounding phrases as 'a woman's right to choose'. Do stealing, lying and cheating help us get ahead in life? Then we must steal, lie and cheat. Does sexual immorality make life more pleasurable? Then traditional morality must be ridiculed as puritanical and naïve, and permissiveness and promiscuity must be labelled as inevitable and even enlightened.

What does our society have to show for our plunge into moral ambiguity? Callousness and vulgarity abound. Crime soars. Drug usage rages unabated. Many schools have become like war zones.

In recent years political leaders, educators and sociologists have begun to express grave concern. They know no society can last if everyone makes up his own rules.

We should not be surprised at the adverse effects of this approach. Every time it has been tried, it has led to darkness and disintegration. To see this, we have to look no further than David's own nation of Israel a few years before he came on the scene. At that time the people threw the notion of moral absolutes to the wind and 'Every man did what was right in his own eyes' (Judg. 17:6; 21:25), and that attitude brought nothing but heartache to the nation.

David's approach

Over against the Amalekite approach to life, we can set the approach adopted by David.

The nature of this approach

And what approach is this? It is the approach that affirms that there are certain moral absolutes to guide us.

The moral absolute that primarily shines out in this chapter is that *we should not live in a self-seeking, self-advancing manner.*

David could have been just the kind of person this Amalekite expected him to be. He could have made his accession to the throne of Israel the supreme priority of his life and rejoiced that the death of Saul had finally cleared the way for him to realize his destiny. But he did not.

Or David could have let personal resentment and animosity control and dominate him. He could have said, 'Saul got exactly what he deserved, and I am not going to shed a tear over him.' But he did not.

There is not a shred of self-seeking to be found in David's response to Saul's death. His song demonstrates that he had a deep appreciation for the good Saul had done and a deep concern for the welfare of the people of God.

The reason for this approach

How did David manage to arrive at such selflessness? How did he come to believe that there was a moral absolute to govern and guide him at this time? Did he just sit down and invent this notion of a moral absolute because it seemed to make sense?

David arrived at the moral absolute of living selflessly because it had been clearly revealed by God. It was God who stated in the law he gave to Moses: 'You shall not hate your brother in your heart... You shall not take vengeance, nor bear any grudge against the children of your people, but you shall love your neighbour as yourself: I am the Lord' (Lev. 19:17-18; see also Deut. 32:35).

In addition to that David had another moral absolute from God. This was that the anointed of the Lord was to be treated with respect (v. 14).

How did David arrive at this particular moral absolute? It was an inevitable deduction from the very meaning of anointing. Anointing meant that someone was set apart for God's special use (Exod. 28:41).

It does not take a great deal of intelligence to draw the conclusion that we had better leave to God those whom he has set apart for his own special purposes.

Why we should embrace the approach of David

This passage of Scripture compels us to look seriously at our own lives to see if we have embraced the approach to life illustrated by the Amalekite or that represented by David. The former is so much in the ascendancy these days that it is very difficult to embrace the latter. But embrace it we must.

Our good in this world

There are two primary reasons for doing so. The first is that our own good in this world demands it. Look back at the Amalekite and David for a moment. The Amalekite's approach ended in death, while David went on to great success and blessing. These outcomes may be considered to be representative of this enduring truth — the Amalekite's approach to life always brings ruin of some sort while that of David always brings blessing of some sort.

A future accounting

The second reason for embracing the approach to life exemplified by David is that the God whose moral absolutes provide the basis for it will some day call us to account. If we have spurned his absolutes and lived on the basis of our own comfort and convenience, we can be sure that we shall experience his wrath.

The example of Christ

There is one more thing. The greatest example of the approach to life illustrated here by David is not David himself, but rather one of his descendants, the Lord Jesus Christ. He spurned self-seeking and freely gave himself so that we might have eternal life (Phil. 2:5-8).

The only way we can truly embrace the approach to life modelled here by David and live selflessly is by bowing in submission before Christ as the only Lord and Saviour. He then takes up residence in our lives, and we can draw power from him each day to put to death the Amalekite that lives within each of us.

19.
Contrasting responses to a sure word

2 Samuel 2-4

Saul was dead. The nation of Israel was without a king. David had been anointed by the Lord to be king over the nation.

With all these things in place, we would have expected to read that the entire nation of Israel joyously crowned David as king and they all lived happily ever after. David did, of course, eventually reign over the entire nation, but it did not happen immediately or easily.

Two little words signal the problem that stood between David and the throne of the nation: 'But Abner ...' (2:8).

Abner's response

Who was Abner? He was the commander of Saul's defeated army and, by virtue of that, a very powerful and influential man. He was also Saul's uncle.

What did Abner do? Although he knew David was God's anointed, he refused to acknowledge him as such and submit to him.

The elders of the tribe of Judah quickly embraced David as their king and anointed him at Hebron (2:4), but Abner evidently used his power and influence to keep the northern tribes of Israel from doing the same.

For the first five and a half years of David's reign in Hebron, Abner apparently prevented the northern tribes from having any king at all. During this time, he seems to have succeeded in slowly pushing the Philistines out of the land, and then he led the nation to anoint one of Saul's sons, Ishbosheth, as king (2:8), an arrangement that was to last for only two years (2:10).

Why did Abner do these things? If he had thrown his support behind David immediately after Saul's death, David would have certainly been anointed as king over the whole of Israel, and that would have spared the nation the agony and bloodshed of a civil war.

What a bloody time it was! Soldiers from both armies were killed in battle, and three prominent men were coldly and brutally murdered: Asahel (2:18-23), Ishbosheth (4:5-7) and Abner himself (3:27-30).

So why did Abner refuse to acknowledge David as the Lord's anointed? Some think it was because he harboured plans ultimately to become king himself over the northern tribes. Others think his actions were taken out of family loyalty.

We remember that the reason why Israel had a king at all was because the people had wanted a king 'like all the nations' (1 Sam. 8:5). Abner may very well have been carrying this sentiment one step further. The other nations had a lineal succession, and he may have thought Israel should have the same.

Whatever his reason, Abner was fighting against God's clearly revealed will — a fight which is always doomed to failure.

How can we be sure Abner knew he was fighting against God? He admitted as much himself. When he and his puppet king Ishbosheth came to a parting of the ways, Abner threatened him with these telling words: 'May God do so to Abner, and more also, if I do not do for David as the Lord has sworn to him — to transfer the kingdom from the house of Saul, and set up the throne of David over Israel and over Judah, from

Dan to Beersheba' (3:9-10). There it is! Abner knew very well that the Lord had 'sworn' to give the kingdom to David. But he still set himself in opposition to God.

David's response

What was David doing all this time that Abner was resisting the plan and purpose of God? He was waiting!

As we look at David during those seven years of reigning over Judah alone, we can see shining prominently from his life patient faith that God would fulfil his promise. We do not see David manoeuvring and manipulating circumstances to bring himself to the throne of a unified Israel. If he ever found himself tempted to force the issue, all he had to do was look back on those instances in which he had tried to take matters into his own hands. When he relied upon his own wisdom and cleverness, he invariably brought heartache upon himself. When, on the other hand, he trusted God, he found himself blessed.

This portion of David's life begins with his seeking the Lord's guidance before he went to Hebron (2:1). That attitude seems to have dominated the whole time he was ruling in Hebron.

What a study in contrast we have in these two men, Abner and David! They both had the same word from God — the word that David was to rule over the nation of Israel — but there the similarity ended. Abner resented and resisted that word while David trustingly waited to see the fulfilment of it.

These contrasting responses to God's Word are still very much with us today.

Our response to God's anointed King

God has an anointed King today just as he did at that time. He has decreed that the Lord Jesus Christ is ultimately going to rule and reign over all. He has declared that every knee is going to bow before him and every tongue is going to confess that he is Lord of all (Phil. 2:9-11).

But just as Abner did not happily embrace the word that David was to be king over all Israel, so many today refuse to embrace the word that Jesus Christ is God's anointed.

The evidence for Christ

Why do they resist God's anointed? It certainly is not because there is a lack of evidence that Jesus is God's anointed King. To the contrary, there is an abundance of it.

His life and ministry indicate his anointing. He spoke as no man has ever spoken. He healed the sick, fed the multitudes, calmed the stormy seas and raised people from the dead. And after he voluntarily laid down his life on a Roman cross, he conquered death himself by coming out of the grave on the third day.

After his resurrection, he was seen by various ones for a period of forty days, a time in which he 'presented himself alive after his suffering by many infallible proofs...' (Acts 1:3).

After that period of time he gathered his disciples together on the Mount of Olives. There he was taken up from them into heaven, and two angels suddenly appeared to assure them that this same Jesus who was taken up from them would come 'in like manner' (Acts 1:9-11).

All these things are not just the clever inventions of clever men. In each case there were witnesses to substantiate and verify them.

Even further proof that Jesus is indeed the anointed of God is available. The Bible tells us all these things that Jesus did were prophesied hundreds of years before.

The rejection of Christ

The proofs for Jesus Christ are massive and irrefutable, but there are millions of modern-day Abners who refuse to accept Christ as the anointed of God. Why do they reject Christ? We can say, of course, that they are, like Abner, filled with themselves and their own schemes and desires, but we must go beyond that to say that they have been blinded by sin. The light of the glory of God is indeed shining in and through the Lord Jesus Christ, but they are unable to see it because of the scales of sin over their spiritual eyes (2 Cor. 4:3-6).

The only hope for these people is that God himself will intervene on their behalf, lift the scales from their eyes and enable them to see that the Lord Jesus is his anointed.

My appeal to the modern-day Abner who persists in stubbornly going his own way even though Christ has been proved to be the anointed of God is this — turn from your foolish course and ask God to have mercy upon you and enable you to see!

The result of rejection

I would add one more word to all those who follow the example of Abner: you cannot possibly succeed in your opposition to Christ. One of the psalms (which may have been written by David himself) is devoted to this very matter of resisting God's anointed. It opens with the rulers of the earth raging against God's anointed and trying to find some way to throw off his bonds. But God responds to their raging and their opposition in this way: 'Yet I have set my King on my holy hill of Zion' (Ps. 2:6).

Of this verse, Charles Spurgeon writes, 'While they are proposing, he has disposed the matter. Jehovah's will is done, and man's will frets and raves in vain. God's Anointed is appointed, and shall not be disappointed.'[1]

And the psalm closes with this solemn word of counsel: 'Kiss the Son, lest he be angry, and you perish in the way...' (Ps. 2:12).

Those who refuse to submit to God's anointed will some day be cut off while they are still walking in 'the way' of rebellion. They will be going along in their hatred, spewing out their venom against God, and he will step in, cut them off and send them away into eternal destruction.

So all modern-day Abners would do well to heed the words of the poet:

Ye sinners seek his grace,
Whose wrath ye cannot bear;
Fly to the shelter of his cross,
And find salvation there.

The response of faith

There is, of course, the other response to the Word of God, the one represented by David. This is the response of confidently waiting on God's promises to be fulfilled. All who have accepted Christ as the anointed of God are now called upon to make David's response to God's promises our response. We live in days of scepticism in which it seems as if God's promises are implausible and impossible, but we are still called upon to trust those promises.

David's circumstances often made the promises of God seem uncertain, but those promises were not uncertain. They all came true, and God's promises to us will prove to be true as well. Therefore, our responsibility is to reject doubt in these days and confidently say with the apostle Paul, 'I know whom I have believed and am persuaded that he is able to keep what I have committed to him until that day' (2 Tim. 1:12).

20.
Flies in the ointment

2 Samuel 3:2-5,13,31,39; 5:13-16

It is not hard to find commendable qualities in David in the early chapters of 2 Samuel. We find him, for instance, not gloating over the death of Saul, but rather mourning over it. We also find him exhibiting a burning desire for justice in executing the Amalekite. We are told that he sought the leadership of the Lord before returning to Judah (2:1). On top of all that, we are able to detect a patient trust in the Lord during those seven and a half years that he reigned over Judah.

But along with these commendable qualities, the Bible also lays before us some things about David that are troubling and deeply disappointing. Even though David had been anointed of the Lord to reign over all Israel, he was far from perfect. We might say there were 'flies in the ointment'.

By the way, one of the most amazing things about this amazing book, the Bible, is that it never glosses over the sins of its greatest characters, but sets those sins in the clear light of day.

David's sins

What sins come to light in David's life in these early chapters of 2 Samuel?

Allowing the expedient to override principle

For one thing, there are instances in which he allowed simple pragmatic expediency to override principle. As a general rule, David lived on the basis of principle, but there were moments when he failed to do so.

David's negotiations with Abner. This fearful element shows up when David had entered into negotiations with Abner to bring all of Israel under David's reign. Abner had installed Ishbosheth as the puppet king of the northern tribes until he was ready to take the kingdom for himself.

Abner finally signalled that readiness when he took Saul's concubine as his own (3:7). Daniel M. Doriani explains the significance of Abner's act: 'In the ancient Near East the concubines of a deceased king were the property of his successor. To sleep with a concubine as Abner had done was, therefore, to claim to be the next king.'[1]

By this act, Abner claimed the kingdom, but he was never able actually to possess it. Ishbosheth apparently retained enough strength to keep him from coming to the throne. So Abner did the next best thing — namely, throw his support behind David (2:8-10).

As part of his negotiations with Abner, David required that his first wife, Saul's daughter Michal, should be returned to him. The problem was that she was by this time married to another man. David did not let this stand in his way. He insisted that she be returned to him, and there is a sorrowful account of her being brought to David with her husband weeping as he followed her (3:13-16).

Why did David do this thing? Was it because he and Michal were madly in love with each other? Subsequent events indicate that they were not (2 Sam. 6:2-23). The probability is that David's demand was a raw political move designed to curry favour among those citizens in Israel who still felt loyalty to Saul's house.

David's refusal to punish Joab. Another example of David putting politics above principle comes when Joab avenged his brother Asahel's death by cold-bloodedly murdering Abner (3:22-30).

This heinous act thrust David on the horns of a dilemma. Principle demanded that Joab should be punished but, because of Joab's influence, political expediency demanded David look the other way.

David dealt with this dilemma by publicly dissociating himself from the crime and by requiring Joab to march with him at the head of the funeral procession for Abner (3:28-29,31-32). David's response to this dilemma found favour with the people (3:36), but David himself admitted that he had been 'weak' in administering the justice this situation demanded (3:39). In other words, he was admitting that politics had won and principle had lost.

We all can certainly understand and identify with David's weakness, but we must also remember that, as William Taylor points out, weakness in a ruler is the same as wickedness.[2]

Multiplying wives

These two episodes in which we see David putting politics above principle are grievous enough, but there is another sin in his life that may be considered to be even greater. I refer, of course, to his sin of multiplying wives.

There are two references to this in the first five chapters of 2 Samuel. The first deals with the period when David was ruling over Judah alone (3:2-5), while the second deals with the period when he was reigning over all Israel (5:13-16).

These passages do not explicitly call David's many marriages sin. They are simply matter-of-fact listings of the names of some of his wives and his children. There was, however, no need for the author of these passages to declare David's marriages as sin. God had already done that through Moses (Deut. 17:14-17). David's marriages, then, amounted to nothing less than a flagrant thumbing of the nose at God's clearly revealed will.

Flagrant sin carries a heavy price tag, and it certainly proved to be so for David. His family turned out to be an unmitigated disaster. His first son, Amnon, brought shame and disgrace by raping his sister (2 Sam. 13:1-14). His second son, Chileab, is not mentioned again. His third son, Absalom, was born to a woman from one of the nations David raided while he was in the land of the Philistines (1 Sam. 27:8). Absalom proved to be the greatest disaster of all, as he eventually tried to wrest the kingdom from his father (2 Sam. 15:1 - 18:18). His fourth son, Adonijah, attempted to take the throne even after his father had designated Solomon as his successor (1 Kings 1:5-53).

Of these four sons, three died tragic, untimely deaths. The other sons in these lists, with the exception of Solomon, are just names of men who failed to figure prominently for God or their nation.

One of the great ironies of David's life is that even though he had plenty of wives and concubines, he still was not satisfied, but took another man's wife and had him killed! (2 Sam. 11:1-27). Sin always promises satisfaction, but it never delivers!

There certainly is no shortage of lessons for us from David's 'flies in the ointment'.

Lessons from David's sins

The ever-present danger of sin

In the first place, we cannot help but conclude that we shall never advance so much spiritually that we do not need to guard against sin. Few men in the Bible can match David in his love for God and his zeal for God's work, but David failed, and failed miserably. The same lesson is written large in the lives of other great men as well: Noah, Abraham, Moses, Simon Peter. All loved the Lord, and all failed.

We are terribly wrong if we use the failures of these men to justify our own sins. Their sins are not recorded to encourage us to sin, but rather to make us more watchful against it.

The inescapable consequences of sin

A second lesson for us to learn from David's failure is not to think we can get away with sin.

Each of David's sins came back to haunt him. Michal and Joab were like thorns in his flesh. His family, as we have noted, brought him untold grief. This lesson is also written large in the lives of the other great men of the Bible.

The exceptional sorrow of sin in family life

In the light of this, we may move on to a third lesson, namely, the exceptional sorrow and heartache produced by sins in family life. Sin of every description does damage, but sin in the family does even more damage.

If much of our happiness is drawn from our families, as most would readily admit, we must be very careful that we do not pollute them with sinful thinking and doing.

We scoff at this today, but it is still true: the way to build a happy family is on the teachings of God's Word. Those who marry and rear their children according to those teachings find their homes to be islands of tranquillity and joy in a world of turbulent storms. On the other hand, those who rebel against those teachings invariably find the turbulence of the world raging within their own homes.

The necessity of the work of Christ

A final lesson for us is this: we must look beyond the sins of David to the Lord Jesus Christ.

David, as we have noted, is in many ways a type of the Lord Jesus Christ — that is, he pictures in advance something of the person and work of the Lord Jesus Christ.

When we come to the sins in David's life, we are reminded that while David was a type of Christ, he was a very imperfect and flawed type. His sins serve to remind us of why it was necessary for Christ to come. Christ, and Christ alone, can finally defeat sin. He was the first and only person ever to live a sinless life. Having done that, he dealt sin a fatal blow by his death on the cross. He did so by taking the place of sinners on the cross of Calvary and receiving there the stroke of God's judgement that their sins deserved. God's holy nature demands that sin be punished, but it also demands punishment only once. If the Lord Jesus Christ has stood in the place of his people and borne God's wrath on their behalf, there is no penalty left for them to pay. Justice has been satisfied and every child of God can join the apostle Paul in saying, 'There is therefore now no condemnation to those who are in Christ Jesus' (Rom. 8:1).

In addition to these things, the Bible also assures us that the Lord Jesus is going to finally and gloriously take his people into heaven itself where they will be for ever free from sin.

21.
Confirmation and conversion

2 Samuel 5:1-6

Worlds of meaning often come folded in very small packages. So it is with those words: 'Then all the tribes of Israel came to David at Hebron' (v. 1).

Confirmation for David

Think first about what those words meant for David. He undoubtedly knew these people were coming and, as they drew near the city, he may very well have gone to a window to observe the arrival of this vast entourage (1 Chronicles 12:23-38 tells us how vast it was). What went through his mind as he saw row upon row of them sweep through the gates to stand outside his residence?

He must certainly have thought about that time, years ago, when the prophet Samuel came to announce that he was to be king over all Israel.

He must also have thought about all that had transpired since that day. There was that grand day when he defeated Goliath, and it looked as if his way to the throne was straight and paved. But David quickly found that coming to the throne was not going to be easy. Fierce hatred sprang suddenly from Saul, and David was forced to flee from him and live as a fugitive.

When Saul finally died, David may very well have expected his path to the throne to be cleared of all obstacles, but it was not to be. Only one tribe, Judah, accepted him as the Lord's anointed. The rest stayed loyal to the house of Saul, and seven and a half years of ugly civil war had followed.

Many times during those years, it must have seemed to David that the promise of God would never be fulfilled, and his faith had on more than one occasion faltered and flickered.

As David viewed the elders of Israel coming through the gates of Hebron, he must have felt a great surge of shame that he could ever have distrusted the Word of God. The arrival of these men trumpeted one truth very loudly and distinctly — God's promises will not fail, no matter how unlikely and tenuous they may seem.

Change for Israel

Think next about what the opening words of this chapter meant for the people of Israel.

These words tell us a profound change had taken place in their minds and hearts. Prior to this they had been unwilling to acknowledge David as their king, but now they come, so to speak, with 'hat in hand' and acknowledge him as their rightful sovereign.

The nature of this change

The nature of this change is detailed in the passage before us and also in 1 Chronicles 12:38-40.

Admitting rebellion. First, it came about only after they had rebelled against what they knew to be the will of God, and only after they saw the utter folly of that rebellion.

In David's presence they admit all of this. They first admit that up to this point *they had been unwilling to accept what they knew to be the truth*. They knew before Saul died that the Lord had designated David as his successor (v. 2), but they had in stubborn pride gone their own way and made Ishbosheth their king.

They also admit *the folly of what they had done*. Their rebellion was foolish because David himself was one of them. He was their own bone and flesh (v. 1). Rebellion against him would have been somewhat understandable if he had been a stranger, but they had been rebelling against one of their very own!

They admit also that their rebellion had been foolish in the light of the way that God had signally used David to give striking victories to the whole nation in times past (v. 2).

Submission. After admitting all of this, the people of Israel gave themselves completely over to David as their shepherd and ruler (v. 2).

The account in 1 Chronicles tells us they came to David with 'a loyal heart' (1 Chron. 12:38). There was no remnant of their former rebellion left in their hearts. It had all been purged from them, and they now embraced David freely, gladly and wholeheartedly as the one who would tenderly care for their needs and as the one who would tell them what to do.

The result of the change

All of this culminated in a grand and gracious reception of them by David. In view of the way they had treated him, he would have been justified in driving them from his presence, but he made a covenant with them and provided a lavish feast for them (1 Chron. 12:39).

Spiritual truths for saints and sinners

The arrival of the tribes of Israel in Hebron represented, then, confirmation for David and change for Israel. This ancient story of what happened in Hebron brims full with meaning for us.

Consolation for saints

Take the confirmation that David felt when the tribes of Israel came to him. All those who belong to the Lord God can draw consolation from the truth that David saw fulfilled and confirmed on that day — namely, God's promises are going to be fulfilled to the letter. Not one of them will fall to the ground.

We badly need this truth. Our circumstances, like David's, often make the promises of God seem uncertain and we, like him, find our faith flagging and faltering from time to time. In fact, flagging and faltering faith seems to be the order of the day.

God's people seem all too ready to embrace the thinking and doing of the world and to disbelieve our own message. Much of our Christianity seems to be of the 'insurance policy' variety. We do not really expect all the Christian message to be true, but we want to be covered just in case it is.

The tragedy is that as long as our faith flags and falters, we miss out on the highest level we can ever occupy in this life. There is absolutely nothing better in this life than the sheer joy and exhilaration of being fully persuaded that God's promises will all come true. As long as we live in doubt, we are unable to mount this high plane.

David and the other great heroes of the faith arise from the pages of Scripture to tell us to lay aside our doubts and rejoice in the certainty that our God is going to perform all he has promised.

Instruction for sinners

But what about the second part of this story, the change that took place in the hearts of the people of Israel. What does that have to do with us? It gives us a very precise and moving picture of the sinner coming to Christ and submitting to Christ.

Just as Israel's change came about only after they had rebelled against David and only after they had come to see the folly of that rebellion, so it is with the sinner.

If we could get into the minds of most of those who are unbelievers and crawl around there for a while, we would find they know that there is a God, that Jesus Christ is the only way to God and that they should receive Christ. But just as Israel knew David was to be king, but refused to openly admit or accept it, so many refuse to accept what they know to be the truth about Christ.

When God moves upon their hearts, however, they are at last able to see the folly of their rebellion against Christ.

Have you come to this point yet? Christ offers everything you need to stand just and clean before a holy God. He offers you an eternal destiny of peace and glory. He offers you the peace and joy of sins forgiven in this life. Why rebel against him?

He has come into this world as our own flesh and bone to make it possible for us to have all these things. Why fight against your own happiness and rebel against him?

We also found that the tribes of Israel, after admitting their rebellion, completely gave themselves over to David as their shepherd and ruler.

This is what each unbeliever must do also if he would end his rebellion against Christ. How we need to understand this! Some think they can come to Christ on their own terms. They think they can take the heaven he offers but continue to live in rebellion against him until it is time to go to heaven.

But salvation consists of breaking with our rebellion, throwing our weapons down and with 'loyal heart' embracing Christ as both our Shepherd and King — the Shepherd of our souls and the King of our lives.

Another parallel between the tribes of Israel coming to David and the sinner coming to Christ is to be found, of course, in that grand and gracious reception David provided for his new subjects. What David provided on that occasion is, however, a very imperfect and feeble picture of the lavish provisions Christ makes for all those who surrender to him as their rightful Sovereign.

22.
Conquering grace

2 Samuel 5:6-12

The keynote of David's life is the grace of God. There is no other way to explain him. Everywhere we look in David's life we see grace. If we could take a pin and scratch David's life at any point we would find grace oozing out.

Every child of God has much in common with David. The same grace that worked in his life is also at work in us. By studying David, we can grow in our understanding and our appreciation of that grace. And we shall certainly grow in our desire to live more for the praise and honour of that grace.

These verses give us the opportunity to admire the grace of God once again. Here we see David taking the city of Jebus from the control of the Jebusites and making it his capital. The Jebusites were among those whom Israel were to drive out when they first entered the land of Canaan (Exod. 33:2; Deut. 7:1; Josh. 3:10; 15:63).

David's conquest of Jebus

Three things stand out about David's conquest of the city of Jebus.

It was seemingly impossible

First, it was accomplished in the face of seemingly impossible odds. The Jebusites were supremely confident that their city was invincible. Daniel M. Doriani says, 'They had lived there since Joshua's conquest of the land, their citadel on mount Zion shut in by deep valleys on three sides and fortified on the fourth.'[1]

As far as the Jebusites were concerned, they did not even need soldiers at all. Even the blind and the lame citizens would be able to defend the city against all attackers, so impregnable was the fortress (v. 6).

Keith Kaynor thinks the reference to the blind and lame may have been in response to David's describing their gods in these ways. He suggests: 'The Jebusites sneered in return, "You say our gods are blind and lame; well, even if they are, they are still strong enough to keep you out." '[2]

If 'the blind and lame' refer to the Jebusites' gods, we can well understand David saying he hated them (v. 8). We live in a day of false gods — gods who are as powerless and unseeing as the gods of the Jebusites, and those who know the Lord should feel as much revulsion towards them as David did. Hatred is not too strong a word for false gods if we love the true God.

David was not deterred by the arrogant disdain of the Jebusites. He knew the city had an 'Achilles heel' — the water shaft — and he offered the generalship of his army to the man who would lead the way through that shaft (v. 8). Joab took up the challenge (1 Chron. 11:6), and led David's army to conquer the city from the inside out.

It led to radical transformation

The next thing we notice about David's conquest is that it brought about a radical transformation and great glory.

We cannot fully appreciate this until we pause to reflect on the nature of the Jebusites. They were a fierce, bloodthirsty people whose insatiable appetite for the worship of false gods drove them to such horrid extremes as child sacrifice (Lev. 18:21,24-28; Deut. 12:29-32). They were also a people who practised sexual immorality and witchcraft (Deut. 18:9-14).

The city of Jebus was, therefore, synonymous with perversity and wickedness of the most repugnant sort.

Everything changed when David took over. He renamed the city 'Jerusalem', which means 'City of Peace'. It also became known as the 'City of David' and 'Zion'. The city, then, went from being Jebus to Jerusalem, and from being synonymous with iniquity to being synonymous with the knowledge of God, the pursuit of God and the blessings of God. The transformation was so stunning and dramatic that David himself would later write of Jerusalem: 'Glorious things are spoken of you, O city of God!' (Ps. 87:3).

It created opportunity for further growth

Another dimension of David's conquest of Jebus is also evident in our text — namely, the opportunity it created for the further growth and expansion of David's kingdom.

After conquering the city, David soon turned his attention to expanding it. Beginning at the Millo, which some scholars think was the town hall, David built 'all around' (v. 9).

The conquest of the city of Jebus also expanded David's kingdom in another way. Hiram, King of Tyre, became aware of David's growing power and influence, and established a relationship with him (v. 11).

The writer makes sure we understand that all of David's successes took place not because of David himself, but solely because the hand of the Lord was upon him (v. 10). It was all of grace.

This passage concludes with another note about David continuing to add wives (v. 13). This lets us know that while the grace of God can, and indeed does, work mightily in his people, its work is never complete in this life.

Lessons from conquering grace

David's conquest of the city of Jebus is full of significance and meaning for us.

Conquering grace, a cause for celebration

First, it should cause all of us who know the Lord to celebrate the mighty, conquering grace of God that has already worked in us and saved us. Jonathan Edwards says Jerusalem was the greatest picture of the church in the Old Testament. He writes of it, 'It was redeemed by David, the captain of the hosts of Israel, out of the hands of the Jebusites, to be God's city, the holy place of his rest for ever, where he would dwell. So Christ, the Captain of his people's salvation, redeems his church out of the hands of devils, to be his holy and beloved city.'[3]

What fortresses God's people were before they were saved! The Bible tells us we were by nature the enemies of God. We came into this world with a nature that was armed to the teeth against God and his ways. As the Jebusites looked with proud disdain upon David, so we looked with disdain upon the ways of God. Our minds were shut against him. Our hearts were filled with affections for everything opposed to God. Our wills refused to accept him.

But, marvel of marvels, God broke in! His mighty, conquering grace penetrated our fortress of sin and he made us his own.

His conquest of us was much like David's conquest of Jebus. It came from the inside out! The Spirit of God used the Word of God to open a tiny shaft of light into our hearts, and the saving power of God poured in through that shaft.

And just as David's conquest of Jebus meant dramatic transformation for that city, so it was with God's conquest of us. Our hearts were no longer citadels of idolatry and arrogance. Our minds were no longer blinded to the truth of God. Our wills were no longer enslaved.

The apostle Paul never tired of emphasizing the greatness of this change. In his second letter to the Corinthians he puts it bluntly: 'Therefore, if anyone is in Christ, he is a new creation; old things have passed away; behold, all things have become new' (2 Cor. 5:17).

In his second letter to the Thessalonians, the apostle spoke of the greatness of this change in this way: 'You turned to God from idols to serve the living and true God, and to wait for his Son from heaven…' (1 Thess. 1:9-10).

Conquering grace, a cause for comfort

David's conquest of Jebus also enables us to draw profound comfort and consolation regarding our present situation.

The truth of the matter is that even though God's grace has conquered our hearts, we are far from perfect. The enemy has been defeated, and the Lord rules and reigns in our hearts, but, if we may picture it in this way, there is still opposition in the city. Stray Jebusites, as it were, remain in our hearts and conduct something of a guerrilla warfare against us. These stray Jebusites can never take control of us again, but they do vex and trouble us.

What we are talking about here is indwelling sin in the life of the believer. God rules in the heart of the believer, but sin still wages war against him. And each time sin rears its ugly head, the believer finds himself crying out in pain and anguish that there is still a battle raging in him.

Where can the believer find consolation in the midst of this situation? In that same grace that conquered him at the first! That grace that saved us will never leave us to ourselves. It will continue to work in us. The apostle Paul assured the Philippians of this truth in these words: 'He who has begun a good work in you will complete it until the day of Jesus Christ...' (Phil. 1:6).

The continuation of God's grace in our lives means God is there to strengthen us in our battles against sin, and it means that the battle will eventually be over, God will be all in all and the grace that made it all possible will be for ever praised.

23.
Breaking the strength of false gods

2 Samuel 5:17-25

The Philistines came against David. David defeated them. The Philistines came against David again. David defeated them again. That seems to be all this passage has to tell us and, if that is all that it says, we probably feel like shrugging and asking, 'So what?'

If we are to derive real benefit from this passage, we must look beyond David, the Philistines and military manoeuvrings to a much larger reality, and one that is still with us today.

The conflict

This reality is set out for us in several ways in these verses. Twice we are told that David 'enquired' of the Lord (vv. 19,23), and twice we are told the Lord granted guidance to him (vv. 19,23). We are also told that David gave the Lord the credit for the first victory — and we may assume for the second as well (v. 20).

So the Lord God is prominent in these verses. But these verses also tell us that the Philistines had their gods too and they carried them with them into battle (v. 21). So the larger reality behind the military skirmishing of Israelites and

Philistines is the conflict between the true God and all false gods.

The Philistines were worshippers of the god Baal, a fertility god who supposedly assured the productivity of the land. They were trusting him to give them the victory over Israel, but the true God gave Israel the victory over them and their false god. This explains why David gave the site of his first victory over the Philistines the name 'Baal Perazim'. The word means 'breakthrough against Baal'.

We know all about conflict these days. It is an ever-present phenomenon. We tune in the news and there it is — conflict between nations, conflict between politicians, conflict between individuals. It is present in many homes and even in many churches.

We have a tendency to explain all this conflict in merely human terms: personality differences, philosophical differences, breakdown in communication and so on. But the Bible tells us the conflicts in this world are only half the picture. There is another realm hidden from men's eyes, and there is a conflict going on there between God himself and Satan (and all false gods are a manifestation of Satan's work).

Furthermore, all the conflicts in the human realm are derived from, and linked to this larger conflict. Conflict comes about here because we, instead of adopting God's ways, allow Satan and his gods access into our thinking and our decision-making.

Thank God, this drama has a happy ending. God will in the end triumph over all his enemies, and Satan, sin, sorrow and death will never be able to trouble the people of God again.

But while we wait for that glorious day, we are still involved in conflict against Satan's false gods, and we ought to be fervently desiring to see 'breakthroughs' against them.

The breakthrough

The need for it

Are there really false gods today? Yes, in abundance! It is true, of course, that our gods tend to be more sophisticated today than the crude images of the Philistines, but that does not make them any less false.

Many today worship their own physical desires and fleshly lusts. Many worship the gods of government and education. Many worship the god of possessions. Even Satan himself is openly and increasingly worshipped.

The false gods of this world can be very intimidating to Christians. The worshippers of false gods outnumber the worshippers of the true God, and they often seem to be more committed. Even more disconcerting to the church is the fact that she often finds the worship of some of these false gods cropping up in her midst.

One of these gods is self. Churches that at one time understood that God is to be the object and focus of worship now unashamedly pander to those who sit in their pews. To be perfectly accurate about it, these occupants of the pews cannot be called 'worshippers' because their thoughts are very far from God and his glory. They are focused on themselves and what they want. They come as spectators to see a performance, or as consumers to enjoy a product. If these religious consumers want hilarity and light-heartedness, many church leaders feel obliged to provide it lest the consumers betake themselves and their money elsewhere. The desire of modern-day 'worshippers' for entertainment is matched, it would seem, by the desire of modern-day 'pastors' for church growth — and the notice that comes with it. At the root of both is the god of self.

This worship of self that demands that we always be entertained and have a so-called 'good time' has had a massive effect upon the church. The holiness of God, the law of God, the reality of sin, the coming of judgement and the need of repentance have been either scuttled or significantly toned down lest the devotees of the false god of self be offended.

In his insightful and disturbing book, *Ashamed of the Gospel*, John MacArthur laments the 'grow at all costs' mentality that has gripped so many American churches. He writes, 'Some of America's largest evangelical churches have employed worldly gimmicks like slapstick, vaudeville, wrestling exhibitions, and even mock striptease to spice up Sunday meetings. No brand of horseplay, it seems, is too outrageous to be brought into the sanctuary. Burlesque is fast becoming the liturgy of the pragmatic church.'[1]

He goes on to say, 'Almost nothing is dismissed as inappropriate: rock 'n' roll oldies, disco tunes, heavy metal, rap, dancing, comedy, clowns, mime artists, and stage magic have all become part of the evangelical repertoire. In fact, one of the few things judged out of place in church these days is clear and forceful preaching.'[2]

But we do not exhaust the topic of false gods in the church by merely focusing on the self-centredness that has crept into her public worship. False gods are also present in the church by virtue of what her individual members allow in their own lives.

Many who profess to know the true God keep up a mere outward show of devotion to him while their hearts are very much with the false gods of this age. What are some of these false gods? Material possessions, entertainment, ease, sensuality and self all come to mind.

In addition to the distressing things Christians see in their own midst, they find themselves further distressed by the fact that so many of the crucial elements of society are firmly in the camp of the false gods — the entertainment industry, the secular universities, the news media.

And to cap it all, Christians find themselves vexed over the sight of their children being carried away from the worship of the true God by the seductive appeal of today's false gods.

What are Christians to do in such a time? The devil's wolves seem so wolfish, and the Lord's sheep seem so sheepish. Secular humanism is militant and aggressive, while Christians seem to be halting and timid. The Philistines have in truth arrived in great number and deployed themselves against us.

The answer for this situation is in that word 'breakthrough'. The crying need of the hour is for the strength of the false gods to be broken. But how does such a breakthrough come about?

The means of breakthrough

The answer is given to us in this description of David's breakthrough against the Philistines.

Recognize it as God's work. First, we need to note that this breakthrough was entirely God's work. Yes, God used David and his soldiers as his human instruments, but they were no more than that. God was the one who assured David of victory (v. 19), and he was the one who delivered it.

As God gave David victory over the Philistines and their gods, so he can give victory to us today. But how do we go about this business of getting the Lord to give us the victory?

Renounce our own ability. The answer is that we must do as David did. We must renounce our own ability, and cast ourselves totally upon him as our wisdom and strength.

If we want an explanation for the sad state of affairs in the church today, we have to look no further than this point. All too often the church has tried to combat the false gods of this age in her own wisdom and power. She has thought she could gain the victory, not by fighting against the false gods of this world, but by imitating the world. She has thought she could gain the victory through putting on all kinds of activities, through entertaining services and political action.

Alas, she has been mistaken! All she has accomplished by such thinking is to make herself weaker while the worship of the false gods flows along unabated. The church's great hope for this hour is in getting her God to fight for her, and this she can only do by seeking his face.

Declare war on our sins. This matter of seeking the face of God is not easy-chair work. If we want the Lord to fight on our behalf, we must first declare war on our own sins because he tells us he will not hear us if we 'regard' iniquity in our hearts (Ps. 66:18).

Obeying God. We must also be willing to do what the Lord tells us to do. How he tested David at this point! The first time David sought his guidance the Lord commanded him to lead his forces in a frontal attack. The next time, however, the Lord commanded that David circle behind the enemy, wait for the sound of a stirring in the tops of the mulberry trees, and then strike.

All of this should remind us that our God is sovereign and free. We cannot tell him when to move and how to move, but we should always be ready and eager to do what he tells us to do.

The sad fact is that many of God's people want him to perform the work of making a 'breakthrough', but they do not want to obey his commands. God will not break through the false gods of our day until we break through our reluctance to obey his commands fully.

What I have been calling 'breakthrough' has another name. It is what we know as 'revival'. Revival is a sovereign act of God in which he moves upon the hearts of his people and restores them to spiritual vitality after they have slipped into a moribund, lethargic state. God invariably begins his work of revival by moving his people to humbly seek it with true brokenness over their sins.

While revival pertains to the people of God, it always has a profound effect on unbelievers. In periods of revival multitudes are awakened and swept into the kingdom of God. It should also be noted that true revival exerts a cleansing and ennobling effect upon entire communities. The moral tone of society is lifted and wickedness diminishes. It could be said, therefore, that revival is a time when God puts the enemies of the church to flight.

There have been many instances of revival down through the centuries of the church's history, and we may hope that it is again on the horizon. Many Christians appear to be growing very tired of the powerlessness of the church against the gods of this age and to be giving themselves more fully to the work of seeking God's face and departing from their sins.

Let us pray that these encouraging signs will continue, that we shall soon hear a stirring in the trees and that the revival we so urgently need will soon break with mercy over our churches, our homes and upon whole nations.

24.
Playing fast and loose with clearly revealed truth

2 Samuel 6:1-11; 1 Chronicles 13:1-14

This passage is one of the most troubling in Scripture. David and the people of Israel were engaged in doing a good thing — moving the ark of God to the city of Jerusalem — when disaster struck. The oxen pulling the cart stumbled, the ark tottered and Uzzah reached out to steady it. Quick as a flash he lay dead.

Perhaps it was just a coincidence that Uzzah died at that very instant. Perhaps he died of natural causes. 'Not so,' says the writer. Uzzah died because 'God struck him' (v. 7).

Why would God do such a thing? Uzzah's act not only seems to have been trivial and innocent, but even commendable and laudatory. What could possibly have been wrong with his merely steadying the tottering ark? Would God have been happier if Uzzah had just allowed the ark to fall to the ground? The ark represented the presence of God among his people. What message would have been proclaimed by the ark lying in the mud? Surely, Uzzah was right to prevent this from happening.

Questions abound when we come to this passage, but crucial lessons also abound. Let's see if we can answer some of the questions and learn some of the lessons. We shall do this by looking at an amazing clarity and an amazing casualness.

An amazing clarity

About the sacredness of the ark

God had been wonderfully clear about the sacredness of the ark. The ark, as we have already noted, represented the presence of God among his people. How easily and lightly our tongues trip over those words without realizing the full import of them!

The presence of God is no small thing! The Bible constantly emphasizes the holiness of God. When we say, therefore, that the ark represented God's presence, we are saying it represented his holiness. And the touching of that ark by a sinful man was, therefore, equal to defiling God.

The people of Israel knew about the holiness of God. God had underscored it for them time after time. When they came out of Egypt to Mt Sinai, God came down on the mount to give them his law. Before doing so, he instructed Moses to set boundaries around the mountain and warned that if anyone went beyond them that person would die (Exod. 19:12).

When God gave instructions for the constructing of the tabernacle, he again emphasized his holiness by establishing certain barriers between himself and the people. Keith Kaynor lays these barriers out for us:

> A cloth fence around the outer perimeter of the tabernacle areas (approximately 100' by 50') not only kept the people out but also kept them from seeing in. The small percentage of the nation who were of the priestly class and who were allowed inside had to pass a brazen altar to get inside the tabernacle itself. This altar spoke of sacrifice; animals were slain upon it to atone for man's sin. Freedom to get closer to the object that represented God (the ark) was purchased with blood.

The cloth-like structure that housed the ark — called the tabernacle — was another barrier. It prevented most of the priests and Levites from seeing the ark. For the few allowed inside the 'holy place' — there was a wash-basin that further reminded the people of sinfulness. Finally, only one man — the high priest — went into the curtained-off area called 'the Holy of Holies' once a year. And he could not come into the presence of the ark without the blood of a slain animal or he would be killed. Blood to cover sin was the only means of approach to God.[1]

About the moving of the ark

In addition to these clear indications of God's holiness, the people of Israel also had specific instructions from God on how the ark was to be moved. It was constructed with rings on each side and rods inserted into those rings, and it was to be moved by the Levites bearing those rods on their shoulders (Exod. 25:10-15; Num. 7:9).

Another clear instruction from God on this matter was that the priests were to cover the ark with heavy badger skins before it was moved (Num. 4:6). All of this was to be done with the full awareness that the ark must not be touched, and that if anyone did touch it he would die (Num. 4:15).

The people of Israel even had a precedent on this matter. The Philistines seized the ark in battle and took it home with them, but they soon found they could not live with it and devised a scheme to return it to Israel. The people of Beth Shemesh received the ark from the Philistines, but some of them looked into it and were instantly killed! (1 Sam. 6:14-19).

With all this in place, we are now in position to note the amazing casualness exhibited in this passage.

An amazing casualness

David knew all these things. So when he decided to bring the ark to Jerusalem, we would expect to read that he instructed the Levites to make sure they followed the laws of God. And the Levites certainly knew these things. So at the very least we would expect to read that they themselves insisted that the laws of God be minutely followed.

But David and the Levites both failed. In some form or fashion it was decided that the best way to move the ark was by oxen and cart!

Of course, nothing but the best is good enough for God, so they built a new cart! (v. 3). Ahio and Uzzah (who were Levites themselves) would drive this new cart, with Ahio in front and Uzzah in the rear (v. 3). Such a significant occasion deserved a proper display of enthusiasm and emotion, so there was plenty of music (v. 5).

Everything was proceeding just as they had planned when the oxen took that fateful step, stumbled and jostled the ark. Uzzah reached out to steady it and was immediately stricken.

Poor Uzzah lay dead (vv. 6-7). David became angry — some say at himself, but I think at God (vv. 8-9) and the ark was taken aside into the house of Obed-Edom (vv. 10-11). What had begun with such pageantry and exhilaration ended in disaster and dismay.

What possessed David and the Levites to take such a casual, nonchalant approach to moving the ark? A clue is found in the account of the Philistines returning the ark to Israel during the early days of Samuel. They did it by cart, a new cart, and they did it successfully (1 Sam. 6:7-8,14). If it had worked for the Philistines, it would surely work for the people of Israel! But it did not.

Vital truths

For the unbeliever

The 'Uzzah incident' is not a dead letter in the dustbin of history. It confronts us with the living and vital truth that we had better not be casual or careless about clearly revealed truth.

In Scripture, God has clearly revealed his holiness to us, even as he did to Israel of old. Because of his holiness, he cannot dwell with sin and will not allow sinners to enter heaven. He is on record as saying that nothing that defiles will be allowed to enter there (Ps. 5:4; Rev. 21:27).

This spells trouble for us because we are all sinners. We have broken the laws of God in innumerable ways. We have thought wrong thoughts, spoken evil words and committed foul deeds. How can guilty sinners ever hope to stand before such a holy God and be pronounced fit for heaven?

We should rejoice that there is in Scripture another clear truth — that is, God himself has done what is necessary for our sins to be removed so we can enter heaven at last. He sent his Son, the Lord Jesus Christ, to this world to do two things. First, he lived the life of perfect obedience that we all have failed to live. Secondly, he died on the cross to pay the penalty for our sins.

Now the glad word goes out to all that if we will repent of our sins and place our faith and trust in Christ alone, our sins will be forgiven and Christ's perfect righteousness will be put to our account.

It is good news, but the unspeakably sad and tragic thing is that so many treat this clearly revealed truth with casual carelessness. Instead of embracing Christ as Saviour, they fancy that they can be saved by their own good works. Or they fondly imagine that simply being sincere is all that is necessary for them to be admitted into heaven.

But just as God would not countenance Uzzah's casualness about clearly revealed truth, so he will not countenance casualness about the gospel, and all who practise such casualness will one day be stricken with eternal judgement just as surely as Uzzah was stricken with temporal judgement. That is the great lesson of 'the Uzzah incident' for all those who have not yet fled to Christ.

For believers

But there is also a great lesson here for those who have accepted Christ — namely, that God's people invite disaster when they lay aside the clear teachings of God's Word in order to embrace the thinking and doing of the world around them.

The bottom line for both unbelievers and believers is this: God is no threat if his laws are obeyed.

25.

Ageless principles from an ancient episode

2 Samuel 6:12-23

These verses give us the sequel to David's failed attempt to move the ark of God to Jerusalem. He and the Levites had played fast and loose with God's clearly revealed truth, opted for the ways of the world and paid a fearful price. Uzzah was dead, David was upset and angry, and the ark of God was in the house of Obed-Edom.

Three months passed. Then the report came to David that God had richly blessed the house of Obed-Edom. We do not know in what form God's blessing came. It could very well have been that Obed-Edom had been very poor before the arrival of the ark, and God had now given him substantial riches. Whatever form the blessing took, it was obvious to all.

David submits to God's demands

That report spurred David to action. The ark must be brought to Jerusalem! But this time there would be no casualness, no new cart, no oxen! This time things would be handled the right way!

Isn't it amazing how we accept the need for precision so easily in other areas of life, but chafe when God demands it? Medications demand precision, and lack of precision can be deadly. We accept that without a whimper. Driving a car requires precision, and we accept that without protest. But let God demand precision, and we are offended.

This time David did not protest against God's right to demand precision, but gladly embraced it. First, he carefully instructed the Levites in the proper handling of the ark (1 Chron. 15:2-3,12-15). He even went so far as to offer sacrifices to God after the Levites had taken only six steps with the ark (2 Sam. 6:13). What was this about?

Any time that we find sacrifice to God in the Old Testament, we have an awareness of sin. David and the people had been blissfully careless at this point in their first attempt to move the ark. There was no keen sense among them of the holiness of God, of their own sinfulness and of the awful gulf between the two. But things were different now!

After offering the sacrifices to God, David led the procession to Jerusalem, not in fear and trembling that someone would be struck dead, for there is nothing to fear when God's laws are obeyed, but rather with great rejoicing. David, clothed in the common garb of the priests, 'danced before the Lord with all his might' (2 Sam. 6:14).

David and his people rejoice in the Lord

It is hard for us to grasp adequately just how great was the joy on this occasion. The twenty-fourth Psalm is regarded by many as one that David composed specifically for this occasion. As the procession approached Jerusalem a choir probably sang:

Lift up your heads, O you gates!
And be lifted up, you everlasting doors!
And the King of glory shall come in

(Ps. 24:7).

A choir stationed on the wall of the city then cried out: 'Who is this King of glory?' (Ps. 24:8). And the processional choir responded:

The Lord strong and mighty,
The Lord mighty in battle. Lift up your heads, O you
    gates!
And lift them up, you everlasting doors!
And the King of glory shall come in

(Ps. 24:8-9).

The choir on the wall would then repeat the question: 'Who is this King of glory?' And both choirs would join in the triumphant conclusion:

The Lord of hosts,
He is the King of glory

(Ps. 24:10).

After the ark had been set in its place, there was more sacrificing (2 Sam. 6:17). The burnt offerings represented the complete devotion of the worshippers to God, while the peace offerings represented fellowship with God.

The joyous occasion came to an end with David distributing 'a loaf of bread, a piece of meat, and a cake of raisins' to the great multitude that had attended the festivities (2 Sam. 6:19).

Michal resents David's joy in the Lord

It all made for an extremely satisfying and delightful day. Then a dark shadow fell across it.

David's wife, Michal, had taken note of the common garb he wore and his exuberant dancing before the ark. To her it was all very unbecoming for a king, and she could not wait to 'vent her spleen'. David had scarcely crossed the threshold of his house before she let loose this barrage: 'How glorious was the King of Israel today, uncovering himself today in the eyes of the maids of his servants, as one of the base fellows shamelessly uncovers himself!' (2 Sam. 6:20).

David saw through her words to her real problem. She really subscribed to the same frigid view of spiritual things that had plagued her father Saul, and she resented the fact that David and his brand of spirituality had been elevated to the throne of Israel at the expense of her father.

After offering this diagnosis, David defended himself by saying, in effect, 'If the glory of this day had anything to do with my being undignified, let me be even more undignified!' (2 Sam. 6:22).

God did not take Michal's criticism of David lightly. Because she had the spirit of Saul, she was denied the ability to bring an heir of Saul into this world (2 Sam. 6:23).

Timeless principles

Timeless principles leap to the surface as we read about David successfully moving the ark to Jerusalem.

God's presence equals blessing

First, we must say that wherever God is there is an outpouring of blessing.

The ark, as we have noted, was the emblem of God's presence among his people. Yes, God was present with them in a sense even without the ark, but his presence was connected to that ark in a special way.

We might say that God is present in different ways with his people. It is possible for him to be present and be so grieved at what he finds among his people that he withholds much of his power and blessing from them. But it is also possible for him to be present in such a way that he pours out his blessing upon his people.

Obed-Edom experienced the blessing of God in the latter sense, and every child of God ought to desire the same thing. In other words, we should not be content with anything less than the fulness of God's blessing.

Gordon Keddie writes, 'God's blessings are real...This is not merely subjective feeling about ourselves or about life. There is hard evidence to support it: marriage, children, the love of God's people, kindnesses, career openings, recovery from illness, preservation from harm, daily bread — all sorts of tangible realities that point to the loving hand of our heavenly Father.'[1]

It should also be noted that when God pours out a fulness of blessing upon his people, it is obvious to those around them, even as the blessing of God on the household of Obed-Edom was obvious to all.

How all of this tests us! Are we as God's people, on the individual level and the corporate level, experiencing such a fulness of blessing that those around us have to take note?

God's blessing is tied to obedience

This leads us to a second principle — namely, that God's blessing is tied to obedience.

We must never forget that the ark came to be at the house of Obed-Edom because of the disobedience of David and the Levites in moving it the wrong way. The blessing of Obed-

Edom could have been the blessing of the whole nation had obedience to God's commands been given priority.

Do we desire the blessing of God? Let us look to this matter of obedience. A psalm attributed to the sons of Korah says of the Lord, 'No good thing will he withhold from those who walk uprightly' (Ps. 84:11).

Obedience to God leads to joy

A third principle that arises from this account is this — wherever obedience to God is, there is cause for great joy.

One of Satan's greatest lies is that obedience to God brings misery. David discovered in a painful way that just the opposite is true. When he disobeyed God, he brought misery and woe upon himself and his nation. When he obeyed God, his own heart was filled with rejoicing and so were the hearts of all the people.

We have even more reason for rejoicing than David and the people of Israel did on that occasion because we have something better than the ark. The Lord Jesus Christ is the supreme manifestation of the presence of God among us. His name is 'Immanuel', which means 'God with us' (Matt. 1:23).

Tragically, many professing Christians are strangely lacking in this area of joy and zeal. This sad reality compelled Gordon Keddie to write, 'Lukewarm water in the kettle argues that the flame is low — or out!'[2]

Joy in the Lord leads to opposition

All did not rejoice when David moved the ark. His wife did not. And that brings us to yet another principle — wherever we find true joy in the Lord we will find deep opposition.

Those who do not know God gladly put up with nominal religion, but they resent anything that gives evidence that God is real and that calls people to genuine faith and devoted service. Zeal is acceptable to modern-day pagans in every other area of life, but let it show up in religion and they despise it.

Opposition to God leads to barrenness

The final principle we may deduce from these passages may be put in this way — wherever we find opposition to God we shall ultimately find barrenness and deprivation.

Michal paid a high price for her hatred of divine things, and the Bible assures us that those who share her hatred will suffer the worst kind of deprivation imaginable — being deprived of the things of God for ever.

All of these principles converge to powerfully put before us one central question: when it comes to the things of God, are we like David or like Michal? This is an extremely important question. The greatest good life has to offer comes from being like David — knowing God, obeying God and enjoying God. The greatest misery comes from opposing God. May God help us to follow the example of David!

26.
A good desire restrained

2 Samuel 7:1-17

This passage gives us a rare glimpse of David. By this time we have probably come to associate him with a whirlwind of activity. This man seems always to have been doing something — fighting Philistines, writing psalms, moving the ark, administering the affairs of the kingdom. David was indeed a vigorous, energetic man. But here we find him in a different mode. The whirlwind of activity has ceased and David has, at least for a time, a breather, or a respite. No enemy threatens. Everything is peaceful and tranquil.

We can tell much about a man by observing him in his hours of leisure, and there is certainly much for us to learn from this episode in David's life.

The passage inevitably falls into three distinct and discernible parts. First, there is what we may call a commendable desire (vv. 2-3). That is followed by a gracious refusal (vv. 4-11) and a glorious promise (vv. 12-17).

The commendable desire

The commendable desire of David was to build a permanent temple for the Lord. Since the days of Moses, the ark of God had dwelt in a tent. This did not seem proper to David in view of the fact that he himself was living in exquisite finery in a house of cedar. David shared his thoughts with the prophet Nathan, whom we meet for the first time, and Nathan encouraged him to pursue what was in his heart.

It may seem that there is nothing terribly profound for us in these verses, but that is not the case. These verses call us to think seriously about ourselves and our desires. Let's look at what these verses tell us about David, and then test ourselves.

First, they tell us that in moments of leisure David's mind and heart naturally gravitated towards the things of God.

Secondly, these verses also tell us David was not content simply to occupy the spiritual plateau he had reached. Matthew Henry says, 'Gracious, grateful souls ... never think they can do enough for God, but, when they have done much are still projecting to do more and devising liberal things.'[1]

Thirdly, these verses also tell us that David was made ill at ease by the thought that he was personally prospering more than the work of the Lord. Matthew Henry adds this about those he calls 'gracious, grateful souls': 'They cannot enjoy their own accommodations while they see the church of God in distress and under a cloud.'[2]

Can we identify with David at each of these points? Do we find ourselves so occupied with God that our thoughts naturally gravitate towards him? Do we find welling up within us a discontent with what we have done and a burning desire to do more? Do we find ourselves upset and distressed if we are prospering while the work of God is languishing? Or are we, like so many today, content to prosper ourselves without the slightest concern for the cause of God?

Nathan provides a test for us as well. Here was a man who was by nature a great encourager. When he heard of David's desire to build a temple, his immediate response was to encourage him. Are we like Nathan? Do we look for ways to encourage others to advance in the work of the Lord?

Nathan's approval probably filled David with intense resolve to immediately prosecute the matter of building the temple. But it was not to be. That very night, the Lord spoke to Nathan on this matter and Nathan, in turn, conveyed the Lord's word to David.

What did the Lord have to say to Nathan? It amounted to a gracious refusal (vv. 5-11).

The gracious refusal

The absence of God's command

Through Nathan, the Lord pointed out a couple of things to David. First, he had not at this point commanded a temple to be built (vv. 6-7).

There is a great principle here for us to consider — namely, that a good desire to serve the Lord and be useful to his kingdom must always be governed by what God has clearly revealed. This is what is known as 'the regulative principle' of Scripture. Gordon Keddie summarizes it in these words: 'In the things of God we must be content to do his will as he has specifically revealed it and not add things, however good they may seem to us to be in themselves.'[3]

Churches badly need this reminder in these days. God has revealed that we are to be advancing his kingdom through the preaching and teaching of his Word and prayer for his power. But many these days have decided that such things can no longer be depended upon and must, therefore, be replaced with entertaining activities. Would to God we could learn the truth of Matthew Henry's statement regarding David: 'Better a tent of God's appointing than a temple of his own inventing.'[4]

God's purpose for David

Secondly, the Lord pointed out that a temple would eventually be built, but that he had a different purpose for David (vv. 8-11).

We each have our own place in the plan of God. God had called David as a shepherd and had elevated him to the kingship (v. 8). God had blessed him and used him, particularly in the area of defeating Israel's enemies (vv. 9,11). All of this meant that David already had a great name and great standing (v. 9).

All of these things had come about because God had ordained them. Notice the emphatic use of 'I' as God speaks to David in these verses.

But God had not ordained that David should build the temple. Later David was to attribute God's refusal to allow him to build the temple to the fact that he had been a man of bloodshed (1 Chron. 22:8). Some have taken this to mean that the Lord refused to allow David to build the temple because he had sinned by shedding so much blood. But the wars David fought were the Lord's wars, and his victories were the Lord's victories (2 Sam. 8:6,14). Furthermore, it was David's wars that allowed his son and successor, Solomon, to have the peace necessary to complete the temple.

But while David's wars were necessary, they still disqualified him from building the temple. Perhaps the issue was, as the *New Geneva Study Bible* suggests, ritual defilement.[5] Or, as Matthew Henry suggested, it could very well be that God was protecting a type. By reserving the building of the temple for a man of peace, the Lord could very well have been prefiguring the building of his church through the preaching of the gospel of peace.[6]

Whatever our understanding at this point, it is evident that God has different roles for his people to fulfil. David's role was to achieve peace for the glory of God. Solomon's role was to use that peace for the glory of God. Through such instances God teaches us to be happy with what he has appointed for us, and not chafe and complain if it is not as large as we would like it to be. Our call is to be faithful to God, and a faithful life, no matter how unnoticed in this world, will not be forgotten by God.

David probably felt some disappointment over God's refusal, but that disappointment must have quickly melted away under the bright sunshine of the glorious promise God gave him (vv. 12-17).

The glorious promise

God's final word to David on this matter amounted to this: 'David, instead of your building me a house, I am going to build you one.'

A son to sit on David's throne

There are two tracks to this promise. David's house would initially be established through David's son, Solomon (vv. 12-15).

God promised two great things about the reign of Solomon. First, the temple David desired would be built. Secondly, God pledged to treat Solomon differently from the way he had Saul. When Saul sinned, the Lord punished him by not allowing any of his descendants to reign after him. When Solomon sinned, God would chastise him severely, but would never completely withdraw his mercy from him.

Permanence for David's throne

The second track of the promise guaranteed permanence for the throne of David (v. 16).

David's descendants proved to be so faithless and wicked that the nation had finally to be punished by being sent into captivity in Babylon, but that only constituted an interruption, not an end, of the reign of David's seed. As the New Testament opens, the people of Israel are back in their land, and a husband and wife are on their way to the village of Bethlehem. There was born the one who fulfilled the promise of permanence to David. He was none other than the Lord Jesus Christ himself. He sprang from David's line, and by virtue of his redeeming work on Calvary's cross, all authority in heaven and earth have been granted to him, and that authority will never be relinquished. He is reigning now at the right hand of God, and he will continue to reign for ever and ever.

David was overwhelmed at the goodness and grace of God to him. That grace that offered permanence to David's throne offers a glorious permanence to us as well. It holds the crucified Christ before us and assures us that if we will turn from our sins and embrace him as Lord and Saviour we will 'dwell in the house of the Lord for ever' (Ps. 23:6).

27.
The workings of a happy heart

2 Samuel 7:18-29

David was a happy man. One of his sons would succeed him as King of Israel and would build the temple he wanted to build, and David's kingdom was to be permanently established (v. 16).

David understood the meaning of that. He knew, from the promises God had given to the fathers of his people, that a Messiah was to come to his nation. This Messiah was to be no ordinary man. He would be nothing less than God himself in human flesh. Now David learns that this Messiah would spring from his descendants, and take his throne. All other kings and kingdoms are temporary, but the Messiah would rule and reign from his, David's, throne for ever.

The one blessing — a son reigning in David's stead and building the temple — was in and of itself a sizeable blessing. But God was not satisfied to leave it there. So he added a second blessing that dwarfed the first.

Yes, David was a happy man. He was fairly reeling under this load of blessing. He was overwhelmed by it all.

A description of David's happy heart

How does a mere mortal properly respond to such a magnificent outpouring of the grace of God?

Sitting before the Lord

The passage before us tells us how David responded. He 'went in and sat before the Lord' (v. 18). I take that to mean David went into the tabernacle and simply sat down in sheer delight and enjoyment of the presence of the gracious God who had so wondrously blessed him.

How long did David merely sit and bask in the wonder and glory of it all before he began to pray? The text seems to indicate that he began to pray as soon as he went into the presence of God but, on the other hand, there is nothing in it that forbids us to visualize him spending some time silently reflecting on, and basking in, the goodness of God.

Praying

After sitting in the presence of the Lord, David began to pray. God had spoken to him through Nathan the prophet, and now David speaks to God. How often we skim lightly and easily over passages which teach enormous truths! God speaks to us, and we can speak to him. The almighty God who created all things and rules over all things condescends to speak to us. And he allows us to come into his presence by means of prayer and speak to him. There are no greater privileges in this mortal realm than hearing God and speaking to God.

David's prayer can be divided into two major parts.

Thanksgiving. First, there is the element of thanksgiving (vv. 18-24). This portion of the prayer can be sub-divided into three parts: thanksgiving for the blessings God had bestowed upon David (vv. 18-21), thanksgiving for God's sovereign greatness (v. 22) and thanksgiving for God's expression of his sovereign greatness in making the people of Israel his own special possession (vv. 23-24).

Petition. That brings us to the element of petition (vv. 25-29). In this portion of the prayer, David asks God to do as he had promised and, in so doing, to bring glory to his name (v. 26).

The whole prayer is offered to God with an attitude of worship and reverence.

A prescription for the happy heart

The prayer of David is not some interesting titbit that has survived for us merely to scan with the same curiosity we might have towards anything of great antiquity. It gives us insight into how the heart of a true child of God works and how he prays. It may be considered to be something of a primer in spirituality.

There are several lessons I would lift from this particular slice of David's life.

Reflecting on the goodness of God

First, we should certainly learn to reflect seriously on the goodness of God towards us and to practise enjoyment of it.

How many of us have ever done as David did in this passage? Do we know what it is to bask in the goodness of God, to toast ourselves in sheer delight in, and enjoyment of, his blessings?

I am not sure whether this is not our area of greatest deficiency. Many of God's people give very little evidence of being unusually blessed of God. We have a tendency to read this account of God's blessing on David and make excuses for ourselves. We say we could be as thankful as David was if we were to be blessed as greatly as he was.

The thing we fail to see is that we who know the Lord have been blessed even more than David was. David was given the

promise of a permanent throne through a coming Messiah.
Every child of God has received permanence — eternal life —
through the Messiah who has already come. How long has it
been since we have sat before the Lord in sheer delight and
amazement over his gift of eternal life?

Expressing gratitude

A second lesson we learn from David is not merely to reflect
on God's blessings but to thank him for them.

David was not content to excuse himself from prayer by
saying, 'The Lord knows I'm thankful.' He believed true
thanksgiving in the heart will spill out the mouth. So he prayed
with what we might describe as 'amazed gratitude'.

Look at how he begins his prayer: 'Who am I, O Lord
God?' (v. 18). When we get down to the nub of the matter, we
have to say the reason why so many of us are deficient in joy
and thanksgiving is that we do not have a keen awareness of
our unworthiness to receive any of his blessings.

We live in a time in which people constantly think they deserve more than what they have. Perhaps this attitude has clan-
destinely invaded the church and distorted the thinking of many
Christians. The truth of the matter is that we do not deserve
the smallest of God's blessings, but he has, in grace that stag-
gers and boggles the mind, bestowed the greatest of all possible
blessings upon us, the blessing of eternal life through his Son.

It should not escape our notice that David went beyond
thanking God for blessings bestowed upon himself to thanking God for his own greatness. We should always prize God
for who he is and not just for what he does for us.

David's thanksgiving also extended to the redeeming work
of God in creating a people for himself (vv. 22-24). God delights in his people, and we should delight in his people as
well. There is too much 'Lone Ranger' Christianity today. We

are each saved as individuals, but God does not intend us to journey to heaven as individuals but as part of the family of the redeemed.

Petitioning God

A third lesson that arises from this passage is that we should petition God along the lines of what he has promised to do.

This always puts some in a quandary. Why should we ask God for something if he has already promised to do it? The answer is that it pleases God for us to do so. He delights in having his people remind him of his own promises.

God has determined to release much of what he has promised in response to the faith of his people. We might say faith is the channel through which the promises of God flow. When God's people remind him of his promises, it demonstrates that they have faith in those promises, and this pleases God.

Keeping the glory of God as our priority

A final lesson for us here is to remember that the glory of God is to be our motive in everything we say and do.

As he prayed, David cried out, 'So let your name be magnified for ever...' (v. 26). God had promised David a 'for ever' — namely, that his kingdom would be established for ever. But David was more concerned about another 'for ever' — that God's name should be glorified for ever. In other words, David was saying this: 'What counts is not that my name should be remembered for ever, but that your name be magnified for ever.'

Christians are far from perfect while they are in this life, and there are times, therefore, when they get 'off track'. When the Christian is 'on track', the great, consuming desire of his heart is to see God glorified.

How could it be any other way? The Christian owes everything to God. There he was in the pit of sin and condemnation,
and God graciously lifted him out, adopted him into his own
family and has given him title to eternal glory. The only proper
response to such grace is to magnify God. David put it this
way in one of his psalms:

And let those who love your salvation say continually,
'Let God be magnified'

(Ps. 70:4).

There can be no doubt that David was a very happy man at
this particular point in his life, and we are privileged to see the
workings of his happy heart. But we also should note that
there is not only a description of the happy heart here, but also
a prescription for it. On the basis of this passage, we can say
happiness comes from reflecting on the goodness of God, expressing thanks for it, resting on God's promises and desiring
God's glory. No one who has ever seriously and sincerely tried
this prescription has found it to fail.

28.
The inner workings of outer success

2 Samuel 8:1-18

This is a chapter about David's success as King of Israel. It tells us that David succeeded at home and abroad. On the foreign front, he scored remarkable victories against the Philistines (v. 1), Moab (v. 2), Zobah (v. 3), the Syrians (vv. 5-6) and Edom (v. 14). Under his reign the nation of Israel finally possessed the land that God had promised to them.

David's success abroad was matched by his success at home. Verses 15-18 tell us that justice was his driving concern in domestic affairs, a concern that was guaranteed to increase the affection and esteem of the people for their king. These verses also indicate that David was skilled in the organization and administration of all the affairs of the nation.

The mere reading of these successes may give us the impression that success came easily to David, that all he had to do to secure victory was toss his sword on the field of battle or, to use a popular phrase, 'name it and claim it'.

It was during this time of brilliant success that David wrote Psalm 60. The heading of this psalm indicates that it was written in conjunction with the event mentioned in 2 Samuel 8:13, David's resounding victory over the Syrians in the Valley of Salt.

Psalm 60 enables us to peer into what went into that victory. It relates a prayer that David offered to God as he and his forces were engaged in conflict with the Syrians. Verses 1-3 consist of David's sad lament before God. Verses 4-8 consist of his solemn pleading with God. The final section, composed of verses 9-12, consists of David's confident rejoicing before the Lord.

These three emphases merge to make it clear that any success enjoyed by a child of God must ultimately be traced to our gracious Lord who is constantly at work in the lives of his children.

David's sad lament before God (Ps. 60:1-3)

The opening words of David's psalm cast a far different light on David's victory over the Syrians from that given by the account in 2 Samuel. It was not an easy triumph at all. It evidently came only after an initial defeat at the hands of the Syrians.

David did not attribute this defeat to 'bad luck', or poor military strategy. He and the people of Israel were in a covenant relationship with God. One aspect of this relationship was God's promise to give them victory over their enemies if they, the people of God, would walk in obedience to his commandments (Deut. 28:1,7). Defeat at the hands of an enemy had, therefore, to be understood and interpreted in terms of the spiritual condition of the people. Perhaps the string of successes under David's leadership had created a false sense of security that caused the people to take for granted the blessing of God apart from their obedience.

This much was clear to David: God had allowed his people to suffer a humiliating defeat because he was sorely displeased with them. He writes:

O God, you have cast us off;
You have broken us down;
You have been displeased...

(v. 1).

This defeat was of such a staggering nature that it seemed to David as if God had made the earth itself to tremble (v. 2). It was so overwhelming that it had left the people of God as disoriented as a man who was reeling under the influence of wine (v. 3).

David's solemn pleading with God (Ps. 60:4-12)

All of this made it most urgent for David and his people earnestly to seek the Lord, and in the remaining verses of the psalm we find David, as the head of the nation, doing exactly that. It is very likely that he also led the nation to join him in his heartfelt seeking of God.

David's personal pleading with God is composed of three strands of argument.

The Lord's banner

First, David holds the thought of a banner before the Lord. He says:

> You have given a banner to those who fear you,
> That it may be displayed because of the truth
>
> (v. 4).

God had special purposes in making the people of Israel his special possession. One of these was that the nation might be a banner to surrounding nations. In other words, Israel was to be a banner that proclaimed God's truth. Others were to be able to look at them and see the truth about God's redemption. The Israelites were to placard before the surrounding world the reality of that redemption and the difference it had made in their lives.

When the people of God suffered defeat at the hand of their enemies, these enemies would be inclined to conclude that there was nothing to the faith of Israel. Israel's defeat would, as it were, cause the banner of truth to be dragged along behind them rather than fly victoriously over them. David's prayer was, therefore, that the Lord would now grant victory to his people so the banner he had given them would again fly high and the truth would be known.

Moses employed the same argument with the Lord. When the people of Israel refused to enter the land of Canaan, the Lord said to Moses, 'How long will these people reject me? And how long will they not believe me, with all the signs which I have performed among them? I will strike them with the pestilence and disinherit them, and I will make of you a nation greater and mightier than they' (Num. 14:11-12).

Moses responded to these words by saying, 'Now if you kill these people as one man, then the nations which have heard of your fame will speak saying: "Because the Lord was not able to bring this people to the land which he swore to give them, therefore, he killed them in the wilderness"' (Num. 14:15-16).

Having made that point, Moses proceeded to remind the Lord of his promise to pardon the sin of his people (Num. 14:17-19). Their sin had made their banner trail in the dust, but pardon would lift it up again.

The Lord's beloved

David further appealed to the Lord by reminding him that he had been chosen by the Lord as the king of the nation. David realized that this was all due to the Lord's having set his love upon him. David recognized that he, the beloved of the Lord, had been placed over a nation beloved by the Lord. As the head of that nation, he pleaded with the Lord to deliver him and the nation from the hardship that had come upon them.

He prays:

> That your beloved may be delivered,
> Save with your right hand, and hear me
>
> (v. 5).

Charles Spurgeon says of this portion of the psalm: 'Here is one suppliant for many, even as in the case of our Lord's intercession for his saints. He, the Lord's David, pleads for the rest of the beloved, beloved and accepted in him the Chief Beloved; he seeks salvation as though it were for himself, but his eye is ever upon all those who are one with him in the Father's love.'[1]

As the people of Israel were blessed in and through David as their head, so the blessings of God flow to the church only through that beloved who is foreshadowed by David, the Lord Jesus Christ himself.

The Lord's promises

David adds yet another dimension to his pleading for God's restored favour — that is, the promises of God. He writes:

> God has spoken in his holiness:
> 'I will rejoice;
> I will divide Shechem
> And measure out the Valley of Succoth.
> Gilead is mine, and Manasseh is mine;
> Ephraim is also the helmet for my head;
> Judah is my lawgiver.
> Moab is my washpot;
> Over Edom I will cast my shoe;
> Philistia, shout in triumph because of me'
>
> (vv. 6-8).

The enemies David mentions in these verses (Moab, Edom, Philistia) were those the Lord had spoken about (Gen. 15:18-21; Exod. 23:31; Num. 34:1-12). David knew the promises of God were sure, and he prayed that God would, on the basis of those promises, use his people (Manasseh, Ephraim, Judah) to achieve victory.

We would do well to emulate David's example at this point. Some turn faith into positive thinking that obligates God to do things he has not promised. But faith is not believing anything we want to believe. It is rather believing God will do what he has promised to do, and praying on the basis of those promises.

It may seem foolish to pray for something that God has already promised to do, but it is not foolish. God is delighted when we parade his promises before him, and praying on the basis of those promises gives us assurance that our prayers will be heard and answered in the time and ways pleasing to God.

Spurgeon says of the assurance that comes from resting on the promises of God: 'Faith regards the promise not as fiction but fact, and therefore drinks in joy from it and grasps victory by it. "God hath spoken; I will rejoice"; here is a fit motto for every soldier of the cross.'[2]

That brings us to the final part of David's prayer.

David's confident rejoicing before the Lord (Ps. 60:9-12)

David began his prayer in something of a turmoil, but now the storm has subsided and all is peaceful and calm. David knew the Lord would again lift his banner of truth, that he would deliver his beloved and keep his promises. There was, then, nothing to fear. The God who had momentarily 'cast off' his people in displeasure and had not gone out with their armies (v. 10) would, in the light of the repentance of his people, give them help (v. 11).

Because God is faithful to return to his repentant people, David closes his psalm on this note of triumph:

Through God we will do valiantly,
For it is he who shall tread down our enemies

                                        (v. 12).

David and the armies of Israel, as 2 Samuel 8 indicates, did indeed do valiantly. The initial defeat David described in the opening verses of the psalm gave way to victory. David's dedication of the spoils of war to the Lord (2 Sam. 8:11) shows he knew his successes were not due to his skill and expertise, but to the Lord. The author of 2 Samuel makes this plain by twice saying, 'The Lord preserved David wherever he went' (vv. 6,14). Furthermore, as Psalm 60 so abundantly proves, David understood that success from the Lord's hand comes as his people walk in a manner that is pleasing to him.

Significant pictures

The historical account of David's successes in 2 Samuel 8 coupled with the principles of Psalm 60 has meaning for us on a couple of levels: the kingship of Christ and the warfare of the Christian.

The kingship of Christ

We certainly cannot read about David's victories over his enemies without thinking of that King whom he only faintly represents and pictures, the Lord Jesus Christ. As military victories over the enemies of his people were characteristic of David's reign, so we must say victories over his people's enemies are characteristic of Christ's reign as well.

The prophet Isaiah indicated that the Lord Jesus Christ would indeed be a warring king when he said, 'And his name will be called ... Mighty God...' (Isa. 9:6).

The apostle Paul tells us that through their mighty Warrior-King the people of God have been delivered from 'the power of darkness' (Col. 1:13), the fear of death (2 Cor. 1:10; Heb. 2:14-15) and the wrath to come (1 Thess. 1:10), and they will eventually be delivered from 'this present evil age' (Gal. 1:4).

Darkness, death and evil are all trappings of Satan's kingdom. To say Christ has delivered his people from these things is to say that he has decisively defeated Satan. How did our mighty Christ accomplish this? It was through his death on the cross. Paul writes of Christ's death on the cross, 'Having disarmed principalities and powers, he made a public spectacle of them, triumphing over them in it' (Col. 2:15). By dying on that cross, the Lord Jesus took the penalty of God's eternal wrath against the sins of his people. There God exacted from Christ the penalty for their sins and, in so doing, removed God's wrath from them and Satan's hold on them.

While Satan was decisively defeated by Christ's death on the cross, he was not totally eliminated. He is defeated but not dead, and he unceasingly prowls about 'like a roaring lion' (1 Peter 5:8). He is the adversary of all God's people, but they will never be in bondage to him again because Christ unfailingly shelters his own. In addition to being their delivering warrior-king, he is also their defending warrior-king.

This delivering, defending Christ will eventually complete his victory over Satan and his kingdom of darkness. On that day every knee will be compelled to bend before him and every tongue will be made to confess that he is indeed Lord of all (Phil. 2:9-11). On that day the thunderous cry will go up: 'Alleluia! For the Lord God Omnipotent reigns!' (Rev. 19:6) and his people will reign with him (Rev. 20:4). On that day the earth will be filled with the knowledge of the glory of the Lord 'as the waters cover the sea' (Hab. 2:14).

The Christian's warfare

David's victories over his enemies also cause us to reflect on the fact that Christians are engaged in a warfare of their own. It is not against Philistines, Moabites and Syrians, but rather against the forces of darkness (Eph. 6:10). In other words, it is a spiritual warfare. Our success in this warfare is, as the apostle Paul asserts, a matter of being 'strong in the Lord and in the power of his might' (Eph. 6:10). Picking up on the principles of Psalm 60, we can say our success in this warfare comes from looking to the Lord's banner, the Lord's Beloved and the Lord's promises.

Looking to *the Lord's banner* means we realize the Lord has a grand purpose for us. He intends us to lift high his banner of truth so that those around us will be compelled to admit that he has indeed made a difference in our lives. We find strength for the warfare by realizing that we lift high the banner of truth through godly living.

Looking to *the Lord's Beloved* means we realize that our victory in this spiritual warfare has already been secured by the Lord Jesus Christ. We are not called upon to win the victory over Satan and his forces, but rather to share in the victory Christ has already won. Further, we are to fight in this spiritual warfare with the awareness that God blesses us for the sake of his Beloved, the Lord Jesus Christ. Christians are beloved to God only by virtue of Christ.

Looking to *the Lord's promises* means we draw strength for our spiritual warfare by rehearsing such promises as these: our Lord has promised to be with us in our warfare (Heb. 13:5), to give us sufficient grace and strength for it (2 Cor. 12:9; 1 Peter 5:10) and, finally, to take us home to heaven where we shall never again have to engage in warfare (Rev. 14:13; 21:1-8).

29.
A marvellous manifestation of mercy to a miserable man

2 Samuel 9:1-13

Mercy is the grandest thing in this tired old world. Mercy is showing kindness and compassion. It may be directed to those who are in desperate need and cannot help themselves. It may be directed to those who have offended us in some way. It is always directed to those who have no right to expect anything from us.

If I take a hungry, destitute man into my home and feed and clothe him, that is mercy. If I forgive a person who is unable to pay me the money he owes me, that is mercy. If I forgive someone who has offended me, that is mercy. Mercy is marvellous. There is nothing like it.

In this passage, we have a marvellous display of mercy. Here is Mephibosheth, the grandson of King Saul and the son of Jonathan. What a miserable figure he cuts in these verses!

The miserable condition of Mephibosheth

A forfeited inheritance

First, he was the victim of a forfeited inheritance. Keith Kaynor says Mephibosheth was 'a member of a defunct regime. The house of Saul had little — their possessions had been lost or confiscated.'[1]

Inability

Secondly, he was completely unable to help himself. When he was a mere five years of age, the news of the deaths of his father and grandfather came to his nurse. Stricken with panic, she decided to flee with Mephibosheth. Somehow Mephibosheth fell in the course of their flight, and the fall left him crippled (2 Sam. 4:4).

The name 'Mephibosheth' means 'shameful thing'. Perhaps others began to speak of him in this way. 'Isn't it a shame about Jonathan's young son?' someone would say. 'Yes, it's a real Mephibosheth,' the other would reply. And the name stuck.

Fear

Thirdly, Mephibosheth had a natural fear of David. In the light of the fact that Saul had tried to take David's life, Mephibosheth had every right to expect David to be hostile towards anyone from the house of Saul.

Poor, pathetic Mephibosheth! Even the name of the town where he was living, Lo Debar ('no pasture'), seems to underscore and emphasize his condition.

Then came mercy like a bolt from the blue. Mephibosheth had no hold upon David. He had nothing to offer David. But David, in great, generous mercy, showed kindness to him.

The mercy of David

Note the following things about David's act of mercy:

1. David took the initiative. David made the enquiry about the house of Saul (v. 3).
2. David acted on the basis of the covenant he had made with Mephibosheth's father, Jonathan (v. 1). One

part of that covenant was that David would not 'cut off' Jonathan's house when he became king (1 Sam. 20:15).

3. David compelled Mephibosheth to come to him. David 'sent and brought' Mephibosheth out of the house of Machir (v. 5).

4. David received Mephibosheth by calming his fears and giving him assurance (v. 7).

5. David restored to Mephibosheth all he had lost (v. 7).

6. David guaranteed personal fellowship and communion between himself and Mephibosheth (v. 7).

7. Mephibosheth accepted David's offer with realization of his own terrible condition and with great humility and gratitude (v. 8).

What mercy we have to admire in this passage! Mephibosheth was hopelessly and helplessly destitute, and David stepped in to give his life meaning and value.

Parallels between Mephibosheth and ourselves

Our dreadful condition

I can identify with Mephibosheth at so many points. In fact I can identify with his dreadful condition at every point.

The Bible tells me that I, like him, was the victim of a squandered inheritance. My father, Adam, was given so much. He was made in the image of God, given the privilege of fellowshipping with God and given the opportunity to secure eternal life.

Adam was no ordinary man. As the first man, he was the representative of all men. What he did counted for all — and, oh, what he did! He disobeyed the only command God gave him, and everything he had received went right out the window.

The image of God was now distorted and twisted in him. The fellowship with God was broken. The way to eternal life was barred and in its place he received the sentence of eternal death. And because of his representative capacity, all of this was true of me as soon as I came into this world.

Not only did Adam lose all these things, but he also lost the capacity, or ability, to change them. When I came into this world, therefore, I already had this same incapacity: no mind to understand God, no heart to love him and no desire to seek him. Like Mephibosheth, I not only had no inheritance, but I was so crippled that I was unable to do anything about it.

But that is not all. There was one who had the power to change Mephibosheth's lot in life — David — but Mephibosheth was afraid of him. And there was one who had the power to change my situation as well — God. But as Mephibosheth was afraid of David, so I harboured a fear towards God. Yes, my name was once Mephibosheth. I was in a dreadful, shameful condition.

The mercy of God

I can also identify with Mephibosheth at another point. I, like him, have received mercy. One glad day the gospel of Jesus Christ broke into my dreary world. It came to me. God took the initiative with me even as David took the initiative with Mephibosheth.

That word came to me to announce that God would restore all that I had lost in Adam. This glorious restoration was not because of any good thing I had done or because of any good I could do. It was not because of any hold that I had on God. It was because there was a covenant in place that I knew nothing about. Back there in eternity past, God the Father and God the Son entered into covenant with each other to provide a plan of redemption for Adam's fallen race.

That word that came to me won my heart. It was a powerful, compelling word even as David's message to Mephibosheth was powerful and compelling. It was a word that I could not ignore, one that I did not want to ignore. It offered hope and life to me.

As I look back on that word, I find myself agreeing with the lines of John Newton:

'Twas the same grace that spread the feast
That gently forced me in
Else I had still refused to taste
And perished in my sin.

When that word came to me, I had a fear of God, but that word calmed my fears just as David calmed the fears of Mephibosheth. It assured me that there was no reason to live any longer in fear of God's judgement, that God's purpose towards me was benevolent and kind, that his purpose was to restore my lost estate and enter into a state of fellowship with him.

Robert Murray M'Cheyne celebrated God's calming of his fears in his poem entitled *'Jehovah Tsidkenu'* (The Lord our Righteousness):

My terrors all vanished before the sweet name;
My guilty fears banished, with boldness I came
To drink at the fountain, life-giving and free.
Jehovah Tsidkenu is all things to me.

The truth is that Mephibosheth, in being given the privilege of eating at the king's table, actually became part of the king's family and, therefore, received more than he had lost.

So it is with me. Through the gospel of Jesus Christ, I have received more than Adam lost, and I can, therefore, gladly join Isaac Watts in these lines about Christ:

In him the tribes of Adam boast,
More blessings than their father lost.

I have been lifted out of my dreadful, shameful condition, elevated to heavenly places in Christ Jesus and adopted into
God's own family. I enjoy fellowship with God and I am assured of eternal life with him.

And just as Mephibosheth's heart was filled with joy and
gratitude and wonder at the mercy of David, so my heart is
filled with joy and gratitude and wonder at the mercy of God.
It is all because of the mercy of God manifested in Christ Jesus:

He left his Father's throne above,
So free, so infinite his grace;
Emptied himself of all but love,
And bled for Adam's helpless race;
'Tis mercy all, immense and free,
For, O my God, it found out me.

(Charles Wesley)

Every Christian was once a Mephibosheth. Now, through
the mercy of God, we are no longer. We are now sons and
daughters of God.

If you are still a Mephibosheth, hear the good news of this
passage of Scripture: there is mercy with God to save you
from your sins and make you part of his own family. Cast
yourself upon that mercy now. Don't be a Mephibosheth any
longer.

30.
Mercy abused

2 Samuel 10

Nahash, King of Ammon, had shown kindness of some sort to David. We do not know the details of this act of kindness. Some speculate that Nahash had provided something that David needed when he was fleeing from Saul.

Now Nahash was dead, and his son Hanun had taken the throne (v. 2). As David reflected on what Nahash had done for him, he decided to send some of his servants to express his condolences to Hanun (v. 2).

A despicable deed

It was a kind, generous thing to do. But David's servants were in for a surprise. The counsellors of Hanun insisted that, under the pretence of sympathy, David had sent spies into the land of Ammon (v. 3). These counsellors won the day, and Hanun seized David's servants, shaved off half their beards, cut off their garments at a very indiscreet level and sent them off thoroughly humiliated (v. 4). Hanun, then, not only rebuffed David's act of kindness, but did so in a very vile and insulting manner.

The Ammonites may very well have laughed uproariously as they sent David's servants down the road, but it was not long before they realized David was not laughing (vv. 5-7).

Two resounding victories

The Ammonites knew their army was no match for David's, so they hired several thousand soldiers from the Syrians and other sources (v. 6).

Joab led David's forces into the field and issued this stirring charge: 'Be of good courage, and let us be strong for our people and for the cities of our God. And may the Lord do what seems good to him' (v. 12). The battle was joined, and, although forced to fight on two fronts at the same time, David's army was successful. The Syrians were put to flight (v. 13) and the Ammonites were forced to take refuge within their city walls (v. 14).

The Syrians mustered another attempt to defeat Israel, only to encounter resounding defeat (vv. 15-19).

Pointed lessons

Ammonites and Syrians, beards and battles — it all sounds very bizarre and totally irrelevant. But closer inspection reveals that there is far more in this account than odd names, strange deeds and forgotten battles. In fact, I would suggest there are several points at which this account speaks powerfully to us. Each of these points may be summarized with one word.

Kindness

First, there is that word 'kindness'. Centuries and civilizations have come and gone. Kings and kingdoms have passed away. But kindness is never to pass away from the people of God.

David's kindness flowed from a grateful heart. He realized he had been the recipient of kindness, and the natural outcome of receiving kindness is to bestow it on others.

The apostle Paul made the connection between receiving kindness and expressing it in these words: 'And be kind to one another, tender-hearted, forgiving one another; even as God in Christ also forgave you' (Eph. 4:32). Oh, how much kindness we received when God through Christ forgave us of our sins and made us part of his family for ever! Anyone who has received this greatest of all kindnesses cannot refuse lesser kindnesses to his or her brothers and sisters in Christ.

While Paul was addressing the matter of brothers and sisters in Christ showing kindness to one another, we must understand that our responsibility is not limited to, or exhausted in, that area. We are also called upon to show kindness to those outside the family of faith, a note which is sounded by both the apostle Paul and the apostle Peter in several verses (Rom. 12:20-21; Gal. 6:10; 1 Peter 3:13-17).

Too often Christians have been content to treat the gospel as if it were a hand grenade to be lobbed from a safe distance over the wall of unbelief. What we need is a key that slides into the lock and easily and smoothly opens the door of the heart. Kindness is that key.

The kindness we need is more than smiling pleasantly and speaking cheerfully to those whom we meet. It involves entering into the lives of those around us to the extent that we know what is going on with them. It can be something of a seemingly small and trivial nature. It is taking note of that person who collects something and making a purchase of that item for him to add to his collection. It can be remembering a birthday. It certainly includes doing something to help when sickness or bereavement comes into that family. It is taking time to write that note of encouragement. It is being a good listener.

The more we practise this kind of kindness, the more opportunities we see for practising it, and the more we enjoy life.

Several months ago there was a nationwide flurry throughout the USA of what were called 'random acts of kindness'. I don't know how it started, but people began to look for ways to perform some kindness for complete strangers. The fact that it caught the attention of the national news media tells us something about its impact. Christians should not have to wait for kindness to become a national fad. It should be such a part of the fabric of our lives that no one can hear the name 'Christian' without thinking of kindness.

Contempt

Another word that connects this passage with our day is 'contempt'. David had the purest of motives in sending his messengers to Hanun, but the counsellors of the latter read a dark plot into David's act. Matthew Henry observes, 'False men are ready to think others as false as themselves; and those that bear ill-will to their neighbours are resolved not to believe that their neighbours bear any goodwill to them...'[1]

The treatment David's servants received is not a strange instance that stands alone. History reveals that the people of God have been rebuffed and spurned and treated contemptibly time after time.

In fact it is safe to say contemptible treatment has become the order of the day in modern Western society. Christians can point to a wonderful legacy of good deeds. Hospitals and universities have been built. Organizations for the relief of the poor, the homeless and the hungry have been founded. More organizations have been created to show compassion for prisoners, drug addicts and alcoholics. Christianity has sent out into this society a stream of kindness and benevolence that is quite overwhelming.

But as one watches television and reads the newspapers and magazines, one gains the impression that Christianity is a sinister threat to the well-being of society as a whole. Terms such as 'far right' and 'extremists' are regularly used to describe evangelical Christians, and columnists speak openly of being 'afraid' of a society that is influenced to any large degree by Christians.

Meanwhile we have had plenty of time to see what has happened to our society as Christian principles have been increasingly pushed to one side. Crime has soared. Drug addiction and alcoholism have sky-rocketed. Teenage pregnancies are epidemic. Divorce rages at flood-tide. Taxation spirals. Isn't it ironic that our columnists and pundits do not speak of being afraid of these things, but only of Christianity?

The contempt that exists on the national level is by no means the whole story. It exists on an individual level as well, even to the point where most Americans now say they would rather live next door to almost anyone than an evangelical Christian.

What remarkable times! They cause us to scratch our heads in perplexity. How are we to live in such times? The answer is clear. We are to go right on being God's good people even though we are regarded with suspicion.

Vindication

The third point of connection between our passage and our own time is summed up in the word 'vindication'.

God's people are not only to face this evil age with goodness, but also with absolute trust in God that he will vindicate them at last. As David decisively vindicated the honour of his servants, so God will finally vindicate his people.

The prophet Malachi tells us the Lord is keeping a book of remembrance. He takes note of his people and of every act of abuse. In due time, he calls his people his 'jewels' and promises to some day gather them up out of the mud and muck of this world. On that glorious day, everyone will know that they were right to serve God (Mal. 3:16-18).

That day of vindication for God's people will be a day of wrath for those who are not his. This is the age of mercy. God, through his people, is showing kindness to an unbelieving world. But there is an end to God's patience and kindness, and when that end comes the wicked will be visited with the consuming fire of God's judgement (Mal. 4:1).

In the light of the dreadful nature of that coming judgement, the Bible urges all to accept God's salvation while there is time. It pleads with us not to be like Hanun. It says there is a high cost to refusing God's mercy and, in the words of the poet, urges us to accept that mercy:

Ye sinners seek his grace,
Whose wrath ye cannot bear;
Fly to the shelter of his cross,
And find salvation there.

31.
David's descent into sin and deception

2 Samuel 11

This chapter brings us to David's blackest moment. It shows us the grim truth that even the godliest of men have hidden in their hearts a foul swamp of iniquity that constantly bubbles up within them and is ever ready to emit its stench.

In these verses, we have the sad spectacle of David moving through a distressing sequence that culminated in his arranging the murder of one of his most loyal soldiers and bringing upon himself the fiery thrusts of God's sword of judgement.

A low spiritual condition

We must not assume that this sequence began with David seeing the naked Bathsheba from the rooftop. It has to be traced back to his allowing a coldness and a casual attitude towards God to creep into his heart and settle there. Somewhere — the exact point is hidden from our prying eyes — David allowed the fire of devotion to God to burn low. Sin is always born in a damp, chilly heart.

Omission usually precedes commission. Let a Christian become careless about his church attendance, or let him become half-hearted when he is in church, and he has already set one foot on the slippery slope of sin. Let him become casual about his Bible reading, or let him read mechanically, and he has already hung the welcome sign out for sin. Let him leave off praying, or pray without feeling, and he has already planted the seeds of disaster.

Gratitude is God's great safeguard for us against sin — and, oh, how much David had to be grateful for! God had plucked him from obscurity and thrust him onto the stage of public prominence in Israel. God had preserved him from the evil plotting of the mad Saul. God had brought him to the throne of Israel and given him prosperity and popularity of immense proportions. To crown it all, God had even given him the promise that the Messiah would be among his descendants.

But on this day David is not thinking about any of these things. There he is now in his palace with his cold heart. His army is engaged in a campaign against the Ammonites, and the text suggests it was David's duty to be with his men (v. 1). But instead of being out in the field with them, here he is, absorbed with his own comfort. His men are engaged in the rigours of war while David regales himself with pleasure. He rises from his nap — a fitting symbol, it would seem, of his spiritual condition — and walks out onto his roof. From there he is able to see a very beautiful woman.

The temptation and the sin

There was a time in David's spiritual pilgrimage when he was able to fend off even the most ferocious temptations. Our minds go back to those times when he was tempted to end Saul's life. On those occasions he very quickly and decisively pushed the temptation to one side and dealt with the situation on the basis of principle.

But David does not act quickly or decisively here. He sees the beautiful woman, but instead of quickly averting his eyes

and going back inside his house, he stands and stares. And as
he stands and stares, the desire within him grows.

One cannot help but wonder if much of David's lusting and
scheming should be attributed to peer pressure. The people of
Israel had wanted a king like all the other nations (1 Sam.
8:5), and the way of those kings was to multiply wives for
themselves even if it meant taking the wife of another. Perhaps David, intoxicated with years of success as King of Israel, now fancied that he should be able to enjoy the 'perks' of
his position just as any other king would. If David engaged in
such reasoning, he was guilty of a terrible omission. He was
not just 'any king'. He was anointed of the Lord to rule over
the people of the Lord according to the Word of the Lord —
a word which gave no quarter for yielding to the worldly
pressure to do things as others did them (Deut. 17:14-20).

As David stands there staring and lusting, a scheme is born.
He sends a servant to find out more about this woman. The
report comes back that her name is Bathsheba. (The 'Bath'
part of her name seems most appropriate!)

Along with the servant's report of her name came what
Gordon Keddie refers to as 'a check to his conscience' when
the servant added that she was married to Uriah the Hittite.[1]

The law of God is crystal clear about sexual involvement
with someone who is married. It is adultery, and it is wrong.
But by now David is beyond caring about that. The engine of
lust is racing at full speed, and he is determined to have her at
all costs. So he sends messengers to bring her to him, and
David has his 'one-night stand'.[2]

The focus of the passage is, of course, on David, but
Bathsheba was not blameless. It is very likely that she knew
her bathing could be seen from the king's palace. Perhaps she
even wanted it that way! We can say for certain that she should
have rejected David's advances. The same law of God that
applied to David applied to her. It would, of course, have been

very difficult for her to refuse the king of her nation, but God does not require obedience only if it is easy. He requires it no matter what the cost.

The cover-up

It seemed for a while that David had got away with the whole sordid thing. No one knew what he had done (with the exception of the servants he had employed), so what difference did it make?

But then the shattering word came from Bathsheba that she had conceived. The Bible emphasizes for us that it was impossible for her to have conceived except by David because they had their affair immediately after she was 'cleansed from her impurity' (v. 4).

Now David had a problem. He had to find a way to cover up what he had done. He immediately sent for Uriah. David pretended to want an update on the war with Ammon, but what he really wanted was for Uriah to go home and spend some time with his wife (vv. 8,10).

David knew Uriah was a loyal soldier, but he had no idea just how loyal he was until Uriah refused to go home. He insisted it would not be right for him to do so while his fellow-soldiers were still on the field of battle (v. 11). David was forced to resort to another stratagem. He kept Uriah another day and got him drunk in the hope that he would go home in a drunken stupor, but even in his drunkenness, Uriah refused to go home (v. 13).

By this time it should be obvious to us that David was in a greater stupor than Uriah ever was. As far as he was concerned, there was now only one way to cover up his sin, and that was to have Uriah killed and take Bathsheba as his wife. In incredible callousness, David sent by Uriah's own hand the order to have him stationed in the next battle at the place where he was most likely to be killed (vv. 14-15).

The order had the outcome David desired. Uriah was killed in battle. Bathsheba was a widow. After allowing her a brief period for 'mourning', David took her as his wife (vv. 26-27). At last David was able to heave a sigh of relief. His twisted mind told him he had successfully covered his sin. The child would be born and everyone would think it was the premature fruit of his marriage to Bathsheba. However, the chapter closes on this most solemn note: 'But the thing that David had done displeased the Lord' (v. 27).

Some lessons from David's immorality

There are an abundance of lessons and applications for us to draw from this sad episode.

1. We must be very careful about listening to what our minds tell us about what we deserve. As we see David lounging about his palace while his men were engaged in battle, we can almost re-create what he had said to himself: 'You have worked so long and so hard, you deserve some time just for yourself.' We have no trouble re-creating this because our own minds have generated the same message time after time.

2. We never reach the point in this life where we are entirely through with sin. David was at this time fifty years of age. By this time, he had walked with God for so long that we might have thought he would be too strong for temptation. But he was not. Indications are that many older people are falling prey to sexual sin after spending a lifetime of obeying God at this point.

3. The best safeguard against sin is to keep our hearts hot after God, and the best way to keep a heart after God is to cultivate gratitude for what God has done for us.

4. Men are to be on their guard about what they see, and women are to be on their guard as to what they show.

There are two categories as far as the seeing goes. First, there are those things we cannot help but see. We must fortify ourselves against these things by living close to God and asking him to give us strength to ward off the temptation that comes to us in this way.

The second category is what we deliberately choose to see. Sexually explicit films, suggestive television shows and pornographic magazines create such an insatiable lust that it is almost impossible to refrain from sexual immorality. The looking is sin in and of itself, and it can easily lead us into the greater sin of actually involving someone else in immoral acts.

5. There is no such thing as hidden sin. David thought his sin was hidden, but it came out. All sin will. If it does not come out in this life, it certainly will in the life to come. God is committed to setting sin in the full glare of light.

6. Evil acts always lead to evil consequences. This chapter only introduces David's sin to us. We shall come to all the miserable consequences later. At this point, let us only note that there are consequences. Sin never leaves us where it finds us. It always brings misery and woe.

7. God's law is the standard for our behaviour, and we are to obey it no matter what we feel, no matter what others say or do or how costly obedience is. We have a tendency to lessen the impact of what David did

by referring to it as an 'indiscretion' or an 'affair', but God's law calls it 'adultery' and says we must not commit it.

David's sin is one of the saddest tragedies recorded for us in the Word of God. We have come to admire this man as a great man of God. His fall reminds us that we must always be on guard against sin. We have also come to view David as a type of Christ in many ways. Let it be said loudly and clearly that he is no type of Christ here. Here he is nothing but a miserable sinner who shows us our need for Christ. Christ alone is the truly righteous King. Only through his righteousness are we able to stand before a holy God.

32.
Confrontation and confession

2 Samuel 12:1-15

Months had passed since David had cold-bloodedly taken pen in hand to write Uriah's death-warrant. Bathsheba was now his wife. Their son, illicitly conceived, had arrived, and the vast majority assumed he was the product of the marriage of David and Bathsheba.

David had engaged in a blatant orgy of self. He had put the gratification of his flesh on the throne of his life and had callously trampled on everyone else.

David's misery

David should have been happy. He had got what he wanted and he had seemingly escaped the consequences. But he was far from happy. He was not happy because he knew that inward turmoil that stems from an accusing conscience. That still small voice must have created many a sleepless night for David in those months that followed his sin. When he looked back on that time he could only say, 'My bones grew old through my groaning all the day long' (Ps. 32:3). It is easier to cover sin from the eyes of others than it is to still the voice of conscience.

And that was not all. Conscience had not died in David. But something else had. That light, happy heart that so quickly took fire for the things of God and caused him to feel joyful exuberance and sheer delight was gone. That heart was replaced with one that was cold, heavy and dead as a rock within him. We may rest assured that David continued his worship in the tabernacle, but it was not the same now. A cold heart makes worship a grim, unhappy business.

Perhaps David persuaded himself that it was just a matter of brazening it out. The passing of time would finally silence his conscience and bring the joy back. God knew better. The only way for one of his people ever to get relief from sin is to listen to the voice of conscience, confess the sin and receive forgiveness.

Nathan's message

To help David reach this point, God sent Nathan the prophet. (Some wonder how Nathan learned of David's sin. The answer is simple: God told him!)

Did Nathan tremble at the thought of confronting his king? It is unlikely. As a true prophet of God, he knew there was a far greater King than David, a King that was no mere man such as David was. Nathan dreaded offending that King far more than he did offending David.

The Lord gave Nathan a story to relate to David. The purpose of this story was to get David to pronounce judgement upon himself. It worked to perfection. Nathan came in and told his story. There were two men in the kingdom — one rich, the other poor. The rich man had a guest come for a visit, but instead of preparing one of his many lambs to feed his guest, the rich man took his neighbour's only lamb — a lamb that was the family's prized pet — and used it to serve his guest (vv. 1-4).

It is doubtful whether David had ever been angrier in all of his life. The very thought of a rich man in his kingdom taking the only lamb of his poor neighbour enraged him! He must have leaped to his feet as he roared: 'As the Lord lives, the man who has done this shall surely die! And he shall restore fourfold for the lamb, because he did this thing and because he had no pity' (vv. 5-6).

That was exactly what Nathan was waiting for. Quick as a flash, the prophet seized on these words and exclaimed, 'You are the man!' (v. 7).

Before David could raise an objection, or issue a word of denial, Nathan fleshed out his message. David was indeed the rich man of the parable. God had anointed him as king, had protected him from Saul and given him the house of Saul, the throne of Judah and Israel and, if all that had not been enough, was prepared to do even more (vv. 7-8). But David, in high-handed wantonness and cold-blooded selfishness, had gone over to his poor neighbour's house, and without one meagre shred of pity, had taken what belonged to him and had even had him killed (v. 9).

Because of this David was now about to face some very miserable times. He had committed adultery with Bathsheba in secret, but an adversary would arise to commit adultery with David's wives in public view (vv. 11-12).

David's confession

When Nathan finally took a breath, David at long last blurted out the only words that can finally bring relief to the soul tortured by sin: 'I have sinned against the Lord' (v. 13).

We often admit our sins in a cavalier, nonchalant manner by saying, 'No one is perfect!' or 'I know I have made my share of mistakes.' But David's words belong to a different world. They were born in the depths of a heart that was rent with the consciousness of the depth of its own iniquity and with the knowledge of how infinitely disgusting sin is to the holy God with whom we all have to do.

Up to this point, David had been refusing to face his sin. He would read the law of Moses, and look away from the accusing finger that pointed from it. He would hear the voice of conscience and would, as it were, clap his hands over his ears.

But he is now through with all that. He is no longer defending himself and rationalizing his sin. Up to this point he and God had been at variance about his sin. God was saying one thing and he another. But here he finally stops defending himself against God, walks over to God's side of the dispute and joins him in condemning his own sin.

The complete account of David's repentance is recorded for us in Psalm 51. There we find David openly and honestly confessing the enormity of his sin, throwing himself totally on the mercy of God and pleading for forgiveness of the sin and restoration of the joy he had lost.

Because David's repentance was genuine and deep and because God's grace is infinite and immense, there was forgiveness for David. He deserved to die for what he had done, but God lifted from him the sentence of death (v. 13).

Immense relief must surely have flooded into David's soul as he heard that, but Nathan had not finished with him just yet. He had already announced one ghastly result of David's sin (the public adultery of a coming adversary), but there was to be another. The son that had come from his illicit union with Bathsheba was to die (v. 14).

Why was such a heavy judgement necessary? Nathan's answer was clear. David's sin had been great, so the judgement must be great. Here is how great David's sin was: it had given the enemies of Israel the opportunity to blaspheme (v. 14). David and his people were called into a special covenant relationship with God. There was a 'missionary' dimension to this covenant relationship. In other words, the people of Israel were to demonstrate by their regard for the laws of God that they served a righteous God who is to be honoured and feared by all nations. But David's act — if not already known — would become known and would cause the surrounding nations to conclude that there was really nothing to the religion of Israel after all.

By severe judgement on David, God would show those surrounding nations that he was still a righteous God even when his people failed to be righteous.

Principles for living

As we have previously noted, the Bible never glosses over the sins of its greatest heroes, but lays them bare before our eyes. Its purpose in doing so is to help us learn some very important and vital principles about governing our own lives.

What are we to learn from the part of David's life that we have been examining?

The following lessons emerge with crystal clarity:

1. A true child of God can fall into horrible sin and remain in it for a time, but he will never be happy in it and will ultimately come to repentance.

2. The messenger of God who refuses to tiptoe around our sins but faithfully rebukes them does us a great service and should be prized as a true friend.

3. True repentance is no light matter. It does not shrug off sin, or seek to excuse it in any way, but sees the enormity of it, condemns it and resolves to break with it. This is done with a spirit of true brokenness and deep sorrow.

4. God's mercy is such that he does indeed forgive the sins of his people and restores their joy, but his forgiveness of their sins does not necessarily mean the removal of the consequences. God leaves those consequences so that others will take note and will guard against sin.

These lessons shine like beacons from David's experience. We can look at his experience, accept these lessons and guard diligently against sin in our own lives. Or we can refuse to learn from David's example. We can assure ourselves that we are the exception to the rules — that we can play with the fire of sin and not get burned. The choice is ours. Someone pointed out that those who refuse to learn from history are doomed to repeat it. We might say that those who refuse to learn from David's experience are doomed to find the misery he found.

33.
Chastisement

2 Samuel 12:15-23

This passage fairly brims with intriguing questions and pressing issues. One of these is the so-called problem of 'unanswered prayer'. Here David prays for something very specific — the sparing of the life of his young son — but it is not granted.

We know something about this. We all have experienced this. We have gone flying into the presence of God to urgently press upon him a petition for something we felt we must have. And the thing that we prayed to happen did not come to pass, or the thing that we prayed not to happen did come to pass. God heard our prayer, but answered 'No!' and we wondered why.

The answer is, of course, locked up in the inscrutable sovereignty of God. He has his own purposes and his own ways of achieving those purposes. He knows what he is about, and it is for us to trust him to have a loving purpose even when he allows sorrows to come our way. As the old hymn says, 'We'll understand it better by and by.'

A second issue raised in this passage has to do with the death of children. What happens to the child who dies before he or she makes a profession of faith? This passage gives us a faint glimmer of the answer. A tiny shaft of light breaks through the grey here. After his child died, David was able to say, 'I shall go to him, but he shall not return to me' (v. 23). Matthew Henry writes, 'Godly parents have great reason to hope concerning their children that die in infancy that it is well with their souls in the other world...'[1] And he adds that such children '... are better provided for, both in work and wealth, than they could have been in this world'.[2]

Although this passage raises these important issues, we have to say that these are not the major thrust of it. That can be summarized in one word — chastisement. Here we have the Lord God correcting his child David.

Chastisement is one of those biblical themes that receive short shrift today. But it is very definitely a biblical theme, written there, as it were, in large letters. It is essential, therefore, that we seek to understand it.

The meaning of chastisement

First, we must seek to understand what chastisement is. Here is a definition of chastisement: it is God's way of getting from his children what he wants from them.

It comes as a shock to many, but the truth is that God wants something from his people. In other words, God does not save his people only so they can go to heaven when they die. He does not merely say to the one whom he has saved, 'You just go on now and live any way you want, and I will see you when you die.' There are many people who would like to believe that, and they seem to be conducting their lives as if it were true. But it is not true.

What is it that God wants from his people here and now? The answer is clear in Scripture. He wants us to have a heart of love for him. The Lord Jesus said the greatest of all God's commandments is: 'You shall love the Lord your God with all your heart, with all your soul, and with all your mind' (Matt. 22:37).

Love does not seem to be all that demanding to us. We think it is just having a warm, woolly feeling in our hearts, and from that we deduce that we love God. But God has made it clear that loving him is more than having a sentimental feeling. It is a matter of obeying his commandments (John 14:23).

So what God wants from each of his children is this — a heart of love that manifests itself in lives of obedience. Now God does not just vaguely desire this from us. He actively works to produce it. And the primary way God produces obedience is through his Word. But we do not always listen to his Word. We often become 'dull of hearing' (Heb. 5:11).

What does God do when we do not allow his Word to produce in us the obedience he demands? The Bible says he chastises us. In this passage we see David being chastised. David had allowed the flame of love for God to burn low in his heart, and had plunged headlong off into the terrible sins of adultery and murder. God sent Nathan the prophet to him to confront him with his sinful behaviour and to announce two terrible results of it: the coming of an adversary (vv. 11-12) and the death of the son of David and Bathsheba (v. 14).

We do not like to hear about God chastising his children. We consider it to be at odds with the love of God, but it is, of course, just the opposite. It is the proof of his love.

Chastisement is not God getting even with his children because of sin in their lives. Its purpose is to correct the child of God so he will follow the right path in the future. R. T. Kendall observes, 'Chastening is not God's "getting even". God "got even" at the cross! ... God's chastening is not meted out in proportion to our sins but in proportion to the lesson we have to learn.'[3]

A quick glance at the twelfth chapter of Hebrews shows the purpose of God's chastening. It is that 'we may be partakers of his holiness' (Heb. 12:10), and so that we might be 'trained' by it and enjoy as a result 'the peaceable fruit of righteousness' (Heb. 12:11).

The manifestations of chastisement

A second aspect of chastisement we need to understand has to do with the forms or manifestations of it.

First, God can correct us by bringing calamity or adversity upon us. This is, of course, the form it took with David. The second form — and we may be sure this element was also present in David's case — is withholding of blessing.

I have no hesitation in suggesting that this second form of chastisement is being employed by God to a very large degree today. Even the most casual observer has to admit there is much carelessness among the people of God today about his commandments. The fact that we are not seeing great calamities inclines us to think we are getting away with our sins. But what is the price we are paying in terms of missed blessing? What good might God be bringing upon our individual lives and our churches if we were more scrupulous about his commandments?

There is something else to be said at this point as well. If we will not learn the lessons God wants to teach us through his withholding his blessings, we can certainly expect him to move to the other type of chastisement by bringing calamity and adversity.

Our response to chastisement

A third dimension of chastisement for us to understand is how the child of God should respond to it.

We do not find David complaining about the Lord's dealings with him in chastisement. While his child was still alive, David prayed that the Lord might spare him. He knew the Lord sometimes announces judgement so that people might be stirred to seek him and that he might then in compassion turn from the judgement. The classic example of this is the city of Nineveh (Jonah 3).

But when the Lord did not spare his son, David quietly accepted it. He did not allow anger and resentment against God to take over his heart, but rather 'went into the house of the Lord and worshipped' (v. 20).

There was no point in David's being angry with God. He knew full well that God had dealt fairly with him. God had very clearly forbidden in the law of Moses the sins David had committed, and yet he had forged madly ahead and violated at least six of the Ten Commandments. He had put himself and his desires above God (no. 1), he had committed murder (no. 6), he had committed adultery (no. 7), he had stolen (no. 8), he had lied and deceived (no. 9) and he had coveted (no. 10).

David actually received from the Lord much less than he deserved.

Our consolation in the midst of chastisement

A final truth for us to learn about chastisement is that it does not mean the end of God's grace and blessing. Yes, God often chastises his people by withholding blessing, but he never completely withdraws those blessings from us, and he often brings good out of the evil we have done.

Even though God's chastening of David was severe, the grace of God was still present to bless. One blessing God bestowed upon David and Bathsheba was the birth of Solomon (vv. 24-25), the son who would finally succeed David as king and who would be used by God to usher in a golden age for the nation. After chastening David, God also blessed him by giving him a significant military victory over the Ammonites (vv. 26-31).

Who can measure the grace of God? It is grace that works in our lives to make us God's children. It is grace that forgives us when we sin against the Lord. Yes, it is even the grace of God that will not let us go but chastens us so we will be what God wants us to be. It is grace that grants blessings even after we have miserably failed, and that grace will finally lead us home.

Let's make sure we daily praise God for this saving, renewing, chastening grace. Let's renew our commitment to carefully obey the Lord God from hearts filled with love.

When he chastens us, let's make sure we do not chafe and complain, but rather kiss the chastening rod because we have a Father who loves us enough to correct us.

Yes, every day of our lives let's magnify the incomparable grace of God, singing with George Matheson:

> O Love that will not let me go,
> I rest my weary soul in thee:
> I give thee back the life I owe,
> That in thine ocean depths its flow
> May richer, fuller be.

34.
A recipe for ruin

2 Samuel 13

Some passages of Scripture are so depressingly sad that words seem inadequate to describe them. This chapter introduces us to one such section. It is one of the saddest portions to be found in Scripture.

There are five major characters in this chapter. One, of course, is David himself. Fresh from God's forgiveness of his sin, he here sees the first instalment in the calamity that the prophet Nathan had promised in these solemn words: 'Now therefore, the sword shall never depart from your house...' (2 Sam. 12:10).

The second major character is Tamar, David's daughter. She plays a prominent part in this chapter, but only in a passive way. She walks on to the stage of history as a vibrant young woman, and leaves it a demoralized, devastated wreck — and all of it was through no fault of her own.

That brings us to three of the slimiest, most pathetic characters in Scripture: Amnon, Absalom and Jonadab. The first two were sons of David. The third, Jonadab, was the son of David's brother Shimeah (v. 3).

What we have in this chapter is a disaster, and each of its four men provides an ingredient for the recipe. Wherever we find these same ingredients joined together we find the same wreckage and ruin that they brought about in the episode before us.

Unrestrained passion

First, there was Amnon and the ingredient he supplied —
namely, unrestrained passion (vv. 1-2).

It might seem that this chapter is primarily about Amnon
and we might, therefore, have expected it to open with his
name. But, as we shall find, it is only secondarily about him.
The primary emphasis in the next six chapters is on Absalom
and David. So the chapter appropriately opens with these
words: 'After this ... Absalom the son of David had a lovely
sister...'

Then comes the tongue-in-cheek statement that Amnon,
the older brother of Absalom, 'loved' Tamar. That was, of
course, the word that Amnon would have used to describe
what he was feeling for Tamar. But it was in reality far from
love. Another word, also beginning with 'l', jumps more readily to mind — lust.

Gordon Keddie says of Amnon's 'love': 'The ingredients
of a genuine love are altogether lacking: there is no self-giving
commitment, no seeking of the other's highest good, no sen-
sitive devotion, not even a hint of romance; there is only naked
physical lust and an utterly self-centred disregard for Tamar's
personal integrity, welfare and blessedness. Amnon is consumed, not by what he could do for her, but by what he wanted
desperately to do to her. He wanted sex — it was as simple as
that!'[1]

There are plenty of Amnon's type about today. Consumed
by lust that masquerades as love, they pressurize young women
to satisfy their lust by assuring them that they love them. To
such men, 'I love you,' really means, 'I love myself and I want
you.' Young ladies, listen to this word of counsel. If a man
truly loves you, he will be willing to commit himself to you in
the bonds of marriage and will gladly wait for you until that
time.

We cannot help but wonder at this point about the effect David's own behaviour had upon his son. Amnon, of course, was responsible to do what was right, but the example of a father who had many wives and who had taken another's wife could very well have made Amnon view women merely as means to gratify lust.

Ungodly counsel

That brings us to this sordid character, Jonadab, and the ingredient he brought to this wretched episode — the ingredient of ungodly counsel (vv. 3-18).

Amnon was so obsessed with Tamar that he could think of nothing else and became ill. This was the man who, we assume, was to take his father's place, and here he is so consumed with lust that it made him ill. What would such an undisciplined man bring to the nation over which he was to rule?

Amnon's cousin, Jonadab, realized Amnon's sickness was due to something troubling him and asked him to share it (v. 4).

Amnon readily admitted his desire for Tamar, and Jonadab soon cooked up a scheme by which that illicit desire could be fulfilled. Instead of telling Amnon to resist the temptation, he emphasized his position as the king's son and indicated that this position entitled him to think solely of his own comfort and pleasure (vv. 5-6). Jonadab's counsel completely ignored the commands of God, the rights of others and the consequences of ungodly behaviour.

Jonadab's twisted mind produced a foul scheme that Amnon's twisted mind readily embraced. Amnon pretended to be physically ill, requested his father to send Tamar with some food, raped her and then, in hatred, sent her away despite her pleas (vv. 6-18).

Keddie explains the hatred Amnon felt for Tamar in these words: 'The rapist hates his victim because in the very act of his self-gratification he knows the most profound frustration of all: the humiliation of rejection. Without brute force, he would have nothing at all. And this sense of inadequacy and frustration is all that he has left, after his fleeting passion has subsided.'[2]

Jonadab's counsel led to all this and we should mark this because our own day finds a multitude of Jonadabs about. Television, films, magazines, psychologists, counsellors and even friends seem to merge their voices in one constant refrain that says we are all entitled to live exclusively for our own comfort and pleasure.

One of the things we constantly hear these days is that self-esteem is the most important building-block for happiness. There is, of course, such a thing as a healthy self-esteem, but there is also the kind that will make it easier and easier to justify doing anything that gratifies our selfish desires. We would do well not to accept at face value all that Jonadab says!

Unacknowledged evil

After all this, Absalom enters the picture, bringing with him the ingredient of unacknowledged evil (vv. 19-29). Absalom could easily see the wrong Amnon had done, but he could not see the evil of his own heart.

The evil of deception

First, there was in his heart the evil of deception. Amnon had deceived Tamar, and now Absalom deceives Amnon by pretending to be indifferent to the whole matter (v. 22). He later deceives his father regarding his true intentions towards Amnon (v. 26).

The evils of hatred and revenge

On top of that there were in the heart of Absalom the evils of the murderous hatred and revenge that he nurtured and nursed for two full years (v. 23). Finally, what was in Absalom's heart burst out into the open, and Amnon lay dead (vv. 28-29).

Repentance is the knife God gives us to excise the evil that is within. If we refuse to wield that knife, we invite the cancer of sin to run its full course in our lives. Absalom did not use the knife, but simply let evil camp out in his heart, and ended up paying a fearful price.

Unexercised authority

The final ingredient of this sad recipe is supplied by none other than David himself. It is the ingredient of unexercised authority (vv. 21,26-27,30-39).

It should not escape our attention that the deception, sexual immorality and murder we find in this chapter are the very same things David did in his affair with Bathsheba. Now they have come back to haunt him in the form of his own sons. Sin never pays.

David cuts a pathetic figure in this chapter. As king he was responsible to make sure the demands of justice were served, but he failed. Although he was angered by what Amnon did to Tamar, he took no action against him (v. 21). The law of Moses prescribed death for such an act of incest (Lev. 20:17), but David, acutely aware that he had himself done something worthy of death, was unwilling to mete out justice to his son. After Absalom murdered Amnon, David took no firm action against him either.

All through his later years, David seemed to be incapable of taking any decisive action. Part of it, as we have noted, was due to his fear that his own sin would be thrown up to him, but another part of David's failure must be attributed to his repeating the sin of Eli — namely, having such an inordinate love for his children that he could not bring himself to discipline them (1 Sam. 3:11-13).

This inordinate love is spelled out later in the case of yet another son, Adonijah. As David lay dying, Adonijah plotted to seize the throne, and the explanation given for Adonijah is this terse statement: 'And his father had not rebuked him at any time by saying, "Why have you done so?" ' (1 Kings 1:6).

It is actually a mistake to call this type of thing love. If a parent truly loves a child, he or she will want what is best for that child and will understand that what is best is not always what the child wants.

God himself is our example on this matter of what constitutes true love for children. The author of Hebrews states it clearly: 'For whom the Lord loves he chastens, and scourges every son whom he receives' (Heb. 12:6).

Undisciplined living, ungodly counsel, unacknowledged evil, unexercised authority — this is the devil's brew! He has concocted it many times down through the centuries, and he has served up a big platter-full for our own day and age. This is a day in which we refuse to discipline ourselves. It is a day in which we readily listen to ungodly counsel. It is a day in which we refuse to address the sins nesting in our hearts, but nurture and nourish them. It is a day in which those in authority often refuse to exercise it and, when it is exercised, it is despised.

The more we eat of this brew, the more pain we are going to feel. May God help us even now to turn from it and embrace the wholesome, healthy food of the Word of God.

35.
Bringing back the banished

2 Samuel 14:1-24

Amnon was dead, murdered by his own brother Absalom for raping his sister Tamar. Absalom himself had fled to Geshur, his mother's homeland, to take refuge among his relatives. And David had a dilemma on his hand. He was caught between conflicting demands. Justice demanded that the death sentence be carried out against Absalom (or at the very least that he remain in exile). But David loved his worthless son, and desired to forgive and restore him. Three long years passed, and David's heart yearned more and more for his son.

Joab's shrewd plot

No end of this dilemma was in sight until Joab, captain of David's army, interjected himself into David's personal life.

What concern was David's dilemma to Joab? The Bible does not say. Perhaps he saw David's administration of the kingdom's affairs slipping and attributed it to his yearning for his son. Perhaps Joab envisaged Absalom as his father's eventual successor and wanted to curry favour with him.

Whatever his motive, Joab decided it was time for something to be done about Absalom in exile. But he was afraid to broach the matter with the king. So he decided to try another tack. He may very well have been aware of the parable Nathan used to confront the king with his adulterous affair with Bathsheba, and decided to use the same ploy. He enlisted a shrewd woman from Tekoa to spin a story before the king. It, like Nathan's parable, was a sob story that was designed to arouse the compassion of the king and get him to pronounce judgement before he realized exactly what he was pronouncing judgement on.

A woman's shrewd parable

The woman claimed to be in the vice of conflicting demands herself. Her two sons had quarrelled as they worked in the field, begun to fight and one had killed the other (v. 6). Now she had only one son left, and her family were demanding that he be executed for what he had done, leaving her without any heir and making it possible that the family name would be extinguished altogether (v. 7). This was regarded as a calamity of the first order in Israel, as evidenced by the law of levirate marriage (Deut. 25:5-10).

David listened to her story, without connecting it with his own situation, and promised to consider it (v. 8).

At this point, the woman began to 'turn the screw' on David. She wanted an ironclad assurance that her son would be granted immunity and the unwitting David finally granted it by saying, 'As the Lord lives, not one hair of your son shall fall to the ground' (v. 11).

The bait had been taken and the hook was firmly embedded. All that remained for this clever woman was to reel the king in. This she did by pointing out that the king had failed to do in his own life what he had just pronounced. One of his sons had killed another, and the dead son was 'like water spilled on the ground' (v. 14). Nothing could bring him back. But the son who had done the killing could be forgiven and brought home (v. 13).

She made her argument even more compelling by adding a couple of points. First, she suggested it would be politically wise to bring Absalom back, that public opinion and the nation's interest would both be served by it (v. 13). Secondly, she insisted it would be theologically correct to forgive Absalom. Such an act of forgiveness, to her way of thinking, would imitate God (v. 14).

A moment later, she added a dash of flattery (v. 17), and David was well and truly caught. He finally spied the hand of Joab in this whole affair (v. 19) but, since it all led him to where his heart wanted to go, he felt no rage. Instead he called Joab in, and without so much as a single word of rebuke, ordered him to bring Absalom home (v. 21).

David's failure

David had finally resolved his dilemma of conflicting demands, but had he done the right thing? Of course not. He decided to bring Absalom back on the basis of a completely fallacious argument. He came to the conclusion that Absalom should return by accepting a line of reasoning that made different things alike.

The story of the woman was completely unlike David's own situation. Her son was guilty of manslaughter, while Absalom had committed premeditated murder. Her son was persecuted by members of her family, but this was not the case with Absalom. Her son was the only remaining heir, but Absalom was not.[1] Comparing her supposed situation to David's was, then, like comparing apples and oranges, but David accepted the faulty logic and treated the two as equal.

After the woman dropped her story and spoke openly to

the king about his son, there were more holes in her argument. She suggested the nation would be served by bringing Absalom back, but she did not provide any details to back up her suggestion. Just how would Absalom's return advance the nation? The mind gropes in vain for an answer to that, but David let it pass. (We shall soon see what Absalom's return really meant for the nation!)

But the weakest point in her argument was likening the forgiveness of Absalom to God's forgiveness of sinners. She was right in saying God 'devises means' to forgive, but she was wrong to suggest that God forgives in the same way she was asking David to forgive Absalom — namely, by subjugating the demands of justice to the demands of love. She was completely wrong. When God forgives, it is not at the expense of his justice, and it is never apart from our own repentance — and, by the way, there is in Scripture not so much as a single shred of evidence that Absalom ever repented of anything.

Let's examine this in more detail.

God's conflicting demands

I began by suggesting that David faced the dilemma of having to deal with conflicting demands. We may speak of God in the same way. The Bible says we, like Absalom, have broken God's laws and stand under the sentence of eternal death. God's just and holy character demands that sentence be carried out. But even as David loved Absalom and desired to forgive him, so God loves guilty sinners and desires to forgive them.

David had, it would seem, only one way or the other to go on this matter, but here is the wisdom of God — he found a way to honour the demands both of his justice and of his love. He found a way to punish our sin and, at the same time, allow the sentence of eternal death to be lifted from the sinner. That way was in and through his Son, Jesus Christ, and his death on the cross.

David resolved his conflicting demands by satisfying the demands of love and letting justice go begging. God resolved his conflicting demands by sending his Son to that cross to satisfy both demands. So God is the just justifier (Rom. 3:26). He is just in that he punished sin. He is the justifier in that he allows the believing sinner to go free. And it is all through his Son, Jesus Christ.

Important conclusions

What is there for us to learn from David's action in bringing back Absalom?

A word of caution

First, God's people today must be on constant guard against fallacious reasoning that makes wrong seem right. David knew what God's Word demanded in the case of Absalom, but he was willing to skirt round it because of clever reasoning.

How many of us do the same! We know God's Word speaks clearly on certain issues, but it is ever so tempting to ignore what it says because of the clever reasoning of our day. Here's one example: 'Yes, I know God's Word says life is sacred, but surely God does not want children who would not be loved and cared for to come into this world.'

A call to gratitude

Secondly, God's people should be filled with gratitude that God has indeed devised a way in which our sins can be forgiven and we can be brought into fellowship with him. That way is the death of his Son on the cross. But that cross represents a way of forgiveness that is radically different from the one adopted by David in his dealings with Absalom. God's forgiveness is not mere leniency. It does not ignore the demands of justice but honours them. God's way of forgiveness represents a perfect blend of both his grace and justice. His grace is certainly reflected in his Son's death on the cross because, through that death, believing sinners are indeed forgiven of their sins. But justice is equally reflected by that same cross because there God punished sin as justice demands. Christ there assumed the sins of his people and received the stroke of God's justice in their stead. Justice demands that sin be punished only once and, since God punished it in his Son, there is no penalty left for the sinner to pay. Justice rejoices, then, because sin has been punished, and grace rejoices that the believing sinner has been freed from condemnation.

Jesus paid it all,
All to him I owe.
Sin had left a crimson stain,
But he washed it white as snow.

Such a glorious plan of redemption should cause God's people to make sure our hearts are constantly filled with worship of him, and our hands are filled with deeds of service to his kingdom.

I also have a word for those who have not accepted God's way of salvation. God's way is the only way of salvation. Don't turn from it to embrace the specious reasoning of a sinful world, but be glad for it, and embrace it through repentance of your sin and faith in Christ.

36.
The tragic results of a false love

2 Samuel 15

Many of us have a love we would do well to let go, a love that threatens to bring us great harm if we persist in clinging to it. Drinking, pornography, an adulterous affair, drugs, money — there is no shortage of dangerous loves.

David's dangerous love was for his son Absalom. He should have let go of him. Absalom was a truly despicable human being. He thought of no one but himself. He was proud and arrogant. He was deceptive and dishonourable. He was a cold-blooded killer. But David refused to let go of this dangerous love. He sold principle down the river in favour of his personal feelings for this deadly viper of a son. How many today are repeating David's error! How many subject principle to feeling!

David picked up a dreadful price tag for his unworthy love, and there is a fearful price for all who refuse to break with a false love. This chapter documents it for us. Here we find Absalom requiting his father's love by attempting to seize his father's throne.

Given David's love for Absalom, it would seem likely that the latter would have eventually been his father's successor. But Absalom was not willing to wait for his father to pass off the scene. He wanted to help him on his way!

Absalom's campaign

Absalom was a very shrewd man. He knew he could not possibly wrest the kingdom from his father by simply announcing
that he wanted to be king. He knew he would first have to
wage a successful campaign for the hearts of the people —
that is, he would have to turn their hearts from his father to
himself.

Absalom wasted no time in launching this campaign. He
first cultivated a very attractive and appealing image: chariots
and horses and fifty attendants — quite enough to impress the
average citizen (v. 1).

In addition to this, Absalom began to build the reputation
of being a man of the people. He always made sure that he
was at the gate of the city very early in the morning. The gate
was the place where the elders heard and settled various cases
and grievances. Evidently the duly appointed officials were
not always there early in the morning (perhaps they had grown
careless in discharging their responsibilities), and this gave
Absalom an opportunity. He would talk to the aggrieved par-
ties gathered at the gate, assure them that their claims were
valid (even though he had heard only their side of the story),
and casually observe that it was a shame that the king's officials were not even there to hear the case (vv. 2-3).

All in all, Absalom made the case that justice was going
down the drain in Israel, and that he was the lone champion
who was seeking to stem the tide (v. 4).

In addition to all this, Absalom perfected a very person-
able, winsome approach with all those who approached him.
Refusing to let them bow before him, he rather treated them
as dear friends and equals (v. 5).

All this had its desired effect. The author summarizes it in
one terse sentence: 'So Absalom stole the hearts of the men of
Israel' (v. 6).

Absalom may very well have been the first in a long line of politicians who place style over substance and distort truth to achieve their own ends.

The complicity of the people

While Absalom was the chief villain in all this, the people themselves were not without blame. Absalom did the duping, but the citizens allowed themselves to be duped. They, in effect, repeated the tragic mistake of David by refusing to act on principle and embracing an unworthy love.

At no time had God given the slightest indication that Absalom was even to succeed David, let alone overthrow him. On the other hand, God had clearly revealed that it was his will for David to reign. He had said nothing about it being his will for David to be replaced. If the people had carefully considered what God had revealed and had determined to be faithful to it, they would have seen through Absalom's scheme and rejected it. Instead they allowed themselves to be captivated by Absalom's charm.

Why would these people allow their regard for the Word of God to be overriden by Absalom? The answer is obvious. Absalom said what they wanted to hear. In particular, he talked to them about their personal problems and sympathized with them (v. 3) In choosing Absalom, then, the people were essentially placing their own personal concerns above the Word of God.

The complicity of the people of Israel in Absalom's evil comes as a solemn reminder that God gives people the leadership they deserve. If they insist on disregarding the principles of his Word and being swayed by personal charm, God will see to it that they get leaders who seek to exude charm and who manifest little concern for principle and character.

In a day when a former president's golf clubs can fetch a million dollars at an auction, one cannot help but conclude that many people today have lost sight of what is truly important in our leaders. Sin is flourishing in our day, and the easiest way to explain it is by pointing to an Absalom over here and one over there. But Absaloms cannot succeed where people embrace the Word of God with a true and living faith.

Absalom's bold stroke

Finally, Absalom decided the time was right to 'make his move'. Hebron, the place where his father was anointed as king over all Israel (2 Sam. 5:1), was to be the place where he would proclaim himself king.

This man knew no shame. He pretended to want his father's approval to go to Hebron to fulfil a vow he had made to the Lord (vv. 7-9), when he cared nothing for his father or for the Lord. It is doubtful whether Absalom ever had a truly spiritual thought in his head the whole time he was on this earth.

Nothing was left to chance. Spies were sent throughout the land to announce his kingship at the appropriate moment (v. 10). Two hundred men, who we may safely assume were prominent citizens, were caught in Absalom's net (v. 11). These men went along with him to Hebron without suspecting that he was about to rebel against his father. Once there they were caught in a vice. If they refused to go along with him, they would probably have been executed, but, on the other hand, if they pretended to go along with him they appeared to be guilty of treason. The presence of these prominent men made it appear that Absalom was backed by Israel's leading citizens.

Lines of application

Several lines of application stretch from Absalom's rebellion to our own lives.

The unerring Word of God

First, we see again the complete dependability of the Word of God.

After David sinned, the prophet Nathan declared that the sword would not depart from David's house. That sword pierced David's heart when his son Amnon raped Tamar. He felt the thrust of that sword again when Absalom murdered Amnon. And now he feels its thrust again as Absalom rebels against him.

We may scoff all we want at the Word of God, but its truth will finally be verified even in our own circumstances.

The cost of sin

Secondly, we see here the terrible cost of sin. The sword in David's house was not just an unfortunate twist of circumstances, or his stars lining up in an unfortunate configuration. That sword was there because David, in flagrant disregard of God's laws, had committed adultery and murder.

Sin always has painful circumstances. The devil always tries to hide these from our eyes. He dangles the pleasure of sin before us in one hand, while holding its consequences behind his back with the other. If we learn to look past what he offers to what he seeks to hide, we shall save ourselves many a heartache.

The importance of principle

Another lesson that emerges from Absalom's rebellion is the importance of living on principle rather than on emotions. If David had dealt with Absalom on the principle of justice rather than on the sentiment of his own heart, he could have spared himself the agony of Absalom's rebellion. If the people of Israel had acted on the principle of what God had said and what he had not said about the kingship of Israel, Absalom's scheme would have unceremoniously fallen to the ground.

David's greater son

The greatest lesson that emerges from this sordid chapter is this — David had another son, his greater son, and this son did not rebel. This son was the Lord Jesus Christ who 'was born of the seed of David according to the flesh' (Rom. 1:3).

This son came from heaven's glory to purchase redemption for sinners. All of this was in accordance with the mission God the Father had sent him to fulfil. Because the Lord Jesus did not fail in that mission or rebel against it, we can have forgiveness of sins and eventually be received into that perfect world where no Absaloms will ever arise.

37.
At the bottom of the barrel

2 Samuel 15:13-37

We are accustomed to thinking of David as standing on the pinnacle of success. Riches, fame, power, recognition from other kings, respect from his enemies, the love of his people, spiritual power and vitality — David enjoyed them all in abundance.

But he toppled from that high plane, and in this passage we find him at his lowest ebb and in his darkest hour. Here he finds himself at the bottom of the barrel and the end of his tether. His pampered, undisciplined son Absalom had risen up in rebellion against him and David was obliged to leave the city of Jerusalem in shame and sorrow.

All of God's children know something about what it means to be at the bottom of the barrel and the end of one's tether. We have all found ourselves in situations in which all our resources seemed to be depleted, and in which we seemed to be able only to hang on by the skin of our teeth.

What does one do in such situations? How is the child of God to respond to them? If we listen carefully to what the passage before us is saying, we can hear David speaking to us from the bottom of the barrel and the end of his tether to help us.

The folly of disobedience

One of the things that he speaks to us about is the folly of disobedience to God. Absalom's treachery was a direct result of David's flagrant violation of the law of God by committing adultery with Bathsheba and arranging the death of her husband.

Sin always promises us that we can enjoy its pleasures and avoid its consequences — that we shall be the exception to the rule. But it never works out that way. The apostle Paul says, 'Do not be deceived, God is not mocked; for whatever a man sows, that he will also reap' (Gal. 6:7).

This is not to say our trials and sufferings are always a result of sin. Sometimes they are sent to us from our Father's loving hand to help us to mature. They may be designed to wean us from the world and to cast us more on our heavenly Father. But, as David's life abundantly shows, there are also instances in which we bring suffering upon ourselves through disobedience.

The truth of the Word of God

This brings us to a second truth that David speaks about — the truth of the Word of God.

After David sinned God sent the prophet Nathan to him with a stern message of rebuke. This message included some very precise and specific predictions: 'Thus says the Lord: "Behold, I will raise up adversity against you from your own house; and I will take your wives before your eyes and give them to your neighbour, and he shall lie with your wives in the sight of this sun. For you did it secretly, but I will do this thing before all Israel, before the sun" ' (2 Sam. 12:11-12). As time passed David may very well have assured himself that this part of Nathan's message would be forgotten, but it was not.

When David fled from Absalom, he left ten of his concubines to keep his house (v. 16). The first thing Absalom did upon his arrival in Jerusalem was to pitch a tent on the top of the house and have those concubines in one at a time for sexual relations with him (16:22).

The Word of God came true to the letter. And that Word, though scoffed at and scorned by so many today, will ultimately prove again to be true. Its promises of judgement will be carried out in minute detail, but its promises of forgiveness and cleansing for those who repent of their sins will also be carried out. And its promises, which tell us that God has a purpose in our trials and is with us in the midst of them, can be completely trusted.

The sufficiency of the grace of God

That leads us to a third truth. David also speaks to us about the sufficiency of the grace of God.

No trial could possibly be more severe than that which David was facing in these verses. His own son had turned against him and was seeking his life. But while the trial was severe and crushing, it was not the only thing David experienced at that time. The grace of God was also there to soften the trial.

That grace is manifested in the loyalty of all those who remained true to David. There was a sizeable number who not only accompanied David, but showed their deep distress over his distress by weeping loudly as they journeyed with him (v. 23). Ittai the Gittite (vv. 19-22), Zadok, Abiathar, their sons and all the Levites (vv. 24-29) and Hushai the Archite (vv. 32-37) are singled out for their devotion. Ittai's loyalty is especially notable because he had joined David only the day before (vv. 19-20).

Life's most bitter afflictions are made easier by kind, sympathetic friends. The fact that David had such friends at such a time shows us the marvellous truth that God's chastisement of his children is always mixed with the oil of his grace.

The priority of looking to God

David also speaks to us about the priority of looking to God.

The account gives us three very important details about David as he fled from Jerusalem.

Submitting to the Lord

For one thing, we are told that David placed his trust completely in God. Even though Absalom's conspiracy was very strong (v. 12) and there appeared to be little hope of withstanding it, David knew it was God, not Absalom, who would ultimately decide the outcome (v. 25). Realizing this, David was able to say of God, 'Let him do to me as seems good to him' (v. 26).

David's attitude at this time was one of complete submission to God. He was not embittered and resentful towards God for allowing these difficulties to come upon him. He recognized that he had brought them upon himself through disobedience, and he left Jerusalem with a spirit of humble repentance over the folly of his sin (v. 30). There was no anger or resentment towards God, only loving submission and trust.

Worshipping the Lord

This comes out even more clearly as we see David pausing during his flight to worship God (v. 32).

The child of God has one great, overarching priority in every situation of life — worshipping God. Our circumstances change, but that priority is always to remain in place.

Life is greatly simplified when we understand that the priority of the child of God is the same, no matter what his circumstances are. When he is in the midst of prosperity, he is to worship God. When he is in the midst of adversity, he is still to worship God.

Praying to the Lord

A third thing we are told about David during this time is that he prayed for God's help (v. 31). What relief comes to the tried, weary child of God through prayer!

What a friend we have in Jesus,
All our sins and griefs to bear!
What a privilege to carry
Everything to God in prayer!
Oh, what peace we often forfeit,
Oh, what needless pain we bear,
All because we do not carry
Everything to God in prayer!

Have we trials and temptations?
Is there trouble anywhere?
We should never be discouraged,
Take it to the Lord in prayer.
Can we find a Friend so faithful,
Who will all our sorrows share?
Jesus knows our every weakness,
Take it to the Lord in prayer.

David's priority when he found himself at the bottom of the barrel and the end of his tether was God himself. He trusted

God, he worshipped God and he prayed to God. The more engrossed with God we are, the more bearable our trials will be.

The consequences of disobedience to God, the reliability of the Word of God, the sufficiency of the grace of God, the priority of trusting and worshipping God — these are truths of which we need frequent reminders. We can remind ourselves of them, or God can remind us of them by bringing us to the bottom of the barrel and the end of our tether.

There is another dimension to David's experience here that we must not neglect. It is the picture he paints of our Lord Jesus Christ. Centuries later the Lord Jesus Christ left Jerusalem by way of the Mount of Olives. He also was deeply and profoundly burdened and distressed with sin and looking to God the Father in prayer. But, thank God, the sin he was burdened with was not his own, but rather ours. Because of that sin-bearing work, we who believe in him are delivered from sin's terrible sentence.

38.
Three faces of evil

2 Samuel 16:1 - 17:4

This passage brings before us three evil men — Ziba, Shimei and Ahithophel. How do we know these men were evil? They all rejected God's anointed servant David in one way or another.

Ziba

At first glance Ziba, Mephibosheth's servant, seems to have accepted David's rightful rule over Israel. But in reality Ziba only had one king — himself — and he was willing to do whatever was necessary to advance and gratify that king. Had Ziba thought he could have served himself better by going to Absalom, we may rest assured that he would have done so. But he gambled on David winning back his kingdom from his rebellious son Absalom.

Ziba knew David was possessed of a generous spirit that rewarded those who helped him. So he intercepted David on his flight from Jerusalem with his own personal show of welcome in the form of a lavish supply of provisions: donkeys on which the king's family could ride, bread, raisins, fruit and wine. Ziba had not overlooked a thing. He pretended to be motivated by a genuine desire to help the king in this distressing time, but his true motive was to win the king's favour (16:1-2).

When David asked him about his master Mephibosheth (and
we may be sure Ziba would have brought the subject up had
David not asked), Ziba brazenly lied. He said Mephibosheth
had stayed in Jerusalem in the expectation that the kingdom
would now become his (16:3). Ziba did not take the trouble to
explain how Absalom's rebellion would translate into kingship for Mephibosheth, or how a man in Mephibosheth's physical condition could realistically expect the people to abandon
both David and Absalom to rally around him.

And David did not ask. He accepted Ziba's pathetic story
at face value and rewarded him for his 'loyalty' by transferring
all of Mephibosheth's property to him (16:4).

Only after Absalom's rebellion had been crushed and when
David returned to Jerusalem did he see the other side of the
story. Three factors indicated that Ziba had viciously misrep-
resented Mephibosheth and had deceived David. First,
Mephibosheth's appearance indicated that he had truly been
in mourning from the time David left Jerusalem (19:24). Secondly, Mephibosheth's answer to the king's enquiry, 'Why did
you not go with me, Mephibosheth?', was not only plausible
but also came from a heart that was still filled with sincere
gratitude for what David had done for him (19:25-28). Finally, Mephibosheth's response to David's reversal of his previous decision (16:4) by now dividing the property between
him and Ziba indicated his unswerving loyalty. 'Rather, let him
take it all' bespeaks a heart that treasured the king himself
more than what the king could give (19:30).

As David reflected on this matter he may very well have
found himself saying the very words his son and successor,
Solomon, would include in the book of Proverbs: 'The first
one to plead his cause seems right...' (Prov. 18:17).

He may have also found himself wincing with pain as he
looked back on his foolish decision to divide the land instead

of totally restoring it to Mephibosheth. David's failure to act justly at this point may have caused these words to well up within his heart: 'Give the king your judgements, O God...' (Ps. 72:1).

This is a sad episode in the life of David. Ziba wore the face of deceptive evil that hypocritically says whatever will advance its own cause. And David failed to recognize it.

Shimei

The second face of evil was worn by Shimei. There was nothing deceptive about this man. While Ziba clothed the iron fist of selfishness in the velvet glove of kindness, Shimei simply allowed his true colours to show.

He had long nursed hatred against David. He regarded the kingdom as properly belonging to Saul, and he regarded David as being responsible for Saul's downfall. As far as Shimei was concerned, Absalom's rebellion was nothing less than David getting back exactly what he himself had done (16:8).

Shimei was sadly mistaken. David had not lifted a finger to take Saul's kingdom from him. When given the opportunity to kill Saul, he had refused to do so because Saul was the Lord's anointed. Saul's downfall was due to his own refusal to obey God, and David's ascending to the throne was the Lord's doing and not his own.

This was so well established that it was beyond dispute. But Shimei refused to believe the truth. We can say, therefore, that he refused to believe the evidence in order to believe what he wanted to believe. He coupled wilful ignorance with deep malice and hostility.

David responded to Shimei's cursing in a remarkable way. He knew he was not guilty of the crime of which Shimei was accusing him, but he also knew he was at this time under the Lord's chastisement for sins he had committed. He refused, therefore, to allow Abishai to execute Shimei on the spot, but rather accepted his cursing as part of the Lord's chastisement of him (16:10). He also expressed confidence that this chastisement was temporary and would eventually yield blessing (16:11).

The trials of life become less bitter when we see them as coming from the Father's hand for our good.

Ahithophel

Ahithophel brings before us yet another type of evil. We might call his the destructive evil that seems invincible.

Ahithophel had been one of David's counsellors, but he had now cast in his lot with Absalom. This constituted no small problem for David. Ahithophel's counsel made it seem that he had a direct hotline to God (16:23).

Ahithophel did not take long to show the type of evil of which he was capable.

First, he counselled Absalom to engage in sexual relations with the concubines that David had left in Jerusalem (16:21). This was to be done in broad daylight in a tent set up for that purpose (16:22). It did not matter to Ahithophel or to Absalom that the law of God declared this to be a capital offence (Lev. 20:11). All Ahithophel was interested in was assuring Absalom's followers that his break with his father was radical and final.

This counsel alone proves Ahithophel was a depraved, vile man. But there was more to come. He also counselled Absalom to rapidly pursue David that very night with the intent of finding him and killing him (17:1-3). This counsel was very wise. David and his men were exhausted physically and emotionally and a quick strike by Absalom would have been very difficult for them to withstand. And David's death would have left his followers so dispirited and demoralized that they would have quickly abandoned their resistance to Absalom.

The response to Ahithophel's counsel was favourable (17:4), but there was an invisible hand at work in these proceedings, a hand that can turn the heart of the king without his even being aware of it. This invisible hand belongs to the sovereign God who works all things according to his will (Prov. 21:1). On this occasion, this sovereign hand caused Absalom and his leaders to accept the counsel of David's friend Hushai rather than the counsel of Ahithophel (17:14).

The relevance of these men

The three types of evil David faced have relevance for us along a couple of lines.

Rejection of Christ

First, we can see them expressed in connection with that anointed King whom David foreshadowed — the Lord Jesus Christ.

Many, like Ziba, seem to accept Christ and the salvation he offers, but theirs is only a sham acceptance. The truth is that they have never truly broken with the god of self to embrace Christ with a true and living faith.

Others, like Shimei, are openly hostile to Christ because they adamantly refuse to consider the evidence for him. The evidence is there. The incredible number of fulfilled prophecies, the resurrection from the dead (substantiated by a great number of witnesses) and the miracles (also substantiated by witnesses) all prove Jesus Christ to be the Son of God.

But many refuse to look at the evidence. Why is this? Because if they were to take a long, hard look at the evidence, they would have to abandon their hostility to Christ. They do not want the evidence to be true because it would interfere with the way they want to live. So they choose to ignore it, even as Shimei ignored the evidence about David.

Some carry hostility to Christ beyond the Shimei stage of openly expressing it to the Ahithophel stage of actually trying to eliminate any vestige of his teaching.

Rejection of Christ's people

The hostility that is expressed towards Christ is also experienced by those of us who know him and follow him. Evil comes to us in the appealing garb of Ziba to persuade us to embrace sinful thinking and doing and, to our shame, we, like David, often fall for it. We also experience the hateful hostility of Shimei that refuses to listen to the evidence for our message but accuses us of posing a threat to the well-being of society. And many Christians in many parts of the world experience the hostility of Ahithophel that actually seeks to take their lives.

How are Christ's followers to stand against evil and hostility? David's responses to the evils posed by Ziba, Shimei and Ahithophel can serve as beacons for us.

The proper response to evil

Responding to deceptive evil

David did not respond well to the evil Ziba. He acted impulsively and jumped to an unwarranted conclusion in the case of Ziba. When he later found that Mephibosheth had been slandered by Ziba, David did not act justly. Instead of reversing his decision to give Ziba all of Mephibosheth's property, he miserably bungled the matter by dividing the land between the two men (19:24-30).

David's failure in this matter is still helpful to us. It teaches us to be ever watchful and discerning so that we are not deceived.

Responding to hostility

David's handling of Shimei was at this point much better. His refusal of Abishai's suggestion that Shimei be killed teaches us not to retaliate against those who hate us.

But David bungled again when it came to leaving Hushai in Jerusalem. As great a man of God as he was, David had the distressing tendency to resort to deceitful subterfuge when he thought it would further his cause (1 Sam. 21:1-15; 27:1-12; 29:1-11).

It was always God's faithfulness to his promises that secured his future, but David often wavered in faith. Gordon Keddie astutely observes of David's deceitful employment of Hushai: 'There is no reason to believe that David would have lost his kingdom had he simply given himself to prayer and kept Hushai in his camp. The fact that Hushai succeeded is no proof that God could not, or would not, have overthrown Absalom by less deceptive means.'[1]

Responding to seemingly invincible evil

David's deceitful response to the threat of Ahithophel is not defensible, but it is instructive in that it teaches us to refrain from fighting evil with evil (Rom. 12:17) and to rest in the confidence that evil is under God's sovereign control. Such confidence enables us to rejoice that evil cannot go beyond

the bounds God allows for it and that it will finally be frustrated and destroyed.

David's bungling and wavering show that he was as much
a sinner as Ziba, Shimei and Ahithophel. But there was a difference. David was a sinner who knew his sinfulness, grieved
over it and looked to the Lord for forgiveness and cleansing.

39.
Sovereignty and responsibility

2 Samuel 17

God had ordained that David should rule over the people of Israel. David, therefore, represents the will and rule of God. Absalom, aided by the evil Ahithophel, had a different plan. He wanted to drive his father from the throne and reign in his stead. Absalom, then, represents the evil that seeks to overthrow God's will and rule.

When we approach this passage with these connections in mind, it becomes powerfully relevant. We are surrounded by Absaloms who would, if possible, eliminate the very last vestige of God from our society. Often it appears as if they are perilously close to succeeding. The cause of God often appears weak and frail, and evil seems robust and strong.

As the people of God observe the situation, they find themselves given to despondency and despair. Will the cause of God fail? Is there anything to encourage and comfort us when evil runs rampant?

This chapter gives us reasons to rejoice as it points us to truths that will help us cope with this day of flourishing evil.

Evil is under God's sovereign control

First, it assures us that evil is under God's sovereign control, and it cannot pass the boundaries he has set for it (vv. 1-14).

The reality of this truth is powerfully brought home to us by the account of this man Ahithophel. Here is a man who was a legend in his own time. His reputation was so great that his counsel was usually equated with God himself speaking (16:23).

The opening verses of 2 Samuel 17 show us that Ahithophel's reputation was well deserved. He suggested that an army of twelve thousand men be sent out for the purpose of eliminating David while Absalom remained in Jerusalem.

This was very wise for several reasons. First, it would have taken advantage of the time when David and his men were most vulnerable, when they were both physically and emotionally exhausted. Secondly, it focused on the crucial issue. Ahithophel knew that if David were killed, the opposition to Absalom would quickly melt away and the nation would unite around their new king. Thirdly, it protected Absalom from any possibility of being killed in battle.

This counsel was enthusiastically embraced by Absalom and the elders (v. 4). Ahithophel was an evil man, and it looked as if he had won the day.

But there was, as we have noted, another counsellor there. Hushai, loyal to the hilt to David, had been sent back to Jerusalem by David for the express purpose of undermining the counsel of Ahithophel (15:31-34). Now it was his turn to speak. What a formidable task was his! He had to give counsel that would negate Ahithophel's counsel, and had to do it in such a way that his loyalty to David would not be obvious and the counsel would be accepted. His was no small task!

So Hushai began to speak. Absalom and his men knew very well that David was a great warrior, and Hushai appealed to that reputation. He suggested that David and his men were furious over this turn of events and were even now lying in wait for Absalom to do the very thing Ahithophel had suggested. If Absalom followed this advice, the initial victory would belong to David, and that victory would cause Absalom's followers to be disheartened. Absalom should, then, move very deliberately. He should take the time to gather a vast army and lead them into battle. They would then pursue David and completely overwhelm and crush him (vv. 7-13).

Hushai's argument was much weaker than Ahithophel's but, wonder of wonders, Absalom and his men fell for it hook, line and sinker (v. 14). Some might be inclined to call this a stroke of good fortune, but the Word of God explains it this way: 'For the Lord had purposed to defeat the good advice of Ahithophel, to the intent that the Lord might bring disaster on Absalom' (v. 14).

Hushai was in the presence of Absalom because David wrongly resorted to deceit. The fact that the Lord used Hushai's counsel to defeat Absalom does not mean God approves of evil. It does mean that he is greater than evil. Without approving of the evil men do, God can and does use it to achieve his purposes.

Do we appreciate what we are seeing in these verses? Here is Ahithophel, whom we may consider to be the representative of evil that is invincible, and yet his evil counsel is put down and negated because God designed it that way.

Absalom and his men thought they were choosing quite freely on this matter, but there was an unseen hand steering their hearts and minds. The author of Proverbs says:

The king's heart is in the hand of the Lord,
Like the rivers of water;
He turns it wherever he wishes
                                                    (Prov. 21:1).

What consolation there is here for us! The evil of our day seems quite as invincible as Ahithophel's counsel, but the same God who sovereignly set the boundaries for Ahithophel does the same with evil today.

We shall never completely understand in this life why God allows the evil that he does, but we can rest assured that he will never let evil pass the limits he has ordained for it, and he will eventually defeat it and destroy it even as he did Absalom.

God controls evil through instruments

The second great truth placed before us by this passage is this — God uses human instruments in controlling and thwarting evil (vv. 15-29).

While God is not responsible for human evil, he is able to use it to promote his purposes. He did so in this case. Hushai's presence before Absalom was due to a lapse of faith on David's part, but this did not stop the Lord from using Hushai to defeat Absalom.

Zadok and Abiathar were also the Lord's instruments in this situation. They received Hushai's message about what he and Ahithophel had counselled (v. 15) and passed the word to a female servant who, in turn, passed it to Jonathan and Ahimaaz to carry to David (v. 17)

In the process of carrying the message, Jonathan and Ahimaaz were seen by a young lad who reported to Absalom (v. 18). But God still had his instruments. A man who lived in Bahurim just happened to have a well in which the two men could hide (v. 18), and a woman pretended to be working with ground grain on a covering over the well (vv. 19-21).

All of these human instruments used prudent judgement. Hushai did not assume his counsel would finally stand, but prepared for the eventuality that Absalom might change his mind. Jonathan and Ahimaaz did not simply say they did not have to worry about being recognized because they were trusting God. Instead they stayed outside the city (v. 17), and when they were seen, they did not merely say they were trusting God to protect them, but they hid in the well (vv. 18-20).

God's sovereign control of all things does not mean his people can and should act recklessly. God's control comprehends the means as well as the end. If God has decreed that someone should live to be a hundred years old, we may rest assured that he has also decreed that the person should properly take care of his or her body.

As we look at the human instruments God employed in delivering David from Absalom, we must surely be impressed with their loyalty to David, with their wise planning on his behalf and with their energetic service to him.

If we would be used of God to combat the evil of this day, we must make sure we are people of the same type. We must be unswervingly loyal to our God. We must be wise and prudent. We must be energetic and diligent in our service.

This passage, then, lays before us a balance in dealing with evil — God's sovereignty and our responsibility. Many of God's people seem to forget the first part of the equation. They leave God out and become either panicky or gloomy and despondent. They think everything depends on us, and they do not see the church having the strength to stand against evil.

Others take exactly the opposite view. They have a strong view of God's sovereign control, and they sit back and do nothing. Talk about Christians acting responsibly and they say we should just leave things to God.

The right way to respond to evil is not to choose between these two options, but to embrace both. We must certainly trust God to be working behind the scenes to control evil, but we also must not hesitate to cope with evil by speaking the message of God (as Hushai did), and by devotedly serving God (as all David's friends served him).

And what about evil itself? There is also a word in this chapter regarding this. After his counsel was rejected, Ahithophel went out and hanged himself (v. 23), the second of only four suicides in the Bible.

Let this last, desperate act of this evil man assure us that all that stands in opposition to God, no matter how strong it may appear to be, will finally and ultimately collapse.

The message of the Bible is that we do not have to live in opposition to God and experience ruin. God himself has provided a way in which we can be at peace with him. That way is through his Son, Jesus Christ, and his atoning death on Calvary's cross. Don't be like Absalom and rebel against this one whom God has ordained as your rightful Sovereign, but rather bow before him now in true repentance and faith.

40.
The death of Absalom

This chapter brings us to the end of the life of one of the Bible's most despicable characters. Here Absalom, who ungratefully rebelled against his father and plunged the whole nation into heartache, comes to his richly deserved end.

Death should never be taken lightly, and this death is especially worthy of careful thought. Here we have a very solemn and instructive picture indeed. David was not the ruler of Israel merely because it had happened that way. He was in that position because God willed it. God had designated him to rule years before, and there is not so much as a single statement to indicate that God had in any way changed his mind. It was still his will for David to rule.

But Absalom cared neither for God nor for David. He was a completely self-absorbed man. So desperately did he want the throne of Israel that he gave no thought at all to the will of God or to the consequences of ignoring it.

We have in David, then, a picture, or representation, of the will and rule of God and in Absalom a representation of wicked rebellion against that rule. This is a miniature picture of a much larger reality. In addition to being God's anointed ruler over Israel, David was also intended to foreshadow that far greater King who was still to come — the Lord Jesus Christ. While David had been anointed to reign temporally over the nation of Israel, the Lord Jesus has been anointed to reign eternally over all. This anointed King puts squarely before each and every one of us an inescapable question: 'Will I bow in submission to him, or be like Absalom and rebel against him?'

Now here is the point of contact between this ancient passage and our own situation: as Absalom came to a tragic end for rebelling against David, so will all who rebel against God's greater King, Jesus. Absalom's end may serve, therefore, as a picture of the end of all those who reject Christ.

This chapter enables us to draw several conclusions about the death of Absalom, each of which has pointed relevance for those who reject Christ.

Determined by God

First, we must say it was irreversibly determined by God. This truth is clearly set forth in these words from the previous chapter: 'The Lord had purposed to defeat the good counsel of Ahithophel, to the intent that the Lord might bring disaster on Absalom' (17:14).

When we come to chapter 18, we find David striving mightily to ensure that no harm would come to Absalom. First, he announces that he himself will go into battle. Yes, David was a brave soldier and he undoubtedly felt responsible, and rightly so, for the crisis the nation was facing, but in this case his motive for going into battle seems to have been to protect Absalom.

Finally convinced that he must not risk the future of the nation by putting himself in harm's way, David strictly charges his commanders to make sure no harm would come to Absalom (v. 5).

But David's attempts to save his worthless son all came to naught. The Lord had determined that Absalom would die, and die he did. As Absalom was fleeing from the servants of David, he 'just happened' to ride under 'a great terebinth tree' and catch his hair in its lower branches (v. 9). Those who are not tuned to God's ways might be inclined to say, 'What rotten luck for Absalom!' But the word 'luck' is not in the Bible. It was God who caused that tree to grow in that very spot and God who steered the mule in such a way that Absalom would be caught.

The same God who determined Absalom would meet death has also decreed death for all those who reject Jesus Christ. But this death is far worse than mere physical death. It is nothing less than eternal death and destruction (2 Thess. 1:8-9).

Ours is a day in which people easily dismiss the theme of judgement and resent anyone mentioning it. As far as they are concerned, it is dead and buried and they do not want it resurrected. But no fair reading of the Bible will enable us to get around this settled truth — God has determined judgement for all those who refuse to embrace his Son. And nothing short of embracing his Son will in any way change or alter his determination.

Shameful and humiliating

This brings us to note that Absalom's death was also exceedingly shameful and humiliating.

What a way for proud Absalom to die! It is one thing to die while heroically wielding a sword, but Absalom could do nothing but hang there and wait for his executioners to arrive. He was utterly helpless. The hair of which he was so proud was his undoing.

Of his hanging there between heaven and earth, Matthew Henry observes that it was as if he was 'unworthy of either', and as 'abandoned by both'. He then adds, 'Earth would not keep him, heaven would not take him, hell therefore opens her mouth to receive him.'[1]

Absalom probably did not continue long in this predicament. An unnamed soldier spotted him hanging there, reported
it to Joab, and the rest, as they say, is history. After administering a sound rebuke to the soldier for not killing Absalom,
Joab proceeded to the spot where he dispatched him into the
next world by hurling three spears into his heart (v. 14). As if
this were not enough, Joab's ten armour-bearers added their
own blows (v. 15).

They then lowered his body to the ground and, as if it were
nothing but a piece of worthless rubbish, cast it into a pit, and
covered it with 'a very large heap of stones' (v. 17). All of his
glory and pride were now gone. All of his ambitions lay in ruins.

Absalom's death is a fitting emblem of what awaits those
who rebel against the Lord Jesus Christ. It is all very easy now
to speak with disdain about the things of God, to pretend that
these things are somehow beneath one's intelligence. It is all
very easy to treat those who serve Christ as being hopelessly
outdated and deserving only of pity.

But death is the great leveller. It respects no one. As Charles
Spurgeon has noted, it takes off the jester's cap as well as the
student's gown and visits the university as well as the tavern.[2]

When it comes those who have gone with pride and arrogance through life and with supreme confidence in themselves
will have to face God, and they will be astonished that they
could have been so stupid as to ignore all the evidence for
God's truth. On that day they will not boast proudly of their
accomplishments but will simply stand in shame. Of the wicked,
Scripture says, 'For when he dies he shall carry nothing away;
his glory shall not descend after him' (Ps. 49:17).

Unnecessary

There is yet another dimension to Absalom's death that we
must note — namely, that it was unnecessary.

Absalom did not have to walk the path he walked. He did not have to rebel against his father. Even after he had chosen to rebel, he did not have to continue in it. He could at any time have broken with his rebellion and sought his father's forgiveness.

Absalom had an abundance of reasons for laying down his arms and being reconciled to his father. He had that law that was such an integral part of the nation's life, the law of Moses. That law clearly called for children to honour their father and mother (Exod. 20:12), and it also promised great blessing to all who lived in obedience to it and terrible calamity for those who refused to heed it. In addition to this, Absalom also had seen enough in his father's own life to convince him that the hand of God was upon him and, therefore, it would be foolhardy to rebel against him.

But Absalom, so filled with himself, ignored all the warning signs and finally ran right into disaster. He could have avoided it, but he fell headlong into it.

The Bible is full of warnings about the disaster that awaits those who refuse to submit to God's greater King, King Jesus. But it also throbs and vibrates with this good news — that disaster can be avoided. It tells us the Lord Jesus Christ himself has done all that is necessary for sinners to be forgiven of their sins, and 'whosoever will' may come and partake of the benefits of what Christ has done (Rev. 22:17).

The plea of the Bible is for us to submit to God's anointed King. It says:

Kiss the Son, lest he be angry,
And you perish in the way,
When his wrath is kindled but a little.
Blessed are all those who put their trust in him

(Ps. 2:12).

41.
Two failures

We must remind ourselves again and again that all Scripture is given by inspiration of God and, therefore, it is all profitable for us. We also must frequently remind ourselves that the redemptive work of the Lord Jesus Christ is the central theme of Scripture. These two truths are shining beacons to guide us as we sail through the great depths of Scripture.

In the light of these things, we have to say that even those passages that seem to be utterly devoid of spiritual truth are not so.

The verses before us consist of two intriguing stories about the aftermath of Absalom's death. One relates the details of how David heard the news (18:19-32). The other relates David's excessive grief and Joab's rebuke of it (18:33 - 19:8). These accounts are interesting enough, but what do they have to do with us? The answer to that question can be put in one word: failure.

Ahimaaz presents us with one type of failure, and David presents us with another type. As those of us who know the Lord read these accounts and analyse these failures, we are compelled to face the distasteful truth that we can also fail in these very same ways.

Ahimaaz' failure to deliver the message

The first failure here is in the area of courageously delivering a message (18:19-32).

After heaping stones over the body of Absalom, Joab sent a Cushite messenger to deliver the news to David. No sooner had the Cushite left than Ahimaaz, the son of the high priest Zadok, pleaded with Joab to let him carry the news to David.

Some think Joab selected a foreigner to deliver the message to David because he was afraid that David would kill any bearer of news about the death of his son. If this was Joab's thinking, he was wrong. The only times David had done anything of this nature was when the messengers themselves took credit for assassinating a king (2 Sam. 1:11-16; 4:5-12).

Initially, Ahimaaz had no such qualms about carrying the news to David. He had a great love for David and, flushed with excitement over the victory, wanted to be the one to tell him the good news. So he continued to beg to be allowed to carry the news even after Joab had dispatched the Cushite. Finally, Joab became so exasperated with his begging that he threw up his hands and said 'Run!' (18:23).

And run Ahimaaz did. Taking a shorter route and evidently being faster of foot, he reached David before the Cushite (18:24-27). Ahimaaz had wanted to be the first one to tell David the news and now he had attained his goal. Breathlessly, he blurted out 'All is well!' (18:28).

But David was interested in only one thing and that was the welfare of his son, and Ahimaaz could only say, '… I saw a great tumult, but I did not know what it was about' (18:28). Perhaps Ahimaaz was telling the truth. Perhaps he had only seen a tumult and did not know that it signalled the death of Absalom. Perhaps he was so excited over the victory of David's army and so eager to carry the news to David that he did not even hear Joab say, 'The king's son is dead' (18:20).

But it is more likely that Ahimaaz simply lost his nerve. When he saw the concern for Absalom etched on David's face and heard the pathos in his voice, Ahimaaz found that he did not have the courage to cough up the news that would devastate the king to whom he was so devoted. That news had to wait for the Cushite's arrival a moment later (18:30-32).

The central theme of this account would seem, then, to be Ahimaaz' lack of courage to tell David what he most needed to hear. It was unpleasant news to be sure, but David had to hear it, and Ahimaaz failed to tell it to him.

The Christian message

All Christians have a message to carry, and we would do well to let this passage speak to us about this task.

Our message is directed to those who do not know our Lord and Saviour. It is a message of glorious victory and eternal hope, but it is also a message about God's unbending holiness, our sin, the need to repent of sin and trust solely in the atoning work of Jesus Christ, and God's eternal judgement on all those who refuse to receive Christ as their Lord and Saviour.

This is the part of the message that our unsaved friends desperately need to hear — because it is the only message that can save them from eternal ruin — but it is also a message they do not want to hear.

And many pastors and churches seem today to be very much like Ahimaaz. They are running very fast with their ministries and activities, but they are strangely silent when the time comes to announce those truths so many find to be distasteful and unpleasant. Let us come away from the story of Ahimaaz with the firm conviction that it does not matter how fast we run in our ministries if we do not have the courage to say those things that are most important.

David's failure to comprehend his calling

That brings us to the second failure in this passage, David's failure in the area of comprehending his own calling (18:33 - 19:6).

Absalom lay dead under a pile of stones. David's throne was now safe. It was good news. Make no mistake about that. David was the man God had anointed to reign as king over the nation. Absalom's rebellion against him was nothing less than a flagrant disregard for the will of God and the welfare of the nation. The fate of the nation was hanging in the balance when the forces of David and Absalom met each other in the field. Had Absalom won, the people of Israel would have had a far different kind of king and would have been a far different kind of nation. But God was gracious to David and to the nation. He thwarted Absalom's grand plans and preserved David.

It was indeed a day for rejoicing, but it almost turned into a day of tragedy and mourning. David almost snatched defeat from the jaws of victory by excessively grieving over the loss of his son.

There was, of course, much for David to grieve about. It was his sin that had set this tragic sequence of events in motion. It was that same sin that had robbed David of the moral authority to discipline his sons, a failure that showed up most notably in Absalom. There can be no doubt about it: David blamed himself for Absalom's death and thought he should have died instead (18:33) — a sentiment that Absalom would undoubtedly have been glad to carry out!

If we learn nothing else from this sad portion of the Word of God, let us at least learn this — sin brings heartache and ruin.

But all this does not absolve Absalom of responsibility. If anything, the sin of his father should have driven home to him the terrible consequences of disobeying God.

And, whatever legitimate reasons there were for grieving, this was not the time or place for David to give himself over to it. And Joab let him know it in no uncertain terms. In rapid-fire fashion, he pointed out certain distinct truths to David.

First, if Absalom had prevailed, David himself would have been executed, as well as his other sons and daughters and his wives and concubines (19:5).

Secondly, by his grief David was showing a profound lack of respect and appreciation for the men who had gone bravely into the field and risked their lives for him and his throne, and was even indicating that he would have been happier if they had died (19:6).

Finally, David's grief was opening the door for even more disillusionment with him as king and further rebellion (19:7).

Joab's sharp words finally penetrated David's stupor, and he went out to greet the people (19:8).

Crucial lessons

The priority of God

There is much for us to take home to our own hearts from all of this. One lesson has to do with the priority of God in our lives.

David was, as we have noted, on the throne of Israel because God willed it, and Absalom, in rebelling against his father, was essentially setting himself against God. Furthermore, David, as the King of Israel, was the 'covenant head' of that nation that was in a special covenant relationship with God.

In allowing himself to be completely overcome with grief, David was obviously showing more concern for his covenant-breaking son than he was for his own calling as the covenant head of the nation. He failed, then, to comprehend what was truly important.

We rejoice in that we can look beyond David to the Lord Jesus Christ himself. He certainly was not devoid of compassion for rebellious sinners and the ruin caused by their rebellion, but he did not allow his compassion for sinners to diminish his zeal for God's just judgement against sin. In fact, his death on the cross was the perfect blending of God's love for sinners and his just judgement on sin. There justice and mercy kissed each other as Christ satisfied the demands of both.

The grace of God

Another lesson has to do with the grace of God to his children even when they fail to live up to their calling. Joab's rebuke to David was the grace of God at work in David's life — a severe grace, but grace none the less.

The words of Gordon Keddie aptly capture this grace: 'Joab was at that point God's instrument to keep David on an even keel and preserve him from throwing away all the fruits of victory because of a disproportionate sorrow for his reprobate son — a son who would not have thought twice about murdering his own father! When you find yourself immersed in the sadness of some trouble — maybe bereavement, separation or divorce — be thankful for the cool heads around you who are able to give the wise advice that you find so difficult to grapple with in the maelstrom of your emotional trauma.'[1]

These truths ought to make it clear that the stories we have looked at are far more than stories. They remind us that in our own day of wickedness like that of Absalom and weakness like that shown here by David, we serve the Lord best if we are courageous in declaring his message and if we truly comprehend his calling as it relates to our own lives.

42.
Sightings of grace

2 Samuel 19:9-39

The grace of God is the dominant note in David's life.

The *electing* splendour of grace was manifested when God sent the prophet Samuel to anoint him as king. The *preserving* splendour of grace was manifested when God preserved his life in his battle against Goliath, in all the times he fled from Saul and in his dealings with the Philistines. The *enriching* splendour of grace was manifested when God elevated him to the throne of the nation and enriched him with honour and wealth, and when God made a covenant with him. The *pardoning* splendour of grace was manifested even when David took his frightful plunge into adultery, deception and murder. God's *preserving* grace was displayed again when God shielded David from the murderous intentions of Absalom.

Wherever the child of God finds grace, he is bound to admire it. The child of God recognizes that he owes all to that grace. He gladly joins with John Newton in singing:

Amazing grace, how sweet the sound
That saved a wretch like me!
I once was lost but now am found,
Was blind but now I see.

'Twas grace that taught my heart to fear
And grace my fears relieved.
How precious did that grace appear
The hour I first believed!

There is certainly much for the child of God to admire in the long section of Scripture before us. Here grace crops up everywhere.

Restoring grace

First, we see the marvel of God's restoring grace (vv. 9-15).

Absalom's insurrection had been crushed, but David knew he could not just casually stroll back into Jerusalem as if nothing had happened. Many of his citizens had supported Absalom's rebellion. To act in heavy-handed fashion would only perpetuate the problem.

So David waited for the people themselves to make an overture to him. Surprisingly, the tribes of Israel were the first to decide to bring David back to the throne. David decided his own tribe of Judah needed a little coaxing, and he provided it by sending Zadok and Abiathar to the elders (v. 11).

When Judah fell into line and it became clear that all the tribes were united in their desire for David to return, he began making arrangements to do so. He selected Gilgal, which means 'rolling away', as the site for his landing after crossing the Jordan River. There the children of Israel, under Joshua's leadership, had the shame or reproach of their years of slavery in Egypt 'rolled away' as they crossed over the Jordan to begin the conquest of the land of Canaan (Josh. 5:9). It was also the place where the kingdom had been renewed under Samuel (1 Sam. 11:14). Gilgal was, then, a place of grace. And David was keenly conscious of the grace of God as he returned to his throne.

It is important for us to recognize that David's crossing of the Jordan was not only an emblem of God's restoring grace to him, but also to the nation as a whole. God is the one who had set David over the nation, and the nation had been blessed under his reign. But the people had, without regard to the will of God in the matter, gone sinfully after Absalom. The people certainly did not deserve such a good king as David, but God gave him back to them.

The restoring grace of God is no mere dead letter as far as the Christian is concerned. The truth is that we all from time to time become infatuated with some Absalom and recklessly pursue it without regard to God's will, even as Israel of old did. But God does not wash his hands of us. He would be justified in doing so, but he patiently bears with us, forgives us and restores us to fellowship with himself.

Pardoning grace

Our second sight of grace in these verses is of the pardoning variety (vv. 16-23).

We have met this man Shimei before. When David was forced to flee from Jerusalem, Shimei took it upon himself to curse him and throw stones at him as he made his way out of Jerusalem. I can imagine Shimei going home that evening with a great deal of satisfaction. His dislike of David had been eating away at him for a good while, and he no doubt felt very good about getting the whole matter 'off his chest'.

Never in his wildest dreams did he imagine that David would once again reign over the land. How he must have trembled in his sandals when he realized that was exactly what was going to happen! He knew he had only one hope for survival and that was by casting himself upon the mercy of the king.

He made sure, therefore, that he was the very first to meet David as he landed on the west side of the Jordan (v. 20). We are told that he hurried to the place (v. 16), and, as soon as he saw David, cried out, 'Do not let my lord impute iniquity to me... For I, your servant, know that I have sinned' (vv. 19-20).

Abishai was quick to suggest that Shimei should be put to death, pointing out that justice demanded it, and many commentators have agreed with his position.

But David was keenly conscious that he himself had been forgiven, even though he did not deserve it, and that he could not withhold from others what he himself had received.

A. W. Pink says of David at this point, 'Divine grace had not only pardoned his grievous sins against Uriah, but had now delivered him from the murderous designs of Absalom; how, then, could he consent to the death of even his worst enemy?'[1]

David, therefore, pledged that Shimei would not be put to death (v. 23), and in doing so pictures for us the glorious truth that God receives even the vilest of sinners and freely pardons them. All he requires is for the sinner to say from the heart, 'I have sinned.'

Testing grace

Our third sight of grace comes when Mephibosheth greets David, and it is the sight of discerning or testing grace (vv. 24-30).

When David fled from Jerusalem, Mephibosheth's servant Ziba had alleged that Mephibosheth had stayed behind in the expectation that the kingdom would finally come back to him, as the descendant of Saul. David had uncritically accepted this report and rewarded Ziba by giving him all of Mephibosheth's land. Now David finds himself greeted by Mephibosheth himself and hears an entirely different version of why Mephibosheth had stayed in Jerusalem (vv. 26-28).

Here, then, David finds himself confronted with diametrically opposed accounts. It should have been obvious to David from Mephibosheth's appearance and demeanour that he was telling the truth (v. 24), but David seems to have been uncertain. He, therefore, reversed his earlier decision and declared that Mephibosheth and Ziba would divide the land (v. 29).

David may not have realized in advance what this decision would do. In effect it provided a test for Mephibosheth and he passed it with flying colours. He responded by urging the king to give Ziba all the land, saying that he was happy just to have the king restored (v. 30). If he had been motivated by a selfish concern for himself, he would have insisted on keeping all the land. Instead he willingly agreed to give it all up.

In David's mishandling of this issue we have a faint picture of one who never mishandles anything. Part of God's gracious work in the lives of his children is to test them from time to time. This is not so that he can determine what is in their hearts (he already knows that), but so they can look at themselves and see whether they, like Mephibosheth, are happy just to have the company of the King! Such a look into our hearts is never pleasant, but in this way we come to grieve over what we find there and resolve to love our Lord more, and it is, therefore, a work of grace.

Rewarding grace

Our final sighting in this passage is of rewarding grace (vv. 31-39).

One of David's most loyal subjects was the aged Barzillai. He had provided David with supplies while he was away from Jerusalem (17:27-29; 19:32), and he accompanied David back to Jerusalem.

To show his appreciation for Barzillai's kindness, David invited him to come and live with him in Jerusalem (v. 33). Barzillai declined the offer for himself but accepted it for one of his sons (v. 37).

David's offer to reward Barzillai reminds us that not even the smallest act of service to God and his cause will finally go undetected or unrewarded.

Some always point out that we should not serve God for reward. True enough. I am sure that what Barzillai did for David he did without any thought of reward, but David desired to reward him. David's generous nature would allow nothing less. So it is with God. His generous nature compels him to reward those who serve him (Matt. 19:29; 1 Cor. 3:14; 2 Tim. 4:8; Rev. 11:18; 22:12).

How good God is to us! It is his grace that enables us to do all we do for him, and then when we have done it, it is grace that rewards us for the doing!

We have looked at many facets of this jewel of grace. Each sighting causes us to agree with the hymn's description of it: 'marvellous, infinite, matchless grace'.

43.
God and wickedness

David's return to the city of Jerusalem has given us some marvellous glimpses into the grace of God, but it also gives us glimpses into the depths of human wickedness.

Where, you may ask, is the wickedness in these verses? It is all over the place. The wickedness of pride and dissension are apparent in the arrangements to bring the king back (19:40-43). The wickedness of rebelling against God's anointed king is apparent in the actions of Sheba (20:1-2). The wickedness of resentment and hatred are apparent in Joab's murder of Amasa (20:4-15).

And the great, recurring question arises: where is God in all of this? Wickedness is cropping up on every hand and God seems to be strangely absent.

Now these ancient verses take on new life. We know what wickedness is all about. We see it on every hand. Crime soars. Wars erupt. Political scandals and scoundrels abound. We look for God and wonder where he is, and he seems to be nowhere to be found. So we question, sometimes doubt and all too often become chilled in our commitment and service to him.

Let's look at each of these instances of wickedness and then look for the hand of God in all of this.

The wickedness of Israel and Judah

The first instance puts the ugly faces of pride and dissension on display (19:40-43).

The tribes of Israel were the first to decide to bring the king back from his exile (19:9-10). David's own tribe of Judah, however, needed a bit of persuading. David provided this by sending Zadok and Abiathar to pose this question to the elders of Judah: 'Why are you the last to bring the king back to his house...?' (19:11).

There is, by the way, a very pointed message in that question for each and every child of God. King David, as we have noted on many occasions, represented the will and rule of God, and Absalom represented rebellion against that rule and the ruin that comes from it. Many of us, if we were completely honest with ourselves, would have to admit that we have often displaced the will and rule of God by embracing some Absalom, and we have brought nothing but heartache upon ourselves. I would urge each Christian who is even now chasing after some Absalom to cease and desist and 'bring the king back' — that is, bow afresh and anew before the will of God.

But we must get back to the point at hand. The people of Judah were swayed by David's overtures and they too invited the king to return (19:14).

Then the problem set in. When it was time actually to receive the king at Gilgal, 'all the people of Judah' were there to escort him back to Jerusalem, but only 'half the people of Israel' (19:40). The fact that the people of Judah had not waited for all their brethren from Israel to assemble was construed by the latter to mean that Judah looked upon David as belonging more to them than to the nation as a whole. The two factions began to quarrel. The situation worsened as harsh words flew back and forth, and it ended when Sheba called the tribes of Israel to follow him (19:42 - 20:2).

What was going on here? A number of things.

First, there was *insensitivity* on the part of Judah. They should have considered their brothers from Israel and waited until all were present.

Secondly, there was wrong on the part of Israel when they *put the worst interpretation* on Judah's insensitivity, making it seem that it was a deliberate attempt to steal the king (19:42).

Thirdly, Judah was wrong in *responding harshly* to the accusation. This was the time when the whole issue could have been defused by a soft, humble answer that admitted their insensitivity. But the words of Judah inflamed the situation still further (19:42).

Harsh words usually lead to *more harsh words*, and Israel responded to those of Judah by calling attention to the fact that they were greater in number and had been the first to suggest bringing the king back (19:43).

All of this seems so childish that we may find ourselves shaking our heads in disbelief. But this childishness has been replayed countless times in the lives of God's people down through the years: insensitivity, putting the worst interpretation on a brother's motives, harsh words, open division. It all has a very familiar and sad ring to it — familiar because it happens so often and sad because it always brings great harm to the cause of God.

May God help us to see such dissension for the wickedness that it is and determine that we will never be a party to it.

The wickedness of Sheba

The second instance of wickedness in these verses stands on the shoulders of the first. It is the wickedness of Sheba's (and Israel's) rebellion against the king (20:1-2).

Here we see the sin of the nation in going after Absalom repeated. David, as we have noted, was not on the throne of the nation by accident. He was there because God appointed him for that rule. When Israel (and Judah) went after Absalom, God had not uttered so much as one syllable to indicate that he had changed his mind about David ruling. In embracing Absalom the people were, therefore, thumbing their noses at God.

Now here we find the people of Israel storming off after Sheba (although it appears that only the Berites persisted to the bitter end — 20:14), and God has still not said one word about anyone ruling except David. So the people are once again thumbing their noses at God.

A large part of the whole problem at this juncture was that the people who went after Absalom had not repented for doing so. When they went about the business of bringing the king back, there was no great, overriding awareness that they had failed God in going after Absalom and no renewed appreciation that David was the anointed of God. It was almost as if they were saying, 'Well, there's no one else, so we might as well bring David back.' This is hardly the raw material from which a healthy new start could be fashioned.

The wickedness of Joab

The third instance of enormously revolting wickedness has to do with David and Joab.

When David made his overtures to Judah, he pledged that Amasa would replace Joab as commander of the army (19:13). This was David paying back Joab for disobeying his explicit order not to harm Absalom (18:5).

But Joab, like a besetting sin,[1] could not easily be swept aside and, as he had done with Abner, he approached Amasa

on seemingly friendly terms only to thrust a sword into his
stomach (20:10). The wretched sight of Amasa wallowing in
his blood on the road is a fitting emblem of the ugliness and
repulsiveness of Joab's sin, and of all sin (20:12).

It is all very depressing and distasteful. Judah and Israel
engage in a feud. Israel rebels. Joab commits murder. Where,
oh where, is God? Well, he is there in the midst of this wickedness, working out and achieving his purpose.

The presence of God

He is there when David returns to demonstrate his grace to an
undeserving people. The people did not deserve such a good
king as David, but God gave him back to them just the same.

He is there in David's return to underscore the point that
his will and rule are ultimately going to be victorious, and the
wickedness of men will not finally be able to thwart or prevent
his purposes.

He is there when David returns to the city and permanently
sequesters the ten concubines violated by Absalom (20:3) to
remind us that his Word always comes true (12:11-12). We
are wise if we heed this and obey that Word!

He is there when Judah and Israel squabble and Israel rebels
to underscore for us that our refusal to repent of known sin
only opens the door to more sin and more disaster. If Judah
and Israel had come to receive David in a repentant spirit,
things would have been far different.

He is there when the wise woman of Abel Beth Maacah
understands that the execution of the wicked Sheba is far better than the slaughter of a great number of innocents and sends
his head flying over the wall (20:22).

All of this should remind us of a rough hill and a cruel cross
outside Jerusalem centuries later. There wickedness so abounded

that it seemed as if God were nowhere near. But that rough hill was the place and that cruel cross the means by which God worked out eternal salvation for all those who believe. Wickedness seemed to have won that day, but in fact it received its death-blow and paved the way for God to become all in all.

Abounding wickedness often obscures our view of God and challenges our faith. But wickedness, however strong it may seem, does not finally defeat God. He works in and through it to achieve his purposes so we can triumphantly say with the apostle Paul, 'And we know that all things work together for good to those who love God, to those who are the called according to his purpose' (Rom. 8:28).

44.
A psalm of praise for deliverance

2 Samuel 22

When we think of psalms, we think of David and the book of Psalms. However, we have here a psalm of David that is found not only in the book of Psalms but, with some variations, here in 2 Samuel.

The fact that this psalm is found in both books indicates that it was sung by David, in the words of Charles Spurgeon, 'on different occasions when he reviewed his own remarkable history, and observed the gracious hand of God in it all'. [1]

Gordon Keddie offers this observation on this psalm: 'It may be that the fuller version in the Psalter was David's final version for public use in the worship of God. The differences are fairly numerous, but the teaching is the same. Both are the inspired Word of God: the one set in a historical context, the other in the manual of praise.' [2]

Certain things bear repeating, and this psalm is certainly in that category. It deals with truths that cannot be repeated too frequently.

Analysis of this psalm must move on, or take into account, two levels. First, there is the personal or historical level, and then there is the prophetic level. In other words, I am suggesting that David first speaks for himself here, but there is another level in which, as it were, the Lord Jesus Christ takes over and speaks through David's mouth. In this chapter we will restrict ourselves to the first of these two levels, and move to the second level in the next chapter.

This psalm of praise arose from David's personal experiences of deliverance from his enemies in general and from Saul in particular (v. 1). In describing these experiences, David constantly shifts from talking about God ('the Lord,' 'he,' 'his') to talking directly to God ('you'). This gives us the mental picture of a man who is so caught up with excitement about what has happened to him that he turns first to tell those around him, turns to express thanks directly to God and then turns back to those around him.

A psalm of praise

Words of praise about God

His first words are to those who happened to be near when he experienced God's deliverance. Deliverance from grave and seemingly inescapable danger is certainly ground for praise and here David, as it were, opens the floodgates and lets out all the praise he can muster. Instead of muttering a mere 'thanks', David multiplies praise by pouring out a torrent of pictures: 'rock', 'fortress', 'deliverer', 'shield', 'the horn', 'stronghold', 'refuge' and 'Saviour' (vv. 2-3).

It should be noted that each of these pictures of God is preceded by the pronoun 'my'. David is asserting in the strongest manner possible that the benefits he had received flowed from a personal relationship with God.

To all of this David affirms his intention always to call upon the Lord, who is 'worthy to be praised', and expresses his confidence that such praise would result in even more deliverances in the future (v. 4).

Testimony of deliverance

From there David proceeds to give a testimony about the anguish he was in before he was delivered (vv. 5-6), his giving himself over to prayer (v. 7), the answer he received from God (vv. 8-20) and the reason why God granted him deliverance (vv. 21-25).

Alternating praise to God and about God

The rest of the psalm alternates between praise directed to God and praise of God directed to those who were on the scene when David experienced God's acts of deliverance (vv. 26-51).

A pressing question

All of this praise about God and to God for deliverance from the crises of life forces us to raise a very important and pressing question — that is, what about those times in which it appears that God has failed to deliver his people?

We all know, do we not, of instances in which the people of God desperately needed deliverance from death, fervently prayed for it and it did not come. How can we praise a delivering God when we can point to so many instances in which he seems to have failed to deliver?

Spiritual deliverance

The trouble we have at this point is due to our assuming that deliverance from distress must always be physical in nature. There are times — many times if we only knew the truth about our earthly pilgrimage — in which God does grant physical deliverance, and such deliverances are indeed marvellous and worthy of great praise.

But there is another kind of deliverance that is just as real and valuable, and that is spiritual deliverance. This kind of deliverance means that while we do not have the physical danger removed we are delivered from fear and anxiety while we face it.

The apostle Paul demonstrated this on more than one occasion. There is that well-known passage in which he details his struggle with a 'thorn' in his flesh. His desire, of course, was for that thorn to be removed, and he pleaded with God to do so. But God did not grant the apostle the physical deliverance he desired. Instead he granted him the grace to bear it and, in doing so, has blessed untold millions of Christians down through the years (2 Cor. 12:7-9).

Who, in the light of all the comfort that has come through Paul's experience, can say the physical deliverance he desired would have been greater than the spiritual deliverance he received?

The great lesson for us to learn, then, is this: there is nothing wrong with desiring physical deliverance, but we must never disparage spiritual deliverance.

Eternal deliverance

While we are on the subject, we should also note that there is such a thing as eternal deliverance. When God refuses to deliver his children physically from some danger, it is not because he has failed to deliver them, but rather because he has, in his grace and wisdom, granted them the greatest of all deliverances by taking them unto himself where no evil can ever touch them again.

Paul also dealt with this matter of eternal deliverance. We find him saying in his second letter to Timothy that the Lord would deliver him (2 Tim. 4:18). At the time of writing those words, Paul was in prison, and that imprisonment ended in the apostle's being beheaded!

Did God fail to deliver Paul, then? Paul would be the first to say the Lord did not fail him. Paul knew he was going to die before he ever said, 'The Lord will deliver me from every evil work.' Earlier in the same chapter we find him saying, 'The time of my departure is at hand' (2 Tim. 4:6).

So what was Paul talking about when he expressed confidence that the Lord would deliver him? It was not physical deliverance from prison, but perfect deliverance by being taken from this world to heaven. Look again at that verse in which Paul says he knows he will be delivered. He goes on to say that the Lord will 'preserve' him 'for his heavenly kingdom' (2 Tim. 4:18). Paul knew he was about to die and go to heaven, and he regarded that as being deliverance. Indeed, he rejoiced in it by saying, 'To him be glory for ever and ever. Amen!' (2 Tim. 4:18).

Our problem always is that we want to dictate to God what he should do in our lives rather than trust in his wisdom to do what is best. In the light of what we have seen about eternal deliverance, I ask which is better — being physically delivered, so we can face another crisis along the way, or being eternally delivered, so we never have to face another crisis at all?

If we were to stop and think for a moment about the glories of heaven, we would realize Paul was right to say, 'The sufferings of this present time are not worthy to be compared with the glory which shall be revealed in us' (Rom. 8:18). And he was also right to say that it is 'far better' to depart and be with Christ (Phil. 1:23).

When we realize all the ways in which God can and does deliver his people, we shall have occasion to join David in full-hearted praise to God.

The urgency of prayer

We must not leave this psalm without giving due attention to the prominence it gives to prayer.

Gordon Keddie points out the clear sequence here: affliction, prayer, deliverance.[3] Prayer was the connecting link between the affliction and the deliverance. If we want God's deliverance, then, we must be careful to seek it fervently through trusting prayer.

If the channel of prayer is clogged and corroded through disuse, we have no right to feel as if God has failed us if physical or spiritual deliverance do not come in the measure we would like. It is an indication of the boundless measure of his grace that eternal deliverance will come to all his children even though they are all too frequently slack in prayer.

It should also be noted that all I have said about deliverance from trouble presupposes that the person in question is a child of God. The unbeliever may receive instances of physical deliverance as tokens of that common grace that God showers upon all, but he is shut off from the spiritual deliverance God provides to his people. And, as for eternity, the unbeliever has nothing to look forward to except 'a certain fearful expectation of judgement, and fiery indignation which will devour the adversaries' (Heb. 10:26).

45.
A psalm of Christ

2 Samuel 22

We have looked at this psalm on the personal level — that is, on the level at which David praises God for deliverance from his enemies and, particularly, from Saul (v. 1). There is, however, another level in this psalm, the prophetic level. On this level we must picture the Lord Jesus Christ as taking over David's mouth, as it were, and testifying to his own experience of God's deliverance.

What entitles us to hear Christ speaking in this psalm? First, it is quite obvious that David himself could not have experienced any deliverance that would do justice to the language used in this psalm. Secondly, no less an authority than the apostle Paul himself draws from this psalm to present Christ's saving work among the Gentiles (Romans 15:9 quotes 2 Samuel 22:50).

Christ's experience of deliverance

Relating this psalm to Christ does raise certain questions.

When Christ needed deliverance

First, it compels us to ask when Christ needed deliverance. The answer, of course, is when, on the cross, he plummeted into the depths of what it meant to be forsaken by God and, after dying there, was buried in a borrowed tomb.

What a graphic description we have of the intense pain and anguish Christ endured on the cross! He says:

The waves of death encompassed me,
The floods of ungodliness made me afraid.
The sorrows of Sheol surrounded me,
The snares of death confronted me

(vv. 5-6).

What should we understand from such language? The main truth that emerges is this — the humanity Christ took to himself was a real humanity. It was not just a humanity that he, as it were, 'zipped on'. Christ took a humanity that felt all that we feel. The author of Hebrews confirms this when he says of Christ, 'Therefore, in all things he had to be made like his brethren, that he might be a merciful and faithful High Priest in things pertaining to God, to make propitiation for the sins of the people' (Heb. 2:17).

Do we understand that Jesus, in order to be able to do anything for us, had to be like us? He could not represent humanity in the work of redemption if he were not a real man. We should not be surprised, then, that the Lord Jesus Christ not only died a real death, but that he also felt normal human emotions about death. We again find confirmation for this from the author of Hebrews when he says Christ 'offered up prayers and supplications, with vehement cries and tears' (Heb. 5:7).

But we have not fully come to grips with the death of Christ if we say nothing more than that it was the real death of a real man. That death had a special quality about it that no one else has ever experienced, or ever can experience. In the psalm before us, Christ alludes to this with these words: 'The floods of ungodliness made me afraid' (v. 5).

Jesus was not on that cross just because he was a man whose time had run out. He was there by the design of God to be a sacrifice for sin. There he took the place of sinners. He himself knew no sin, but their sin was placed on him (2 Cor. 5:21). And his becoming sin for us led to the greatest agony of the cross — namely, his being forsaken by God. He became sin, and sin separates from God. So Jesus, in order to provide atonement for his people, had to be separated from God. This explains his cry of dereliction: 'My God, my God, why have you forsaken me?' (Matt. 27:46).

In this psalm, then, we hear Christ speaking about his excruciating, painful death on the cross, and that testifies to his humanity and to the atoning nature of that death. It was this experience of death that caused Jesus to cry out to God for deliverance. He says:

> In my distress I called upon the Lord,
> And cried to my God;
> He heard my voice from his temple,
> And my cry entered his ears
>
> (v. 7).

There is a problem here. We certainly have no trouble understanding that the experience of death would cause Jesus to cry out to God, but this verse claims more than that. Here Christ not only asserts that he cried out to God, but also emphatically affirms that God heard him.

How Christ experienced deliverance

The second question we must ask, then, is how did Christ experience deliverance? Christ cried out for deliverance from the cross, but he was not delivered from the cross. He died there! We are surely forced to say, then, that God failed to answer his prayer, and the prophetic confidence expressed by Christ in this verse was mistaken.

No, there is no mistake here. Christ was indeed delivered from death. He was not delivered in the sense of being rescued from the cross, but rather delivered by being raised from the dead. He was delivered from death in the sense that death could not hold him.

So after his resurrection Jesus could truly say of God:

He sent from above, he took me,
He drew me out of many waters.
He delivered me from my strong enemy...
He also brought me out into a broad place...

(vv. 17-18,20).

The resurrection of Jesus Christ is an event of such magnitude and glory that it can only be fittingly described in terms of God causing the earth to shake and tremble (v. 8), kindling a blazing fire (vv. 9,13), coming from heaven to put darkness under his feet (v. 10), thundering from heaven (v. 14) and firing arrows to vanquish his enemies (v. 15). And that resurrection, in turn, led to the exaltation of Christ to the right hand of God and to his ruling over the nations (vv. 38-51).

In this psalm of prophecy, the Lord Jesus Christ could not be content only to affirm his forthcoming death and resurrection. He also speaks very powerfully and forcefully about his relationship to the Father.

Christ's relationship to the Father

This relationship was one of mutual delight. Christ's delight in the Father may be seen in the opening verses of the psalm. We hear him speaking these words about the Father: 'The Lord is my rock and my fortress and my deliverer' (v. 1). We go on from there to hear him refer to God as his strength, shield, horn of salvation, stronghold and refuge (v. 3). Because he has such delight in God, he announces his intention to call upon him 'who is worthy to be praised' (v. 4).

Later in the psalm, Christ refers to his Father as his light in darkness (v. 29) and as the one who enables him to run against a troop and leap over a wall (v. 30). He also asserts that God's ways are perfect, that his word is proven and that he is a shield to all who trust in him (v. 31).

There is much more in this psalm from the lips of Christ about his delight in his Father. But it is also important for us to understand that the Father delighted in his Son. It was because of the Father's delight in the righteousness of the Son that he raised him from the dead (vv. 21-25).

The main subjects Christ speaks about in this psalm are, therefore, his crucifixion, his resurrection and the mutual delight of the Father and the Son.

Applications

But what is there here for the people of God? How can we apply it to our lives?

A call to trust the Word of God

First, this psalm calls us to trust the Word of God implicitly. We have in this psalm a very poignant picture of Christ's death and resurrection. The fact that it was written centuries before Christ came tells us the Bible is no ordinary book. It has, as it were, the divine insignia upon it.

A call to fresh appreciation of Christ

Secondly, this psalm calls us to a fresh appreciation of what Christ did in order to purchase our salvation. He went so far as actually to take our humanity and in that humanity to face the most gruesome death and most extreme anguish imaginable.

If our hearts are cold, it is because we have not been spending as much time in Calvary's school as we ought. This psalm will take us back to that school and will fill our hearts with wonder and praise.

A call to prayer

This psalm also calls us to prayer. The Lord Jesus Christ was a man of prayer. He constantly sought the Father's face. The night before he was crucified, he communed with the Father. On the cross, he continued to commune with the Father until that period of being forsaken by God.

Can there be any doubt at all about the lesson here? If the Lord Jesus Christ found it necessary to devote so much time to communing with the Father in prayer, how much more do we need to be devoting ourselves to prayer?

A call to delight in God

This psalm also calls us to delight in God and offer praise to him, even as Jesus did. It calls us to meditate much on who God is and what he has done, to meditate on these things until the wonder of them grips our hearts and then to openly praise God for these things.

A call to recognize the reign of Christ

Finally, this psalm calls us to recognize that our Lord Jesus Christ is reigning even now. We do not have to worry and fret as we wonder what the world is coming to. Our crucified, risen Lord has been exalted to the right hand of the Father, and he will eventually bring all things to their appointed end, and God will be all in all.

46.
When the time comes to die

2 Samuel 23:1-7

One of the most frequently used phrases of our day is 'I don't have time.' That phrase covers a multitude of situations. When something arises that is not particularly pleasant, we often sidestep it by saying, 'I don't have time.'

There is, however, something on the horizon for each of us that is not particularly pleasant, and our much-used excuse will be of no value when it arrives. That something is death, and when it comes, we shall all have time for it. People sometimes jokingly say, 'I don't have time to die.' But we all have time to die. We have no choice about it.

2 Samuel 23:1-7 presents us with the last words of a dying man. That man is David.

There is a minor difficulty here. The problem is that these so-called 'last words' do not correspond to the 'last words' of David recorded in 1 Kings 2:1-9. I call it 'minor' because a little examination reveals there is no real difficulty at all. The words recorded in 1 Kings are clearly described as words David spoke to Solomon. The last words in the passage before us here are presented in the form of a psalm and, judging from the content of them, were intended for the whole nation. So David had two sets of last words — those addressed to the whole nation and those addressed to his successor.

We do not know how far David was from death when he wrote these words to the nation, but he knew it was not far off. And, wise man that he was, he did not want death just to be something that happened to him. He wanted to prepare for death by thinking about certain things, and he wanted what he thought about to be a blessing and benefit to others.

His wisdom is exceedingly rare these days. We do not like to think about death at all. We just want it to be over with as quickly and painlessly as possible. And if God chooses not to grant us this type of death, we complain about how unfair it is. But the wise person not only believes in preparing for death, but also knows what truths have the power to best fortify him against its terrors.

We see David rehearsing these truths in this passage. He could have chosen to dwell on all the accomplishments of his reign, but instead this man of grace chose to magnify the grace that had made him the man he was. And he could not magnify that grace without a word of warning to those rejecting it.

Grateful reflection on God's grace

First, there is grateful reflection on the magnificence of God's grace in the past (vv. 1-4).

How marvellously kind God had been to David! He had showered his grace upon him in abundant fashion. It was God's grace that took David all the way from being a shepherd boy to serving as King of Israel.

We do well to remember how this came about. Samuel the prophet was sent by God to anoint one of Jesse's sons to be king. Humanly speaking, there was no way David could have been selected above all his older brothers. Each of these men doubtless had many attractive and appealing qualities. But God does not do things the way we do, and he was pleased to bypass all those men and bring David to the throne (1 Sam. 16:1-13).

God's grace was not only responsible for plucking David out of obscurity and making him king. It was also God's grace that made him 'the sweet psalmist of Israel' (v. 2). David was under no illusions about his work as a psalmist. It was not because of his own creativity but rather because the Spirit of the Lord spoke by him.

Many today say they do not believe in the verbal inspiration of the Scriptures. David certainly had no trouble with this doctrine. He says the psalms came about because God had placed his word on his tongue (v. 2).

How gracious God was to David to use him in this way! But there is yet more. That grace that made David king and made him the psalmist of Israel had also spoken to him about the kind of king that he was to be and had, to a large extent, made David a king of that type.

What kind of king was this? It was one who knew that God was 'the Rock of Israel' and one who was just and who ruled 'in the fear of God' (v. 3). It was one who was so godly that his reign dissipated the darkness of sin and sorrow even as the morning sun dissipates the darkness of the night. And it was one whose reign promoted productivity and prosperity among the people just as surely as the sunshine promoted these things after the rain.

While we are certainly entitled to see here a foreshadowing of the kingly office of Christ, we also have to say David had to some degree been that kind of king to Israel. But in so far as he had been successful in being that type of king, David knew the credit went, not to his political shrewdness, but rather to the grace of God.

We must not miss the fact that God's grace had a great purpose in all this. It was for the good of God's people that God did all this with David. It was 'the God of Jacob' who anointed him to be the king and who inspired him to be 'the sweet psalmist of Israel' (v. 1).

All of this was a comfort to David as he descended into death. Let us learn from his experience that our own descent into death will be much easier and more pleasant if we are much occupied with the grace that has worked in our lives and made us useful to others.

Yes, if we are children of God, we must say that the same grace that worked in David has worked in us. No, we are not kings and psalmists in the same sense that David was, but we have been visited by the grace of God, redeemed from sin and elevated to the high level of being spiritual kings and priests (1 Peter 2:9-10).

Remembrance of past evidences of God's grace will help us in the hour of death in this way — it will cause us to realize that God would not have expended such grace upon us in the past if that same grace would not safely carry us through the valley of death.

Dependence on future grace

But David had more comfort for dying than what God had done for him in the past. He also deliberately rested on the sufficiency of God's grace for the future (v. 5).

God's grace had worked abundantly in David, and the working of that grace had caused him to perform admirably as king. But David was still conscious that he had failed in many respects. He and his house had already experienced much trouble, and he knew even more troubles were ahead (v. 5). All of this made David acutely aware that he could not depend on his performance in the hour of death. The good in his life was due to the grace of God, and past grace was a token of sufficient grace in the future. But David had an even greater ground for assurance in the face of death than the past blessings of God, namely, God's 'everlasting covenant'.

That everlasting covenant can only refer to the covenant of grace God has made with his people. It is the only covenant that can truly be described as 'everlasting'. It reaches from eternity to eternity. It is that covenant in which God pledged in eternity past to grant eternal salvation to all those whom he loved before the foundation of the world and gave to his Son. They are those for whom the Son agreed to stand as their surety and whom he purchased as his own by receiving the penalty for their sins. They are also those in whom the Holy Spirit works by convicting them of their sinful condition and enabling them to lay hold of the redeeming work of Christ with a true and living faith. These are the ones who will finally be brought into eternal glory.

That covenant is 'ordered' — that is, it is all carefully planned and arranged by God. Nothing is left to chance. It was designed by God to bring salvation to his people and to do so in such a way as to bring great honour and glory to his name.

That covenant is also 'secure'. It is promised by the God who never changes and never lies.

This covenant of grace is not only that in which David rested his hope for salvation, but it is also that in which David delighted and exulted. He writes, 'For this is all my salvation and all my desire' (v. 5).

Our hope in the hour of death and our peace and joy in this life come from that same ordered and secure covenant in which David rested.

A warning of neglected grace

That brings us to David's solemn warning to those who neglect this covenant of God's grace:

But the sons of rebellion shall all be as thorns thrust
    away,
Because they cannot be taken with hands.
But the man who touches them
Must be armed with iron and the shaft of a spear,
And they shall be utterly burned with fire in their place.

(vv. 6-7).

What a fearful picture we have here! Those who rebel
against God and reject his covenant will be thrust away by
God as a man thrusts away thorns. When men handle thorns
they have to use appropriate tools. They cannot pick the thorns
up with their hands, but deal with them from a distance by
using a tool with a long handle. In like manner, when the time
finally comes to deal with those who rebel against him, God
will, as it were, stand afar off from them, and will cast them
into the fire of eternal destruction.

Gordon Keddie summarizes this portion of David's last
words in this way: 'If David's song ends on this dismal note, it
is only the Lord's way of driving home the point that he alone
is able to save his people and that his covenant is no mere
option for a more meaningful life, but is the great divide between the saved and the unsaved, in time and for all eternity.'

The message of David's last words is clear. If we are to
face death as he did — with peace and tranquillity — we must
not assume it is just a matter of 'the luck of the draw'. Instead
we must cease rebelling against him and embrace that grace
that is offered in God's everlasting covenant.

47.
David loses his senses over a census

2 Samuel 24

We are coming towards the end of David's life. Most of us know the details about his closing months, but let's lay that aside for a moment and pretend we did not. How would we expect this story to end? Would we not expect Scripture to tell us that this man in whom the grace of God had worked so magnificently came to the end of his reign triumphantly and heroically?

We know by now that David was far from perfect. The names of Bathsheba, Uriah, Amnon and Absalom immediately leap to mind. What sordid, sorry episodes David's sin created! But we expect men to learn from their sins, to see their wretched consequences and to resolve never to be caught in sin's web again.

The sombre passage before us reveals the solemn truth that God's people will never be able to lay their spiritual armour down until this life is over. We must keep our weapons against sin in our hands until we die. This David failed to do. His weapon slips from his hand in an unguarded moment, and sin pounces — quickly and destructively.

David's sin

What was David's sin? It seems so innocent. He took a census of the people. We read this account and we shake our heads in amazement. What could possibly be so bad about taking a census?

Pride

The answer is fourfold. First, it was prompted by pride.

David had just come from a string of impressive military victories. Perhaps he wanted to see just how strong a military state he could muster. If so, he lost sight of the fact that Israel's military might lay, not in her numbers, but in dependence on her God. By numbering the people, David was guilty of diverting the people from the Lord and the need to trust him to depending on their own strength.

Attributing this act to David's pride in no way contradicts the statement in verse 1 that God incited David's action, or the statement in 1 Chronicles that Satan incited it (1 Chron. 21:1). We feel the need to choose between these things. It has to be one or the other! Either God caused David to do it, Satan caused him to do it, or he caused himself to do it! But Scripture assures us all three statements are true. David's act was at one and the same time due to God's permissive will, Satan's evil intent and David's excessive pride.

How are we to reconcile these things? A reasonable synopsis would be to say God allowed Satan to tempt David, and David yielded to that temptation. In other words, God read the pride in David's heart and decided to allow Satan to tempt him as a judgement upon him.

We can also say God allowed Satan to tempt David because God had a controversy with the whole nation. Keep in mind that David was God's choice to be king over Israel and that Israel had flagrantly rebelled against God in going after Absalom. Up to this point the people of Israel had not repented of that sin. By allowing Satan to tempt David, God was essentially bringing judgement upon the nation for her sin.

What we have here, then, is essentially the same thing that happened with Job. God allowed Satan to try Job (Job 1:6-12; 2:1-9) and he allowed him to try David. But we must remember that neither the fact that God permitted the temptation nor the fact that Satan carried it out for one moment relieves David of guilt.

Disregard of the Word of God

The second part of the answer to why this was such a serious sin has to do with how David went about it. In other words, he completely disregarded the example and the clear teachings of the law of Moses on this matter.

Moses twice took a census of the people of Israel. So the taking of a census was not inherently wrong. But each time Moses did it, he was commanded by God to do so (Num. 1:1-3; 26:1-2). No mention is made at all of God commanding David to take this census.

If David was set on taking a census without God commanding him to do so, the very least he could have done, it would seem, was take it in the way prescribed by the Word of God. What was that prescribed way? Ransom money was to be received for each person when such a census was taken (Exod. 30:11-16 — Note especially verse 12 in which God says this ransom was to be paid so 'that there may be no plague among them when you number them'). In those instructions we have a powerful picture of the need for atonement. The only way anyone can ever stand before a holy God is by virtue of a ransom being paid for his or her sins.

The apostle John drives this home in the book of Revelation. There he tells us that he saw something of a census being taken in heaven. This census revealed 'ten thousand times ten thousand, and thousands of thousands', and they were all there by virtue of the ransom paid by Christ when he shed his blood on the cross (Rev. 5:11-12).

Refusal to listen and persistence in sin

In addition to these things, we can say David's sin was aggravated by his refusal to listen to the counsel of Joab and the captains of the army (vv. 3-4). It was further aggravated by his persistence in it. At any time during the nine months and twenty days it took to do the census (v. 8), David could have called a halt to it. But he did not.

What seems, then, to be innocent is far from it. Here is pride. Here is disregard for the Word of God. Here is refusal to listen to wise counsel. Here is persistence in all these things. This is indeed a poisonous brew. When we see these four elements in the life of any child of God, we are looking at something that is terribly ruinous and damaging.

Only after the census was complete did David come to his senses. And he did what any child of God ought to do when he has sinned. He cried to the Lord in heartfelt repentance: 'I have sinned greatly in what I have done; but now, I pray, O Lord, take away the iniquity of your servant, for I have done very foolishly' (v. 10).

It is a fine prayer, and we expect to read that nothing evil befell David and the people as a result of his sin. But there is no 'They lived happily ever after' here. God sent the prophet Gad with the sobering word that judgement was about to fall.

God's judgement and grace

Why would God send judgement after David had repented? There is a principle here that we all have great difficulty learning. Repentance removes the guilt of sin, but it does not necessarily remove the consequences of sin. If a person spends years wrecking his body through alcoholism and then repents, God will forgive him of that sin, but he probably will not give him a new body. His body will continue to suffer the ravages caused by his years of sin.

But even when God judges, he does so with grace. His judgements are always tempered with grace. That grace is evident here in several ways.

First, God offered David a choice on the type of judgement that would be sent (vv. 11-12).

Secondly, when David asked to 'fall into the hand of the Lord' rather than 'into the hand of man' (v.14), God mercifully selected the judgement that was shorter in duration, namely, the three-day plague (vv. 15-16).

Thirdly, God brought blessing out of the calamity. The place where the judgement was called to a halt, the threshing-floor of Araunah (v. 16), became the site of Solomon's temple.

Finally, the judgement of God led to true spiritual renewal and healing of the land.

Where do we see renewal in these verses? It is there in David's compassion for his people (v. 17). Compassion of heart and intercession for others are infallible signs of spiritual renewal.

It is also there when David offers burnt offerings and peace offerings to the Lord (v. 24) — the former representing fresh dedication to the Lord and the latter representing renewed fellowship with the Lord.

Some significant lessons

This episode from ancient history embodies several practical principles that are of utmost importance:

1. No matter how long we have been serving the Lord, we never outgrow the temptation to be proud and self-serving.

2. We cannot sin without profoundly affecting others.

3. Clearly forbidden sins are more severely judged.

4. The sins of those in positions of great authority affect others more than the sins of those with lesser authority. The greater the office, the greater the influence for good or for evil.

5. True spiritual renewal is a costly thing. It often comes only through calamity.

6. God's grace is never absent from the life of the child of God. Even in chastisement it is there to soften the blow.

The greatest lesson of all is, of course, the need for those of us who know the Lord continually to order our lives in accordance with his Word. Obedience is the key word for the Christian. The presence of it brings blessing. The absence of it only brings ruin.

48.
Laws for living

1 Kings 1-2

These chapters bring us to the end of David's long life and the transfer of the kingdom to his son Solomon.

This portion of David's life is far more than a mere historical account of various political manoeuvrings. In fact, I have no hesitation in suggesting that David's last appearance on the stage of human history forms a kind of summary of his whole life. It is something of a microcosm of the whole.

This account is also filled with practical wisdom for the people of God. How desperately we need such wisdom! Life is a very challenging business at best, and it takes many 'living skills' to cope with it. These skills flow from wisdom, and wisdom flows from God. Some never master these skills. They always intend to, but they never do. The sad truth is that there are multitudes who are going to be just as unskilled at living ten years from now as they are today.

What I am about to say may sound shockingly strange — the final instalment of the life of David can help us with this very matter of skills or principles for living. We can look at the twilight of David's life and discover certain laws that will serve us well in this matter of facing life.

Sowing and reaping

The first is a very well-known, but frequently forgotten law, the law of sowing and reaping.

How poignantly this law was driven home to David before he died! He had planned for many years to make Solomon his successor, and it probably seemed for a long while that nothing would prevent that plan from becoming reality.

But another of David's sons, Adonijah, had another plan. When it became obvious to him that his father was near death, he decided to make his move. He gathered his supporters, some of whom had been loyal to David (Joab and Abiathar), and declared himself king.

This brazen attempt to seize the throne was not just a freak outcome of chance events. It was the inevitable result of certain things that had been put in place years before. It was, in other words, the reaping of what David had been sowing.

David's polygamy

For one thing, David had practised polygamy from early manhood. Polygamy was, of course, the common practice of those days, but the fact that something enjoys popular acceptance does not make it right. God's law defines what is right and what is wrong for his people, and God had distinctly said the king was not to 'multiply' wives for himself (Deut. 17:17).

When we disregard the laws of God, we may be sure that sooner or later we shall have to eat bitter fruit. One of the bitter fruits polygamy produced was rivalry among the sons of different mothers. David had tasted it before, and before he died he had to taste it again.

Adonijah's attempt to seize the throne was also the result of David's weakness as a father. The Bible tells us David had never rebuked Adonijah by saying, 'Why have you done so?' (v. 6). The New American Standard Bible says David had never 'crossed' his son. The picture here is of a son who is headed down the wrong path. It is the responsibility of the father in such a case to 'cross' his son, to intercept him, to put himself between his son and the disaster towards which he is headed. But David never did this. He just let his son go. What a pointed lesson there is here for us! If we let our children go, they will go — down the wrong road, down to dreadful consequences, and maybe all the way down to eternal destruction.

David's adultery

The act of Adonijah also demonstrates the law of sowing and reaping in another way. It takes us back to that sorry episode when David committed adultery with Bathsheba and had her husband, Uriah, killed in battle.

God sent Nathan the prophet to David at that time to announce that the sword would never depart from David's household. David's sin would affect his family life! This is not to say Adonijah was not responsible for his own actions. He was. But, as was the case with Judas Iscariot's betrayal of our Lord, Adonijah's act was at one and the same time his free choice and the fulfilment of what God had predicted!

As I look at the moral wreckage that is strewn across our society today — and all the heartache that goes with it — I am driven to say that there is no principle that is more desperately needed at the present moment than the one which we have been looking at. We reap what we sow! Our choices have consequences. Good choices lead to good consequences, and evil choices lead to evil consequences. Nothing is more important, then, than this matter of making good choices.

How do we go about this matter of making good choices? It is not a matter of guesswork and hocus-pocus, but rather, as we have already noticed, following the Word of God. In his better moments, David knew this and wrote:

Your word is a lamp to my feet
And a light to my path

(Ps. 119:105).

Having learned this afresh from Adonijah's rebellion, David
would pray for his son Solomon: 'And give my son Solomon
a loyal heart to keep your commandments and your testimo-
nies and your statutes...' (1 Chron. 29:19).

God's overruling grace

That brings us to a second law for living — namely, the law of
God's overruling grace. This law or principle, as we have had
many occasions to note, is the keynote of David's life. As we
look at him, we see a monument to the grace of God.

When we look at David's life we see that grace constantly
overruling. It overruled Samuel when he went down to Jesse's
house to anoint a king. Samuel went looking on the outward
appearance, but God channelled him towards David. It overruled all expectations when David went out to meet Goliath.
All bets would have been on Goliath that day, but God gave
David the victory. It overruled King Saul's jealous rage and
protected David from all his murderous plots. God's grace
overruled Jonathan's natural bent, and caused him to embrace
David as God's anointed king. God's grace overruled David's
own follies. When David, in dependence on human wisdom
rather than on God's promises, went down to the land of the
Philistines, God protected and preserved him.

We can even see God's overruling grace at work in David's
immoral liaison with Bathsheba. God's grace rebuked David
and brought him to repentance. God's grace granted forgiveness to him when he repented. And God's grace brought good
out of evil by giving Solomon to David and Bathsheba.

We see that same overruling grace at work at the end of David's life. Adonijah rebelled against God's will and his own father's will, but God overruled Adonijah's evil designs and brought Solomon to the throne just as he had promised.

Now we need a word of caution here — we are not to jump to the conclusion that God's overruling grace means we can and should live any way we want. The law of sowing and reaping and the law of God's overruling grace must be held in tandem. The fact that God can bring good out of evil does not mean evil is good. The evil we do will bring heartache and pain just as David's evil did, but God is so great that the evil we do will never thwart his purposes.

God's purpose all through the Old Testament period was one and the same. It was to fulfil the promise that he made to Adam and Eve — that is, to send his Son into this world to provide redemption for sinners.

Everything leading up to that ultimate purpose was carefully arranged. David was part of that plan. The Christ was to spring from his line. And Solomon, not Adonijah, was also part of that plan. Why? Simply because it pleased God to make Solomon part of that plan.

What about God's plan? Was it in danger of being thrown off course when Adonijah decided to seize the throne? Was there panic in heaven? No. There was no way Adonijah's evil could destroy or thwart the plan of God. All his evil could do was thwart his own happiness and well-being.

What comfort there is in all this for our own day! As God had a plan then, so he does today. His plan today is part of that plan. It is a continuation of it. The Christ who was coming to this earth to provide redemption will one day return to consummate it.

Christians are often discouraged by all the evil that constantly goes on around them. Evil is so widespread and so militantly aggressive that it may seem that God's plan will fall to the ground. But the God who calmly worked all things out then will not be defeated today. He will continue to work his plan — no matter how many Adonijahs arise — until every knee shall bow and every tongue confess that Jesus is Lord.

I cannot think of any truths that are more serviceable to us than these. We reap what we sow and we can trust God's grace to be at work in every situation we face. It is our responsibility to be aware of these laws and to live in the light of them. It is our responsibility to sow the right crop and to trust in the daily sufficiency and the ultimate victory of God's grace. Our refusal to live according to these laws will not ultimately defeat or destroy God, but it will defeat and destroy us.

Notes

Introduction
1. Daniel M. Doriani, *David the Anointed*, Great Commission Publications, p.9.

Chapter 1
1. Thomas J. Nettles, 'A Better Way: Reformation and Revival,' *Reformation & Revival*, John H. Armstrong, ed., vol. i, no. 2, pp.23-4.

Chapter 2
1. Gordon J. Keddie, *Dawn of a Kingdom*, Evangelical Press, p.166.
2. As above.
3. S. G. DeGraaf, *Promise and Deliverance,* Presbyterian and Reformed Publishing Co., vol. ii, p.111.
4. As above.

Chapter 3
1. Doriani, *David the Anointed*, pp.29-30.

Chapter 6
1. Quoted by Erroll Hulse, *Give Him No Rest*, Evangelical Press, p.10.

Chapter 8
1. Bob Jones, *Bob Jones' Revival Sermons,* Sword of the Lord Publishers, p.51.

Chapter 9
1. Keddie, *Dawn of a Kingdom*, p.203.
2. Doriani, *David the Anointed*, p.51.

Chapter 11
1. Dale Ralph Davis, *Looking on the Heart: Expositions of the Book of 1 Samuel*, Baker Book House, vol. ii, p.93.
2 . C. F. Keil and F. Delitzsch, *Commentaries on the Old Testament: Samuel*, Wm B. Eerdmans Publishing Co., p.229.

3. Matthew Henry, *Matthew Henry's Commentary on the Whole Bible,* Fleming H. Revell Company, vol. ii, p.404.

Chapter 12
1. Davis, *Looking on the Heart*, p.97.
2. Keith Kaynor, *When God Chooses*, Regular Baptist Press, p.100.

Chapter 13
1. Kaynor, *When God Chooses*, p.115.

Chapter 14
1. Quoted by Davis, *Looking on the Heart*, p.113.
2. Doriani, *David*, p.63.
3. Davis, *Looking on the Heart*, pp.113-14.

Chapter 15
1. Davis, *Looking on the Heart*, p.129.

Chapter 16
1. Davis, *Looking on the Heart*, p.164.

Chapter 19
1. Charles Spurgeon, *Treasury of David*, MacDonald Publishing Co., vol. i, p.11.

Chapter 20
1. Doriani, *David the Anointed,* p.90.
2. William M. Taylor, *David, King of Israel: His Life and its Lessons,* Harper & Brothers Publishers, p.198.

Chapter 22
1. Doriani, *David the Anointed,* p.92.
2. Kaynor, *When God Chooses,* p.173.
3. Jonathan Edwards, *The Works of Jonathan Edwards*, The Banner of Truth Trust, vol. i, p.554.

Chapter 23
1. John MacArthur, *Ashamed of the Gospel*, Crossway Books, pp.xxvii-xxviii.
2. As above, p.46.

Chapter 24
1. Kaynor, *When God Chooses,* p.193.

Chapter 25
1. Gordon J. Keddie, *Triumph of the King,* Evangelical Press, p.52.
2. As above, p.54.

Chapter 26
1. Henry, *Commentary,* vol. ii, p.478.